RADICAL HOPE
Poverty-Aware Practice for Social Work

Michal Krumer-Nevo

First published in Great Britain in 2020 by

Policy Press
University of Bristol
1–9 Old Park Hill
Bristol
BS2 8BB
UK
t: +44 (0)117 954 5940
pp-info@bristol.ac.uk
www.policypress.co.uk

© Policy Press 2020

British Library Cataloguing in Publication Data
A catalogue record for this book is available from the British Library

ISBN 978-1-4473-5490-1 (paperback)
ISBN 978-1-4473-5489-5 (hardcover)
ISBN 978-1-4473-5493-2 (ePub)
ISBN 978-1-4473-5492-5 (ePdf)

The right of Michal Krumer-Nevo to be identified as author of this work has been asserted by her in accordance with the Copyright, Designs and Patents Act 1988.

All rights reserved: no part of this publication may be reproduced, stored in a retrieval system, or transmitted in any form or by any means, electronic, mechanical, photocopying, recording, or otherwise without the prior permission of Policy Press.

The statements and opinions contained within this publication are solely those of the author and not of the University of Bristol or Policy Press. The University of Bristol and Policy Press disclaim responsibility for any injury to persons or property resulting from any material published in this publication.

Policy Press works to counter discrimination on grounds of gender, race, disability, age and sexuality.

Cover design by Robin Hawes
Front cover image: Viki Itzhaki, vikistudio.com

To Gideon

Contents

List of illustrations		vi
Acknowledgements		vii
Update: COVID-19		viii
Introduction		1
1	Poverty-aware social work: a paradigmatic proposal	15
Part I:	**Transformation**	**43**
2	How to speak critically about poverty	45
3	How to write a critical case study	55
4	How to teach poverty critically	75
5	Frequently asked questions about poverty and poverty-aware social work	83
Part II:	**Recognition**	**91**
6	Poverty, recognition, therapy	93
7	On needs and knowledge: Sarit's story	105
8	On emotional pain	123
9	On minor movements of resistance	137
Part III:	**Rights**	**149**
10	What is active in the active exercising of rights?	151
11	Material help and a flexible budget	169
12	Active rights exercising: advanced	179
13	In the face of social injustice: a panel	191
Part IV:	**Solidarity**	**201**
14	When Douby looked for a home: 'standing by' within the establishment	203
15	A babysitter for a dollar: community development	211
16	Between Othering and solidarity: crisis intervention with children at risk	215
17	'I'm not that kind of person': solidarity in a group intervention	229
References		239
Index		259

List of illustrations

Table

1.1	The three paradigms	19

Figure

1.1	The poverty wheel	31

Boxes

3.1	Guidelines for writing a critical psychosocial report	69
7.1	Sarit's story	110

Acknowledgements

The list of people who accompanied me during the development of the Poverty-Aware Paradigm (PAP) is too long to include here. It includes service users, activists, social workers, policymakers, students, colleagues and members of human rights organisations. I am deeply grateful to all of you. In particular, I thank the social work students and supervisors who participated in the programme Casework for Social Change and the social workers who participated in the PAP courses initiated by the Ministry of Welfare and Social Services for sharing with me so many anecdotes from their practices, many of which found their way into this book. Thank you for teaching me and learning with me.

The Ministry of Welfare and Social Services, with the collaboration of the National Insurance Institute, JDC-Ashalim and the Rashi Foundation, led the development of the PAP programmes and the implementation of the PAP in social services departments on a national scale from 2014. Part of this process consisted of implementing a project aimed at developing digital materials on the PAP. Chapter 5, 'Frequently asked questions on poverty and poverty-aware social work', was originally written with the Center for Educational Technology as part of this project. I also thank Sivan Russo-Carmel and Iris Socolover-Yaacobi for their contribution to the writing of the Hebrew version of Chapter 10, 'What is active in the active exercising of rights', which appeared in the journal *Social Security* in 2019. Many thanks also to Ruth Buzaglo, Rina Bartz, Shlomi Michael ben Hamo, Adam Cohen, Idit Zamir-Yaffe and Sivan Russo-Carmel for approving the publication of the panel discussion in Chapter 13, 'In the face of social injustice – a panel'. I also thank Semadar and Nurit (pseudonyms) who gave me permission to publish their stories of practice. Finally, I thank Lindsay Talmud for his careful editing and Nur Shimei, Yuval Saar-Heiman, Shachar Timor-Shlevin, Eynat Vager-Atias and Sivan Russo-Carmel for their ongoing comradeship. I appreciate it very much.

Update: COVID-19

The coronavirus burst into our lives as this book was in the final stages of proofreading. It is impossible to evaluate, at the present stage, what the long-term effects of coronavirus on our lives will be. What is clear is that this medical crisis carries heavy social and economic costs. The crisis exposed the ailments of neoliberal policy which, in recent years, changed the structure of the employment market and gnawed at the health, welfare and education systems. It seems that the pandemic exposes the deficiencies of the economic right, and the weakness of the ideas of personal responsibility and extreme individualism. Suddenly it is clear to everyone that the state has a crucial role as a safety net for its citizens, and that solidarity and mutual responsibility are the order of the day.

Coping with the pandemic has raised the question whether Western states can allow themselves to continue weakening the public systems, cutting the social safety net and abandoning citizens each to her own lot – or will be able to show responsibility towards the citizens, to safeguard their physical and economic security and to build social institutions based on the principles of equality and social justice. This debate is important and precious. It constitutes an opportunity for social work academics and practitioners alike to take part and make a stance. It reminds us of the social basis of the discipline and strengthens the radical and critical ideas informing it from its inception.

Nonetheless, a poverty-aware stance compels us at all times to examine specifically the implications of the new situation on the weakened and excluded group of people living in poverty. Without ignoring the situation of millions of people around the world who experience firsthand a lack of economic security, it is important to remember and remind others of the material and symbolic implications of the situation on those who live in poverty and experience economic hardship for a long time. A poverty-aware stance in times of lockdown means a specific consideration of the implications of the crisis on those who live in small flats with no yard or porch to offer some refuge from overcrowdedness and physical and emotional suffocation, those who are not eligible for allowances in the form of unemployment benefits, those who do not have health insurance, those who do not have an internet connection in their house (vital for connecting with other people), and those who do not have a computer for every child in their house and cannot make use of the services of online teaching. An awareness of poverty enables us to remember that the lockdown has brought about an abrupt job termination for all those who worked in undeclared work, that is, all those who managed to work in temporary, unstable jobs, and who are not entitled, in the wake of the lockdown, to compensation for losing their income.

Not less important is examining critically the processes of decision-making taking place vis-a-vis the crisis and the policy measures that are being decided upon. Such an examination will enable us to discern the lack of representation of the interests of people in poverty in the decision-making processes. In Israel, the decision on the lockdown and the dialing down of the economic activity to the bare minimum as a coping mechanism with the pandemic has rapidly brought about massive lobbying action on the part of various elements in the organised work sector. But the sector of workers at the bottom of the employment market did not get representation. In this way, policy resolutions can be reached that ignore the interests of those who live for many years on minimal wages. In the same vein, the interests of those who do not work but live on benefits alone did not get meaningful representation. Policy-makers do not recognise the implications of the pandemic on the most weakened and excluded groups, be it workers, non-workers, people without status, refugees, and, given the lack of political power, the voice of these groups is shoved to the side in the hectic public debate developing these days.

In this hour, we do not know what will happen the following day. Will the pandemic constitute a turning point in the ongoing history of neoliberal ideology? Will we see a return to a social-democratic policy on the model of a developed welfare state that does not shirk its responsibility of providing social services? Will we see a change in interpersonal discourse and practice in the direction of strengthening democracy and social solidarity? Or will the social crisis only toughen individualistic and conservative positions, divisiveness and exclusion? What is certain is that in this hour the voice of poverty-aware social workers is a necessary, crucially important one.

March 2020

Introduction

> 'When I came to the social services department and asked for material assistance, they said, "We don't have money." When I asked for somebody to talk to, they said, "We don't have time."' (Tania, the Families Meet Opportunities [MAPA] programme)

With a handful of words, Tania eloquently summarises the shortcomings of social services departments in the current neoliberal era in Israel and other welfare states, when poverty is not recognised as a material predicament or an emotional and relational experience. The transition made by social work since the turn of the millennium from social care to care management has reframed the interactions of social workers with service users. These interactions are now based on information gathering, risk management and surveillance in a shift away from both the ethical foundation of the profession and relationship-based interactions (Jones, 2001; Schram and Silverman, 2012; Cummins, 2018; Ferguson, 2008, 2017a, 2017b). Given this neoliberal context, keeping alive against all odds the hope and belief that relationships matter – that social workers are able to imagine a world without injustice and willing to stand by service users to ensure that such a world will come into being – has become both a basic necessity and a radical choice.

This book offers hope for those who want to see social work as a profession that is rooted in critical thinking and fighting for social justice. It does so by presenting the Poverty-Aware Social Work Paradigm (PAP) – a paradigmatic way of thinking about social work with people in poverty that has been developed through 30 years of my involvement in research, teaching and activism, and implemented in Israel on a nationwide scale over the last five years. The uniqueness of the paradigm lies in the connections that it makes between poverty as a material predicament and poverty as an emotional and relational experience, as well as in its integration of the ways in which social work sees (its ontology), knows (its epistemology) and commits itself (its axiology) to people in poverty. Enriching these connections and making them part of actual practice is a theme that runs through the book.

Personal positioning: social work and the political

Many social workers in today's world feel that their profession is being stolen from them (Jones, 2001; Ferguson, 2017a, 2017b). The original motivation that brought them to the profession, which entailed a desire to have close relationships with others and to change the world for the better, seems to have been lost in procedures, paperwork, regulations and a narrow perception of professionalism. Ferguson (2017a, 2017b) describes social workers who protest against these trends. The PAP is an example of such a protest. Moreover, it represents an attempt to construct a comprehensive theoretical and ethical framework for practice in the field.

The PAP is grounded in the tradition of critical social work, which sees social work as a political activity that involves the exertion of power.[1] As such, social work requires social workers to position themselves vis-a-vis hegemonic notions regarding social problems and marginalised groups.

I came to understand social work as a political activity relatively late, while I was working on my PhD. My dissertation dealt with the life stories of women in poverty and those stories and lives revealed the unjust and immoral nature of the existence of poverty. At the time, I believed that expanding the body of knowledge on poverty would be enough to make a change in the world. I thought that the findings of my research would bring about a change at least in the profession, if not in general public discourse and policy. I soon realised how naive I had been. I understood that the absence of certain stories from the public and the professional discourse was not the result of people keeping their stories to themselves or waiting for a researcher to expose them, but rather stemmed from the fact that no one wanted to hear them and treat them as repositories of valuable knowledge. Bruno Tardieu (1999: 5), a French activist of the ATD Fourth World Movement, an international movement committed to the eradication of chronic poverty, stated that 'The main thing is not to give the poor the chance to make their voice heard, but to open our ears. It is not about empowering the poor, but about humanizing citizens and institutions.'

With time, I realised that while listening to the stories of people in poverty, different people hear different things. These stories may be heard as tales of social injustice, unbearable living situations, pain and struggle, or as a catalogue of the faults, mistakes and immoral behaviour of individuals. The realisation that listening to the stories of people in poverty gave rise to *interpretive battles* shattered my naivety.

I began to ask myself who dominated the public discourse and how this domination was constituted and maintained. What was the role of language in processes of domination? What made the suffering of some people 'legitimate' while the suffering of others remained their own problem? What role did social work as a discipline and a profession play with regard to society's dominant discourse on marginalised groups? Was social work an instrument of power and surveillance, or an instrument of emancipation? How should social work be shaped in order to become an instrument of emancipation?

In attempting to answer these questions, I began to perceive the political dimension of society as a matter of power relations that pervade and shape personal behaviours and relationships, radiating from language to policy and then to people. I began to see the political everywhere, not only in the remote sphere of policymaking, but in the subtle ways in which exclusion, discrimination and oppression are used to create social hierarchies and justify them in the intimate, personal and interpersonal lives of individuals. This insight was the beginning of the development of the PAP.

Over the years, the paradigm has gained attention beyond the academic world. In 2015, the Israeli Ministry of Welfare and Social Services decided to adopt the PAP as a leading paradigm in its programmes on a national scale.[2] This book describes the paradigm – its theoretical and practical aspects and the crucial turning points in its development. In order to contextualise this process, it is important to briefly review the background of poverty and the welfare state in Israel.

Poverty and the welfare state in Israel

Since its inception in 1948 and throughout the first decades of the state, Israel had a strong social-democratic orientation. Beginning in the 1980s, this situation gradually changed as social-democratic trends gave way to a neoliberal orientation (Gal, 2017). In 1948, Israel was a small state of 650,000 citizens characterised by a high degree of equality. Since then, Israel has had large influx of Jewish immigrants and an on-going military conflict with its neighbouring Arab states. In 1967 Israel occupied territories populated with Arab-Palestinians. The population of the occupied territories does not share citizen rights with the rest of the Israeli population and does not receive services from the Israeli welfare systems. In contrast, Arab-Palestinians who live in the area that was part of Israel before 1967 are Israeli citizens and comprise about 20% of the Israeli population, now standing at 8.5 million citizens.[3]

The current neoliberal orientation manifested in an accelerated process of managerialisation and privatisation of the public sector, alongside a steep increase in rates of poverty and inequality. Since 2003, the size of the population living in poverty in Israel has been estimated at approximately one fifth of all families and one third of all children. This is one of the highest rates among Organisation for Economic Co-operation and Development (OECD) countries, even after a slight decline in recent years (NII, 2018). Some populations are more affected by poverty than others, and the Arab-Palestinians and ultra-Orthodox Jews are the two groups that suffer from poverty the most. Old people, Mizrachi Jews (Jews whose origins are in Muslim countries), single mothers and immigrants are also highly vulnerable to poverty.

The state offers assistance to families in poverty through two channels. The first of these is the National Insurance Institute (NII), which directly allocates cash benefits to families by law. These include, for example, social assistance (a means-tested benefit, termed 'income support'), child benefits and disability and old-age pensions. The second channel is municipal social services departments, which provide psychosocial treatment. Social workers in these departments serve as caseworkers, performing various functions, from counselling, mediation and advocacy, to child protection.[4] These departments and the work undertaken in them constitute the main focus of this book.

At the beginning of the 21st century, the process of neoliberal entrenchment was exacerbated by certain welfare policy decisions that adversely affected people in poverty. These included the harshening of the entitlement conditions for income support benefit, a sharp reduction in assistance levels and an increased emphasis on the legalisation of social work practice, in particular, with regard to children at risk of abuse and neglect. These changes also worsened working conditions in the social services departments. Instability and occupational insecurity, heavy caseloads, limited resources, and a lack of regular supervision (Gal, 2017) all contributed to the distancing of social workers from service users.

Tania's statement that comprises the epigraph of this introduction is an indication of service users' perspectives regarding these processes. Her perception of social workers as having neither time nor money is supported by various studies in Israel (Sharlin and Shamai, 2000; Krumer-Nevo, 2006; Krumer-Nevo and Barak, 2006; Strier and Binyamin, 2013; Lavee, 2016; Lavee and Strier, 2018). A similar picture arises from studies conducted by various authors in England (Cummins, 2018; Gupta and Blewett, 2008), the US (Reisch, 2013), Australia (Healy et al, 2011) and Canada (Dupere et al, 2012). Service users' encounters with social workers are accompanied by experiences of shame, a lack of respect, alienation and discrimination (Chase and Walker, 2013; Walker et al, 2013; Sutton et al, 2014; Walker and Bantebya-Kyomuhendo, 2014; Gupta, 2015; Beddoe and Keddell, 2016). In this context, the blurring of the political nature of poverty and the denial of the role that social work plays with regard to poverty has intensified.

Nonetheless, in recent years, there have been signs of a reaction against these trends in Israel. A wave of mass protests in the summer of 2011 placed social protection high on the public agenda and led to some policy changes. The public sentiment expressed in the protests resulted in the establishment of the National Committee to Combat Poverty in 2013 (Gal, 2017). The committee, on which I served as a member, recommended that policymakers adopt a perspective of 'poverty awareness' and a series of far-reaching changes on housing, education, health, employment and welfare policy in order to cut poverty in Israel in half within a decade. An examination of the implementation of this plan three years later revealed that the government had put some of the recommendations into effect and added approximately 54 per cent of the recommended amount of funding to the relevant budget areas. Most of the increase was devoted to welfare and social security through work grants (negative income tax), an increase in old-age income supplements and the establishment of the Child Development Account programme. However, these steps still seem insufficient in terms of reducing the poverty rate significantly (Gal and Madhala-Brik, 2017).

The development of the PAP in Israel

The PAP was developed in opposition to the process of the rise of neoliberal ideology and the changes that this phenomenon has brought to social policy and the social work profession. After I completed my PhD and became a full-time academic, I was involved as an activist with the Forum for the Eradication of Poverty and various initiatives with local social services departments. After 15 years of academic research and activism, in 2010, I established a critical fieldwork training programme for social work students at Ben-Gurion University, called Casework for Social Change. This small-scale local student programme served as a laboratory for the development of the theoretical principles of the PAP. Simultaneously, through a process of mutual influence that took place between the theoretical ideas and the experiences of the students in the programme, three PAP models were developed: pedagogical, organisational and practical.

Concurrently with the establishment of Casework for Social Change in the second decade of the 21st century, the public climate that called for strengthening the welfare state placed people in poverty at the centre of the attention of the Ministry of Welfare and Social Services. In this context, the PAP gained attention as an alternative to mainstream professional practice. The recommendation of the National Committee to Combat Poverty (2014) to develop poverty-aware policy and practice contributed to this process and led to the decision of the Ministry of Welfare and Social Services in 2015 to adopt the PAP as a leading paradigm for social workers in social services departments. Currently, the paradigm is being applied in five different programmes that serve more than 5,000 Jewish and Arab families, and are run nationally in about half of the local authorities in Israel.[5]

The first of the five programmes was MAPA, where I met Tania. This was a pilot programme that targeted families that had been beyond the reach of social workers for many years. The second programme – Families First – is the largest one, and its focus is on families who have good chances of improving their income through employment. The other three programmes serve families in the child protection system, with the aim of preventing the removal of children from their homes or bringing children who have already been removed back to their families. The five programmes work according to similar PAP organisational and practical principles, with specific variations put in place to tailor them to specific population groups and local contexts. Some 3,000 social workers in various positions and with varying levels of seniority, including caseworkers, Social Workers to the Youth Law,[6] team directors, supervisors, instructors, directors of social services departments and policymakers, underwent PAP training in order to implement and support this work. The stories I heard from these social workers and the families with whom they work appear in every chapter of this book.

Following another recommendation of the National Committee to Combat Poverty (2014), rights centres have been established in all authorities where a PAP programme is running. Each of these rights centres has a designated social worker whose role was developed according to the principles of the PAP practice of the active realisation of rights. In order to work according to the PAP's organisational model, in addition to the rights centres, every social services department that implemented one of the PAP programmes received a part-time additional worker, a flexible budget to cover families' immediate needs, a PAP training course and ongoing PAP supervision. The book covers all of these aspects of the PAP.

From an evaluation of the five programmes that are running and still being evaluated, we know that the PAP has helped social workers to reach out to families that were previously beyond their reach (Ben-Rabi, 2019). An evaluation of the largest programme, Families First, which serves more than 4,000 families, shows improvement in the material situation of the families derived from salary or cash benefits (Leibovitch et al, 2019). Another study shows an increase in service users' satisfaction with the social work treatment they received (Brand-Levi and Malul, 2019). All the evaluations indicate an essential change in the ways in which social workers perceive their relationship with service users and conduct practice, as manifested in more frequent and regular meetings, in social workers knowing much more about their service users – their histories and social contexts – and in social workers getting closer to them.

Families First: what next?

One may get the impression that the PAP has made a successful, smooth entry into the establishment. Yet, not surprisingly, the story is much more complicated than it seems. These developments come with a heavy price. Not all professionals at all levels have understood or accepted the political nature of the paradigm. Some of them have focused on the part that relationships play in the paradigm, ignoring poverty as a mechanism of power that has a major influence on these relationships, asking what poverty has to do with it and claiming that the PAP is 'just good relationship-based social work'. I perceive this kind of response as indicating a depoliticised understanding of the encounters between social workers and service users living in poverty. Experience teaches us that those who think that 'only good relationships' are necessary are unable to stand by service users when they do not do what social workers expect them to do or do not 'cooperate' with them. In fact, they are not able to stand by service users in the complex situations in which they find themselves.

Another problem arises when professionals ignore poverty as a material predicament. Doing so leads to disregarding the political nature of rights-oriented practice. This can happen when social workers think that 'empowering' service users means avoiding providing them with assistance or making them exercise their rights on their own while ignoring the structural faults in the system that prevent them from succeeding. It can also happen when social workers are so loyal to the system that they are not able to talk with service users about the systemic injustice that the latter are experiencing. In fact, it has reached the point where for some professionals, the PAP is a token, co-opted for neoliberal purposes.

Problems have also surfaced at the level of macro-practice. The designated Rights Exercising Social Workers have not adopted policy practice as enthusiastically as they have direct assistance in rights exercising. Moreover, despite the additional workforce, the PAP has not changed the reality of social services departments being overburdened with large caseloads. The flexible budget, which has been part of all PAP programmes and has assisted social workers in responding to families' acute needs, is still under discussion between the Ministry of Welfare and Social Services, which supports it, and the Ministry of Finance, which objects to it.

More problems exist within the Ministry of Welfare and Social Services itself. High-level officials in the child protection system argue fiercely against the idea that poverty is associated with child abuse and neglect. Data pertaining to the links between poverty and child abuse/neglect, for example, data on the socio-economic status of families whose children have been removed from their homes, are unavailable.[7] The same officials also argue that the PAP supports parents but does not fully take into account children at risk, and they cannot agree with the analysis according to which interventions in this field involve oppressive power.

The adoption of the PAP as 'a leading paradigm for social workers in social services departments' (Ministry of Welfare and Social Services, 2016), as first declared in 2015, is still a distant objective. Putting in place the organisational changes necessary to make the PAP feasible – for example, reducing caseloads, having a flexible budget that can be used at the family's discretion or providing ongoing supervision – requires fundamental transformation. Such change will not occur as long as policymakers reject the notion that poverty is a societal problem and fail to regard people in poverty as their equals instead of seeing them as 'undeserving' or Other.

Why hope?

The PAP is a radical paradigm. It perceives the social work profession as a means of social criticism, not as an objective or neutral system of expertise (Garrett, 2013). This paradigmatic choice transforms the ways in which social workers think about and work with people in poverty. However, in order for such a transformation to take place, there must be a much larger change in socio-political structures, organisations and policy. In Israel, in addition to the issue of poverty, the political situation and the ongoing conflict with the Palestinians take their toll on the possibility of maintaining hope. For me, my experience with being deeply involved in the implementation of the PAP at the Ministry of Welfare and Social Services highlighted the crucial need for hope.

Very early on in this endeavour, I understood that even if the PAP was fully implemented in social services departments, all social workers stood by service users and all service users overcame the obstacles they faced from within themselves and from the outside world, the struggle to eliminate poverty would still not be over. The war on poverty cannot be won through social workers alone. Integrated efforts are needed to change the housing, education, health and benefits systems, as well as the labour market. Macroeconomic transformation is needed, for example, in the tax system.

Nevertheless, social workers have a crucial role to play in this broad picture. We are obliged to transform the way in which we establish relationships and the way in which we position ourselves in society. We are obliged to follow Cloward and Fox Piven (1975: xii), who said:

> The false choice – of whether we should become revolutionaries or merely be social workers – allowed us to avoid a series of much more important choices; more important because they were choices about actual possible venues of action, and about areas of activity in which we as social workers might make a difference.[8]

Being committed to 'making a difference' in the current socio-political context is not possible without hope. Remaining hopeful is thus a moral choice (Ferguson, 2017a, 2017b). It is a choice to swim against the current and to infiltrate every crack that we can find in the hegemony in order to resist it. It is a choice to create links and build bridges where there are gaps and walls. It is a choice to be involved. James, Este, Bernard, Benjamin, Lloyd and Turner (2010: 27) write that critical hope:

> refers to hopeful action that is based on the critical analysis of a situation and the recognition that wishing alone is not sufficient to make change. It involves an understanding of the forces that produce injustice and an imagining of what the world without these forces, and without the injustice, might look like.

Garrett (2013: 215) has the following to say on the subject: 'In seeking to create this counter-hegemonic project and new bonds of solidarity in hard times, we have much to lose, but everything to gain.'

The book

Poverty-aware social work practice aims to respond to the call implicit in Tania's statement that begins this introduction by facing poverty through two interconnected channels based on the politics of recognition and respect, and the politics of redistribution (Fraser, 1998, 2003; Lister, 2004). As described later, the politics of recognition and respect inspires the PAP's version of relationship-based practice, while the politics of redistribution inspires the PAP's version of rights-based practice. These two are intertwined: the struggle to exercise service users' rights or to provide a response to material needs is a straightforward step towards improving one's material predicament in terms of redistribution, yet, at the same time, it supports and restores one's experience of the self. The effort to create a relationship of recognition is therapeutic in nature but, at the same time, enables social workers to stand by service users in their battle to exercise their rights and improve their economic situations.

The first chapter of the book – Chapter 1, 'Poverty-aware social work: a paradigmatic proposal' – gives a full overview of the theoretical principles of the paradigm. After briefly introducing the concept of the paradigm and discussing its contribution, the chapter goes on to describe the PAP, its ontological, epistemological and axiological premises, and their influences on social work practice. The chapter compares the PAP and the two historically dominant paradigms in social work: the conservative and the structural. The conservative paradigm is strongly challenged in this chapter. The structural paradigm is presented as offering a fruitful analysis of poverty. However, it has not inspired direct practice on a large scale. The chapter builds upon the structural analysis and combines it with concepts from critical theories and current psychoanalytic concepts to present the PAP as a useful paradigm for analysis and practice.

Following this overall review of the paradigm, the book is divided into four parts, each dedicated to one of the four pillars of the paradigm: Transformation, Recognition, Rights and Solidarity.

The four chapters of Part I, 'Transformation', address the transformational nature of the paradigm. Chapter 2, 'How to speak critically about poverty', is devoted to the professional spoken vocabulary regarding poverty. Through a close look at the words that social workers use to describe service users in poverty, links are made between language, attitudes and practice.

Chapter 3, 'How to write a critical case study', continues Chapter 2 and centres on the subject of how to translate the insights of the PAP into the writing of a case study. It is based on a case study written by a senior social worker for the purpose of supervision and the process of deconstructing and rewriting it through the supervision.

Chapter 4, 'How to teach poverty critically', focuses on the challenges of teaching the paradigm to professionals. How do social workers respond to the paradigm? How is it possible to deconstruct conservative attitudes during teaching without attacking or blaming students? What is the role of ongoing dialogue in this teaching?

As its title indicates, Chapter 5, 'Frequently asked questions about poverty and poverty-aware social work', includes ten questions that I am frequently asked by students, practitioners and policymakers, and answers them. Among these questions are the following: are people who are busy with basic survival in order to meet their primary existential needs available for an emotional therapeutic process? If structural aspects have such a crucial impact on poverty, how are we to understand that in the same neighbourhoods, the children of some families manage to escape poverty while others do not? Does the PAP free people from their responsibility for their situations? How can social workers understand the issue of 'welfare dependency'?

Part II, 'Recognition', builds on the concept of 'recognition' in the work of the philosophers Nancy Fraser and Axel Honneth, as well as relational psychoanalysts, mainly Jessica Benjamin. The chapters present 'recognition' as an organising concept for acknowledging the subjectivity of service users in the therapeutic relationship, conceptualising and exemplifying what recognition is in the context of poverty.

Chapter 6, 'Poverty, recognition, therapy', serves as an introduction and provides background on recognition in social work practice in the context of poverty. The three chapters that follow are devoted to the main areas to which recognition should be directed.

Chapter 7, 'On needs and knowledge: Sarit's story', focuses on the recognition of service users' knowledge and needs through a close reading of the life story of Sarit, a 23-year-old single mother of three. Chapter 8, 'On emotional pain', centres on the emotional pain associated with poverty. Through citations from research interviews and self-reflection, emotional pain is explored and the role it plays in the interactions between people in poverty and professionals is discussed.

Chapter 9, 'On minor movements of resistance', is devoted to the daily resistance of people to their poverty and the measures that social workers should take to identify these acts of resistance and reinforce them. The chapter introduces the concept of resistance based on Lister's (2004) taxonomy of acts of agency. It differentiates resistance from the concept of strengths, and conceptualises the difference between agency and resistance. The chapter provides examples of resistance from related practice.

Part III, 'Rights', is devoted to the politics of redistribution in direct practice. It is presented in four chapters. The first, Chapter 10, is titled 'What is active in the active exercising of rights?' and describes the practice of the active exercising of rights. It focuses on the differences between a technocratic realisation of rights based on the assumption that the system works well, and a critical version of it that sees the origin of service users' difficulties in systemic failures. After outlining the ideas behind the active exercising of rights, the chapter goes on to present the practice as it is implemented in the work of caseworkers and in the special role of rights social workers that was developed in the framework of the PAP.

Chapter 11, 'Material help and a flexible budget', focuses on the complex relationship between responses to material needs and responses to emotional needs. My argument is that the emotional (internal) and material (external) realms are closely connected, and that practice should seek to respond simultaneously to both. The chapter argues for a flexible budget as a necessary tool for doing so.

Chapter 12, 'Active rights exercising: advanced', is concerned with the role that social workers adopt when they face situations in which the responses to service users' needs are not recognised as legal rights. Based on examples from the field, the principles of dealing with these situations are explored, with an emphasis on the importance of social workers' analyses of these situations as problems of rights.

Chapter 13, 'In the face of social injustice: a panel', is based on the transcript of a panel discussion held as part of a seminar on the PAP. The panel included one service user, students from the Casework for Social Change programme and social workers who were involved in the development of the PAP's rights practice. The discussion focuses on the participants' personal experiences of the active exercising of rights, their attitudes towards it, the requirements for this kind of practice and its pros and cons.

The book concludes with Part IV, 'Solidarity', which presents four case studies that exemplify the various ways in which solidarity might shape social workers' practice. Chapter 14, 'When Douby looked for a home: "standing by" within the establishment', tells the story of a woman who was evicted from the apartment that she had occupied for 12 years and her social worker's struggle to reverse the eviction order. The chapter addresses the tension between practice that is based on solidarity and mainstream social work practice in social services departments.

Chapter 15, 'A babysitter for a dollar: community development', considers a case in which a fire broke out in the public housing apartment of a woman who had locked her children in when she left for work. Is it the story of one woman – of a neglectful mother? What is the connection between the fire and poverty? What kind of policy and community services can prevent such events from taking place? Chapter 16, 'Between Othering and solidarity: crisis intervention with children at risk' tells the story of a home visit that a social worker conducted following a complaint from the neighbours that young children had been left at home on their own. During the visit, she discovered that the apartment was flooded with sewage. Her response is analysed in terms of building relationships of solidarity.

The final chapter of Part IV and of the book – Chapter 17, '"I'm not that kind of person": solidarity in a group intervention' – is based on the story of a group intervention in which one participant threatened to set himself and his children on fire as an act of protest in order to receive better housing. I was one of the social workers in this group, and I learned a great deal from it.

The presentation and inculcation of a new, critical paradigm has come about through endless dialogues that I have conducted with professionals, from front-line workers, to directors, instructors, supervisors and policymakers. I have found dialogues to be an efficient medium through which to involve people with the re-evaluation of their unquestioned axioms and dogmas, or what Fook and Gardner (2007) call 'critical reflectivity'. Dialogue is also a good medium through which to bring the abstract and conceptual framework of the paradigm to life, linking theory with practice and introducing audiences to the messy and complex world of working with people in poverty. The book attempts to capture the conversational nature of these dialogues. Some of the chapters are based on public lectures that I gave and some are based on pedagogical dialogues that took place in the framework of teaching the paradigm to professionals. This is not a mere collection of lectures, but rather an effort to use specific moments in time that are captured in those lectures in order to present a full picture of the various aspects of the PAP. In addition, some of the chapters in the book were written especially for the book in a conversational style.

Notes

1. See works from the path-breaking *Radical social work* (Bailey and Brake, 1975), to *Radical social work today* (Langan and Lee, 1989), *Radical casework: A theory of practice* (Fook, 1993), *Structural social work* (Mullaly, 1997, 2007), *Rethinking social work: Towards critical practice* (Ife, 1997), *Transforming social work practice* (Pease and Fook, 1999), *Anti-racist social work* (Dominelli, 1997), *Social work: Critical theory and practice* (Fook, 2002), *Human rights and social work: Towards rights-based practice* (Ife, 2012), *Reclaiming social work: Challenging neo-liberalism and promoting social justice* (Ferguson, 2008), *Radical social work in practice: Making a difference* (Ferguson and Woodward, 2009), *Radical social work today: Social work at the crossroads* (Lavalette, 2011), *Re-imagining child protection: Towards humane social work with families* (Featherstone et al, 2014), *Protecting children: A social model* (Featherstone and Gupta, 2018), *Social work and social justice: Concepts, challenges, and strategies* (Reisch and Garvin, 2016), *The new politics of social work* (Gray and Webb, 2013) and *The Routledge handbook of critical social work* (Webb, 2019).
2. The implementation of the PAP into the work of the social services in Israel took two forms: the establishment of five programmes that worked according to similar organisational and practical principles; and the establishment of an organisational infrastructure to support the programmes. The Ministry of Welfare and Social Services collaborated in this initiative with JDC-Ashalim, the Rashi Foundation and the National Insurance Institute.
3. As part of its analytic framework, the book deals with experiences of Arab-Palestinians who are Israeli citizens. The situation of the Palestinians in the occupied territories is beyond the scope of this book.
4. For a comprehensive summary of the structure and history of the Israeli welfare system, see Gal (2017).
5. Half of the localities in which PAP programmes operate are Arab localities. Since PAP programmes entered the most deprived localities in Israel, Arab localities are over-represented.
6. A Social Worker to the Youth Law is a specialist social worker who has legal duties in criminal investigations of maltreatment and represents the child's interest in juvenile courts.
7. Similar obstacles faced Bywaters and his team, who examined the connections between poverty and child abuse/neglect in the four UK countries (see Bywaters et al, 2018).
8. In this regard, Gray et al (2015: 387) state: 'However skeptical one might be of the pernicious effects of neoliberalism, the state is important, and perspectives such as those presented here are needed to increase the diagnostic and analytic capabilities of professional knowledge and experience. These perspectives show not only that the state is important but how it is important, despite the limits, challenges, and opportunities presented by neoliberalism. Working within the state need not necessarily mean blind complicity with its policies and practices. As Lipsky (1980) and Schram and Silverman (2012) remind us, human service professionals are constantly working for and against the state simultaneously, trying to reap the best it has to offer for their clients, while seeking to minimize its harshest effects. They constantly seek to invent new ways of practicing their profession in collaboration with their clients and other social and political actors and agents.'

1

Poverty-aware social work: a paradigmatic proposal[1]

This chapter presents the theoretical and ethical premises of the PAP. It starts with a discussion of what it means to think paradigmatically and continues with a detailed presentation of three paradigms: the conservative, the structural and the PAP. The first two are the dominant paradigms in the field, and they are compared with the third, which I am suggesting. The conservative paradigm, I claim, essentialises people in poverty as Others. Through its focus on the weaknesses and deficits of individuals as the cause of their poverty, it inspires direct practice that aims at changing the characteristics of individuals. Contrastingly, the structural paradigm sees societal failures as the cause of poverty, recommending a politics of redistribution as the solution to poverty. The structural paradigm has had a great influence on macro-practice but much less so on direct practice. Building on the structural analysis, the PAP adds to it the concept of recognition – derived from current relational psychoanalysis – in order to offer a detailed blueprint for direct practice. The three paradigms have strong links of mutual influence between practice and theory.

Introduction

> When I give food to the poor, they call me a saint. When
> I ask why the poor have no food, they call me a communist.
> (Dom Helder Câmara, quoted in McDonagh, 2009: 11)

Asking about the reason for people's poverty causes discomfort in those who call the Brazilian Catholic archbishop who inspired Latin America's 'liberation theology' a 'communist'. Giving food does not evoke a similar response because it seems neutral, apolitical. However, every practice is, in fact, political. What makes the provision of food to the poor seem apolitical is not its essential nature, but its proximity to hegemonic ideas regarding what poverty is and what the ways to combat it are. There is no escape from being political; thinking through the framework of paradigms helps us to expose the political component of practice.

During the last two decades, social work scholars in the UK (Craig, 2002; Jones, 2002; Davis and Wainwright, 2005; Mantle and Backwith,

2010; Parrott, 2014; Cummins, 2018; Featherstone, 2016; Gupta et al, 2017), Belgium (Boone et al, 2018, 2019), the US (Deka, 2012; Reisch and Jani, 2012), New Zealand and Australia (Waldegrave, 2005; Beddoe and Keddell, 2016; Morley and Ablett, 2017), and Israel (Rosenfeld, 1993; Rosenfeld and Tardieu, 2000; Strier, 2009; Krumer-Nevo, 2009, 2015, 2017; Strier and Binyamin, 2010, 2013) have started calling for a restructuring of the relationships between social workers and people in poverty, based on a social justice agenda that emphasises rights, democracy, inclusion and respect. The 'Poverty-Aware Social Work Paradigm'[2] (PAP) translates this agenda into specific theoretical and ethical principles.

Why do we need a paradigm? Or, thinking paradigmatically

A paradigm is a comprehensive 'set of basic beliefs ... that deals with primary principles' (Guba and Lincoln, 1994: 107) and connects ideas regarding the nature of the world (the ontological premise), what is considered valid knowledge and how it is acquired (epistemological premise), and ethics (axiological premise) (Heron and Reason, 1997). The ontological premise is an answer to the question: 'What is the world?' In our case, this is a question of 'What is the nature of poverty?' and 'What are the characteristics of people in poverty?' The epistemological aspect refers to the question: 'How do we know?' Specifically, in our case, 'What kind of knowledge is needed when working with people in poverty?' Finally, the axiological aspect raises the question of 'Why?' or 'For what purpose?' – in our case, 'What is the ethical purpose of our practice with people in poverty?'

The structure of a paradigm emphasises the strong connection between theoretical, epistemological and ethical assumptions, on the one hand, and practice, on the other. This connection makes for a dynamic equilibrium in which theory and practice mutually influence one another. This means that the answers to the three questions – 'What is the nature of poverty?'; 'What kind of knowledge is needed when working with people in poverty?'; and 'What is our ethical purpose?' – stand at the heart of and inform every practice. The paradigmatic structure highlights the relationship between practice and its underlying basic assumptions, and emphasises questions as to 'why' and 'for what purpose' practice is done as crucial questions that shape the way in which it is actually done.

Thinking paradigmatically means carrying out an ongoing, reflexive examination of the theoretical and ethical principles behind every decision regarding intervention. This examination can take place in two ways. One can start with looking at a real-life practice and analysing its theoretical and ethical premises, that is, asking the aforementioned ontological, epistemological and ethical questions about that practice. This process of critical reflection, which starts from practice and analyses its hidden assumptions, helps professionals to develop awareness of actions they take for granted (Fook and Gardner, 2007). Alternatively, one can start from thinking about the paradigmatic questions and imagine practice that is grounded in the answers to these questions. In this case, practitioners might start with asking themselves: 'What are the characteristics of the people I am working with?'; 'What kind of knowledge do I need?'; and 'What is the purpose of my activity?' Based on the answers they give, practitioners might think of different ways of doing practice, and then choose the one that suits them best from among them.

Grounding practice in theory and ethics, rather than seeing it simply as a *module* or a set of actions, has far-reaching implications for social work. Yet, the theoretical and ethical context of practice is seldom discussed or examined. Therefore, practitioners mistakenly think that they can adopt certain practices without considering the paradigmatic assumptions that they imply. However, this is a huge mistake because different paradigmatic assumptions lead to different ways of doing practice, even if the practice looks superficially the same.

As an example, let us take the practice of home visits. Home visits can be approached from a supervisory stance, seeking to gauge the functioning of the family or the risk to their children. This stance will shape the home visit in a particular way that, as we shall see later, is more suited to the basic premises of a conservative paradigm but contradicts the principles of the PAP. Home visits are a staple in the PAP but the paradigmatic principles will shape them in a totally different way than those emanating from the conservative paradigm. According to the PAP, the purpose of the visit is to gain familiarity with the family's actual life context (see Saar-Heiman et al, 2017) and establish a close relationship that will enable the social worker to become relevant for the family and to stand by it in its struggle against poverty and hardship.

Thinking about home visits through a paradigmatic lens leads us to ask: ontological questions, such as 'How do I perceive need or risk?' and 'How do I perceive the problem or difficulty that led me to carry out a home visit?'; epistemic questions, such as 'What kind of knowledge do I seek to gain during a home visit?'; and ethical questions, such as 'What is the set of values according to which I conduct the home visit?'

and 'How do I position myself in relation to the situation?' Different answers to these questions dictate the specific way in which the social worker presents herself to the family, looks at the house and sits and talks to the family members.

Just as a home visit can be carried out in very different ways, and for very diverse reasons, the same applies to material assistance, a therapeutic session or rights-exercising practice. In fact, all the various social work practices, including policy practice, stem from theoretical and ethical principles, whether they are acknowledged or not.

My experience tells me that dealing with poverty raises a surfeit of issues, the critical discussion of which in professional circles is very difficult. Motivation to work, welfare dependency, material assistance and child abuse/neglect are all explosive issues. It is hard to discuss them because they give rise to very strong feelings, and because a professional climate that glorifies evidence-based practice ignores questions of ethics. In contrast, the paradigmatic structure facilitates this discussion because every claim made can be responded to with the questions that comprise the paradigm: 'How do you perceive the problem?'; 'How do you know what the problem is?'; and 'What is the goal of intervention?'

Once it is understood that theory, values and practice are closely connected, two dominant paradigms can be identified in the field of social work in relation to poverty: the conservative and the structural. I will now compare these two paradigms with the PAP that I am suggesting. To facilitate the process, I will describe the three premises of each paradigm – the ontological, the epistemological and the axiological (see Table 1.1) – and the practice that derives from them.

The conservative paradigm

Ontology

The conservative paradigm is grounded in the historic notion of the 'undeserving poor'. The influential historian Michael Katz (1986, 1990, 1992, 1995) claims that American social policy in the 20th century kept the 18th-century distinction between the deserving (mainly disabled people, war veterans and widows with children) and the undeserving poor (characterised by behavioural and moral problems). Although the distinction originally derived from the pragmatic need to allocate scarce resources and did not carry moral judgement, it acquired a moral connotation during the 19th century. The 'undeserving poor' were treated with a mixture of disciplinary, punitive and educational

Table 1.1: The three paradigms

	Ontology	Epistemology	Axiology
The conservative paradigm	Poverty is a culture that is manifested in the psychological, familial and communal characteristics of poor people	Positivist, professional knowledge as objective truth (directed to the pathologies and deficits of human subjects)	The poor exhibit a serious deviation from social and moral norms, and live off the productivity of the normative members of society
The structural paradigm	Poverty is a problem of societal inequality, the consequence of unequal social structures and institutions	Positivist, professional knowledge as objective truth (directed to the deficits of society; at the level of direct practice knowledge, directed to human subjects' strengths)	Poverty is incompatible with a just society Ethics of redistribution
The PAP	Poverty is a violation of human rights. People in poverty are agents who resist poverty under conditions of a severe lack of economic and symbolic capital	Critical-constructivist, obtained through relationship with service users	Ethics of solidarity, minimising otherness and extending the group of 'we'

strategies in order to modify what was perceived as their moral inferiority and negative behaviour.

During the 20th century, rules of public discourse did not allow an explicit distinction to be made between the deserving and undeserving poor. However, Katz (1990) traces how this distinction permeated policies and regulations, for example, in work requirements and eligibility restrictions imposed on welfare recipients. At the beginning of the second half of the 20th century, the concept that prevailed in poverty discourse, though not without controversy, was the concept of 'the culture of poverty'. Coined by the anthropologist Oscar Lewis (1966) in his foundational text 'The culture of poverty', it substantiated the existence of poor people riddled with an accumulation of specific problematic behaviours on the personal, familial and community levels, as well as in their relationships with society as a whole. According to this thesis, in all these spheres, poor people who are part of the culture of poverty have psychological, moral, behavioural and cultural pathologies or deficits. Lewis (1966: 25) summarised it in these words: the culture of poverty 'does not provide much support or satisfaction; its pervading mistrust magnifies individual helplessness and isolation. Indeed, poverty of culture is one of the crucial traits of the culture of poverty.'

Although Lewis intended his research to promote a progressive policy,[3] his text came to be conceived as a classic example of a deficit perspective or stigmatising discourse (O'Connor, 2009), one that focused on portraying people in poverty primarily as 'damaged'. This was strengthened by Lewis (1966: 21) arguing that:

> Once the culture of poverty has come into existence, it tends to perpetuate itself. By the time slum children are six or seven, they have usually absorbed the basic attitudes and values of their subculture. Thereafter they are psychologically unready to take full advantage of changing conditions or improving opportunities that may develop in their lifetime.

At the time it was published and later on, the culture of poverty thesis was critiqued by researchers on both methodological and ethical grounds, as well as for the deterministic nature of the argument (Valentine, 1968, 1971; Gans, 1971; Wilson, 1987; Katz, 1995; Abramovitz, 1996). It was argued that the popularisation of the concept of 'the culture of poverty' mainly emphasised the *difference* between people in poverty and other people in society. Moreover, it constituted a supposedly scientific basis for politicians who had used the 'culture' argument to ignore the need for progressive socio-economic change. According to this logic, since poverty is a question of *culture*, it cannot be reduced by socio-economic steps.

Soon after it appeared, the 'culture of poverty' concept largely disappeared from academic discourse. However, its discursive characteristics, which portray people in poverty as damaged and as 'Others', remained and resurfaces in the discourse on the underclass. This discourse – which evolved in the late 1970s and into the 1990s in the UK (Murray, 1990) and the US (Murray, 1984) – focused on the problem of irresponsibility among the 'underclass', causing them to be involved in violent crime, to feature prominently in unemployment figures and to epitomise single-women-headed families.[4]

Garrett (2018: 80) claims that 'This identification of an underclass can, in fact, be interpreted as central to the naming practices and vocabulary of neo-liberalism in the 1980s and to the interventions of politicians, economists and cultural figures associated with this radical project.' Garrett (2018: 84) cites Bourdieu and Wacquant (2001: 4), who see 'the term underclass and its associated talk ... as a "screen discourse" blocking engagement with more substantial economic and political questions'.

Recent scholarship has reformulated the conservative discourse, with the current scientific trend being to study the cognitive abilities of the poor and their neurological characteristics. Inspired by current 'neuroenthusiasm' (Wastell and White, 2017), medical researchers have found the brain of poor people to be a promising research site. They have shown that poverty and traumas related to poverty have a negative impact on the neurological system and cognitive development (for example, McCoy et al, 2017). By examining the mechanisms by which poverty negatively affects children's brain development, it was found that poverty was associated with particular brain characteristics. Convincing pictures of bigger ('normal', non-poor) and smaller brains (to illustrate the damage to neglected, poor children's brains) became popular in social work training to support the argument that poverty-related traumas are a major disadvantage for children.[5] However, given the absence of critical reflection regarding the role that it plays in the politics of representation, this discourse creates strong links between (negative) types of parental care-giving and poverty that explicitly or implicitly characterise parents who live in poverty as malfunctioning, and lends credence to the responsibilisation of poor mothers, 'positioning them as the architects of their children's poverty and deprivation' (Edwards et al, 2015: 184).

The writing in the conservative paradigm derives from a strong moral stance regarding the assumed essential differences between people in poverty and the rest of society. Most of this writing has the strong neoliberal flavour of a belief in the idea of the autonomous, independent human subject and opposition to the involvement of the state in the free market, as well as to structural interventions to reduce poverty (Featherstone et al, 2014).

The main feature of the conservative paradigm is to portray poverty as an incubator for people's pathologies, deficits and weaknesses, whether they are psychological, neurological, cognitive or moral. Once these personal characteristics are shaped, they tend to be essentialised and to acquire an autonomous entity, especially with regard to older children or adults. The overall picture of the poor invoked by this discourse is monolithic, uniform and cyclic. Personal characteristics are seen as the reason for entry into poverty and remaining in it, and the deficits or pathologies shaping individual personalities are construed to be beyond repair.

Epistemology

In line with its ontological viewpoint, the epistemological premise of the conservative paradigm – that is, the answers to the questions regarding how knowledge is acquired, what kind of knowledge is sought and what counts as valid knowledge – focuses on knowledge regarding the deficits and pathologies of people in poverty. Thus, it forms a crucial part in the process of establishing people in poverty as the ultimate Other. Irrespective of the nomenclature used, whether it is the inhabitants of the 'culture of poverty', the 'underclass' or people with brain deformations, people living in poverty are marked as 'abnormal' and 'non-normative', and a barrier is created between 'them' and 'us'.

Even if some of the conservative literature is written for progressive purposes, with researchers believing that they are promoting social justice by supplying policymakers with the latest data regarding the destructive nature of poverty and its effect on human subjects (as was the case with Oscar Lewis), I claim that they are unintentionally contributing to the portrayal of poor people as Others. In what is ultimately a cyclic process, the Othering of this group contributes to its exclusion and justifies it. Knowing the Other is a basic social work skill, necessary for any process of assessment, diagnosis, evaluation and intervention. The crux of the matter is that the conservative epistemological premise is positivist in nature. Guidelines for the assessment of service users – whether individuals, families or communities – that fall into the positivist matrix are based on criteria assumed to be valid, objective and neutral (Bell, 2012). However, this approach has two main limitations. First, the positivist approach that aims to know reality 'as it is' requires professionals to maintain a neutral and objective position while acquiring knowledge (Anastas, 2012; Witkin, 1991). Professional knowledge is perceived to exist independently of the bodies of the professionals and their interpersonal interactions. Hence, the relationship between social workers and service users is considered irrelevant to the accumulation of knowledge about the issues that service users face, as well as their solutions. Good relationships might be considered as a tool to gain information but they are not supposed to 'get in the way' of 'objective' professional assessment. Moreover, the professional herself – as a social persona with social, ethnic, class and gender identities – is hidden in the process, as is the role that those identities play in the interpretation of the situation.

Second, according to the positivist approach, the professional is the only one who knows, or, at least, the one who knows best. People in poverty are denied the status of being knowledgeable, or if their knowledge is recognised, it is considered as 'mistaken' knowledge and the cause of their problems. The consequence of these limitations is that the analysis of power relations between professionals and service users is also deemed irrelevant.

Axiology

The axiological facet of a paradigm refers to its ethical distinction between 'good' and 'bad'. The conservative paradigm actually differentiates between the 'good' and the 'bad' poor. The 'good' poor are those people who came into poverty against their will through a bad turn of fate, or through natural life events, such as illness, disability or death. Those people do everything that is normative to get out of poverty. They are obedient, hard-working, independent and self-reliant. They choose a life of study or work and stay away from any involvement in non-normative activity. Thus, they are not totally 'Others', and they deserve help in order to improve their lives. To the contrary, the 'bad' poor are those whose immoral behaviour brought them into poverty, and so they deserve to be blamed and punished.

The position that social workers should adopt with regard to people in poverty is that of the representatives of society. They are society's agents, representing society's values and norms, and armed with efficient methods of intervention in order to cure people, to change their mindsets and to help them overcome their weaknesses.

Practice derived from the conservative paradigm

Practice derived from conservative premises treats poverty as only a background variable, not as a target for direct change, while conservative policy emphasises individualised solutions that focus on achieving behavioural change. The state's power plays a major role in these solutions because they are often coupled with sanctions for non-cooperation. The most famous example of this kind of policy is welfare-to-work programmes, participation in which is a condition for being entitled to receive cash benefits. It is based on the assumption that the state should motivate individuals who are otherwise not interested in escaping poverty. Poverty as a social phenomenon is totally ignored in this kind of policy.

It is interesting to examine the recommendation for policy and practice made by recent neurological-scientific research. In my view, they bring the ignoring of poverty to a peak of absurdity, as evidenced in an article published in *JAMA Pediatrics* – a top journal in the field – that is dedicated to the effects of poverty on childhood brain development, which concludes that:

> The finding that the *effects of poverty* on hippocampal development are mediated through care-giving and stressful life events further underscores the importance of high-quality early childhood care-giving, a task that can be achieved through *parenting education and support*, as well as through *pre-school programs* that provide high quality *supplementary care-giving* and a safe haven to vulnerable young children. (Luby et al, 2013: 1141, emphases added)

The absurdity lies in the fact that instead of recommending unequivocally the adoption of a policy to reduce poverty, poverty is masked by the genteel phrases 'parenting education and support', 'pre-school programs' and 'supplementary care-giving'. Although some neurological and brain researchers use their findings to recommend anti-poverty policy that addresses the poverty of children and adults,[6] the more popular usage aims to target children's development through parenting programmes, including: programmes aimed at strengthening parents' acknowledgement and skills in reading to their children; improving their ways of communication; mindfulness/meditation/biofeedback programmes aimed at improving self-regulation; and encouraging a healthy diet and regular exercise to improve the regulation of mood and behaviour[7] (for example, Blair and Raver, 2016; Cates et al, 2016). As Wastell and White (2012) claim, in this context, poverty has become a biological problem, and early intervention that aims to promote neuro-cognitive development is regarded as the next step in the war against poverty, trauma and stress. Meanwhile, the poverty of both children and adults itself remains largely untouched (Wastell and White, 2012).[8]

This discourse also influences social work to ignore poverty and issues of social justice as part of direct practice (Handler and Hasenfeld, 2007; Baines, 2011; Krumer-Nevo et al, 2011). Correcting service users' attitudes and behaviours through re-engineering and surveillance becomes the key role of conservative interventions. People in poverty are treated as objects – the sum of their behavioural characteristics and problems. If the problem is perceived to be 'passivity', the aim of intervention should be to change service users to become active, competitive and industrious. If the problem is service users' 'dependency', intervention should aim to foster independence. A similar logic lies at the heart of intervention aimed to improve parenting, negotiate the labour market or manage anger. Those interventions aim to protect people in poverty from themselves or from one another: children from their mothers; women from their men; and men from their tendency towards violence, addiction and other self-destructive behaviour.

Even if softened by empathy, surveillance impacts the helping relationship (Moffatt, 1999). Surveillance might take the form of conditioning material assistance on service users' active participation in the labour market or their cooperation in counselling, or, in the worst case, the threat to take children out of their parents' custody. In all of these interventions, social workers represent the hegemonic definition of 'good' to the poor while maintaining distance or objective separateness from them (Katz, 1995; Lavee and Strier, 2018; Morris et al, 2017).

Wacquant (2010: 201) claims that the punitive character of interventions in the lives of marginalised groups is 'not a deviation from, but a constituent component of the neo-liberal leviathan'. He argues that the management of marginalised populations and increasing state intervention should be understood as part of an expansion of the dominant, 'thin' conception of neoliberalism as a free-market, small-state ideology.

The thrust of my argument is that much of current social work discourse and direct practice is influenced by the conservative paradigm. It adopts a narrow definition of poverty that focuses on the behaviour of people as the cause of their difficulties, and aims to correct it. These practices often fail. Service users do not want to be the objects of surveillance (Dodson and Schmalzbauer, 2005). They rebel openly by not being cooperative or through aggressive behaviour, or covertly by being superficially obedient. When they do so, social workers feel helpless. Even if social workers understand poverty to be a major obstacle in service users' lives, the conservative paradigm does not provide them with the conceptual tools to devise different, more fruitful interventions. When they do not succeed, they can always summarise their efforts by using professional buzzwords such as 'non-cooperative clients', 'chronic case', 'borderline personality', 'lack of motivation for therapy' or 'lack of capability to internalise norms' (Schnitzer,

1996). Although great effort and large budgets are invested in those interventions, the sentiment that they convey could be encapsulated by the statement of a social worker who once described a service user to me by saying, 'She is a total loss.'

The structural paradigm

Ontology

The answer of the structural paradigm to the ontological question 'What is poverty?' is totally different from that of the conservative paradigm. The main argument of the structural paradigm is that poverty is the consequence of societal inequality: a structure of limited opportunities (Rank, 2005; Wilson, 1987, 1996; Royce, 2018) that is particularly confining for certain groups, such as women or minority ethnic groups. This structure manifests itself in: restricted, isolated, non-unionised, short-term and unsafe jobs (Zeytinoglu and Muteshi, 2000; Quigley, 2003; Karjanen, 2016); unhealthy housing and violent neighbourhoods (Wilson, 1987, 1996; Chetty and Hendren, 2016); low-quality schools (Chubb and Moe, 1996; Peters and Mullis, 1997; Bassok and Galdo, 2016); a lack of access to health services (Bond, 1999; Bywaters, 2007); and weak, stigmatising and privatised welfare systems (Dominelli, 1999). Contrary to the focus of the conservative paradigm on pathological behaviours, inequality is a key component of the structural paradigm, and is understood not only in terms of the conditions of the poor, but also in connection to the rich, as well as in terms of the distribution of wealth in a given society and the paths to social mobility (Wilkinson and Pickett, 2010; Atkinson, 2015).

Viewing poverty as a problem of societal inequality dramatically changes the analysis of service users' situations. Instead of an essentialist perception that regards their difficulties as manifestations of culture or of individual deficits and pathologies, these difficulties are perceived to be an outcome of the limiting context of poverty and the lack of any real alternatives. Adopting a contextual rather than an essentialist perception provides very different answers to the questions that the conservative paradigm is constantly occupied by or, as matter of fact, consumed by: 'Why do people develop long-term dependency on governmental allowances?'; 'Why do women become single parents?'; and 'Why do people prefer not to work when they can work?'

Whereas the long-term reliance of service users on state cash benefits is interpreted in the conservative paradigm as an expression of people's essential dependency, the structural paradigm perceives it to be an expression of the consequence of living in a poor neighbourhood with inadequate schooling and housing that does not provide the inhabitants with the necessary capabilities for an advanced integration into the labour market (for a critical analysis of 'welfare dependency' as a discursive construction, see Fraser and Gordon, 1994). The choice to become a single-parent family, perceived in the conservative framework as an expression of the irresponsibility of women, is interpreted in the structural paradigm as a rational response to the limited availability of men who can become reliable breadwinners in the context of poverty, violence, incarceration and unemployment (Edin and Kefalas, 2005), or as a rational reaction to public housing policy that ignores the needs of childless single women (Krumer-Nevo, 2005). A structural interpretation to the issue of work versus welfare benefits does not regard non-working life as a behavioural or moral pathology, but as a rational preference for a stable and secure, though limited, sum of money rather than an unstable and insecure job under highly unaffordable conditions in the labour market (see, for example, Achdut and Stier, 2020). It is significant that while the conservative approach places the responsibility for both poverty-related distress and emergence from it on people in poverty, the structural approach places it on societal institutions.

Epistemology

Although there are major differences between the conservative and structural paradigms in terms of their ontological premises, they both share a positivist-based epistemological standpoint, which sees the professional as the main source of objective knowledge. However, the structural paradigm does not target the pathologies of people in poverty, but rather the deficits and pathologies of society. Instead of getting to know service users' individual or family characteristics, the structural social worker evaluates social problems through statistical or community-based information regarding societal inequality, such as health, education and housing systems. This knowledge will inform practice.

Social workers who adopt the structural paradigm framework see poverty as man-made evil. In line with the emphasis on societal pathologies in the macro-sphere, in personal social services, they would not evaluate service users' pathologies, but rather their strengths.[9] This epistemic stance takes a softer version of the conservative stance on the position regarding knowledge. Similar to the conservative social workers, social workers who work according to the lines of the structural paradigm aim to gain 'objective' knowledge as the basis of intervention. However, they differ from the conservative practitioners because of the emphasis that they put on partnership with service users in knowledge accumulation. The relationships with service users are important for them but they are limited to the joint fight against unjust policies.

Axiology

In terms of axiology, the structural paradigm relies on values that suit a socialist or welfare state ideology, which sees the 'good' as attaining social equality and justice. Thus, the aim of the structural paradigm is to change society, not the people who take the brunt of its inequality and unjustness. The role of social workers is not to represent society vis-a-vis service users, but the opposite: to be agents of social change. Hence, the aim of intervention is not to improve the conditions of people in poverty alone, but to cure society as a whole. The distinction between 'deserving' and 'undeserving' poor becomes irrelevant in this context, and all poor people are equally worthy of assistance.

Practice derived from the structural paradigm

The perception of poverty as the result of institutional and structural arrangements emphasises the politics of redistribution (Lister, 2004), which aims to change the structural barriers that push people into poverty and prevent them from escaping it. These ideas have inspired a long tradition of macro-practice, defined by Netting, Kettner and McMurtry (2016: 3) as 'the professional directed intervention designed to bring about planned change in organizations and communities'. Macro-practice includes community organisation and development, social planning, social action, social administration, policy practice (Gal and Weiss-Gal, 2013), and community activism (Hardcastle et al, 2004). The perspective of the macro-practice social worker is based on the assumption 'that if the community, with its organizations and institutions and behavior patterns, can function more effectively and be more responsive to its members, the members of the community will be healthier and happier' (Hardcastle et al, 2004: 4).

Although the birth of macro-practice social work, attributed to Jane Adams's Settlement House, had a strong orientation towards social justice, and some branches of macro-practice – especially community activism and policy practice – are loyal to the aim of achieving social justice, current neoliberal ideology has weakened the links between most of the practice undertaken by macro-practitioners and social justice (Reisch and Garvin, 2016). Ferguson (2008: 99–100) differentiates between two approaches of community social work: one is 'primarily concerned with community work as a technique for restoring equilibrium between essentially harmonious social systems'; the other sees 'community action as means both of promoting political change and of securing new resources in poor communities'. The tendency of macro-practice social work towards a conservative-oriented practice is strengthened by the fact that community social workers are often employed, directly or indirectly, by the state (Hardcastle et al, 2004), and hence serve the interests of the state to improve itself through small-scale social reforms without challenging the neoliberal infrastructure. Ferguson (2008: 44) describes the ideology of New Labour in Britain as a 'communitarian philosophy which sees community as first and foremost a mechanism of social control, and a vehicle for disciplining and regulating the behaviour of its more wayward members'. Moreover, the increased reliance of voluntary organisations on government-funded projects limits the freedom of community social workers to act as agents of social justice.

Why do we need a third paradigm?

Evidence shows that social work practitioners do adopt structural explanations of poverty (Weiss, 2005, 2006; Weiss and Gal, 2006).[10] Moreover, over the years, significant efforts have been made to translate structural analysis into direct practice (Fook, 1993; Dominelli, 1997; Ife, 1997; Pease and Fook, 1999; Lundy, 2004; Goldberg Wood and Tully, 2006; Mullaly, 2007). However, the influence of these efforts on mainstream direct practice has remained marginal (Ferguson, 2008; Hill et al, 2010; Rothman and Mizrahi, 2014), leaving social services to the dominant conservative paradigm that has inspired a rich agenda of social work interventions (Specht and Courtney, 1994; Figueira-McDonough, 2007; Ferguson, 2008; Kam, 2014).[11] Indeed, after many years of teaching poverty, I know that structural analysis does not translate well into the analysis of individual service users and fails to inspire direct practice. Often, social workers do not see the connections between the interpersonal relationships of direct practice and the politics of redistribution that is negotiated and determined at the level of policymakers. Hence, they find it hard to integrate the notion that poverty is a manifestation of inequality into an understanding of the micro-level of specific service users' behaviours and choices. Again and again, I have heard my students saying:

> 'I know that poverty is the result of unequal and unjust societal arrangements, but with Alia, my client, it's different. She really is responsible for her poverty because she got married too early, has too many children, will not take the job offered to her, or spends money on hair dye instead of buying food.'

The PAP is an attempt to bridge this gap between structural analysis and micro-level behaviours and relationships. It is an updated critical paradigm that builds on structural analysis and adds to it a detailed analysis of the impact of poverty not only as a material condition, but also as a condition that has shaped the interpersonal realm of life. It aims to develop a complete and comprehensive way of doing direct practice with people in poverty.

The Poverty-Aware Paradigm

Ontology

The PAP conceives of poverty as a violation of human rights. The United Nations (UN) has supported this approach through the 2012 Resolution 21/11, which calls upon states to eliminate extreme poverty in a human rights-based manner (United Nations, 2012). This approach builds on and extends the structural analysis of poverty, viewing poverty not only as a lack of material resources and social opportunities (for example, adequate housing, education and health), but also as a lack of symbolic capital, manifested in stigmatisation, discrimination and the lack of voice. Based on the inspiring work of Ruth Lister (2004: 8), we conceptualise poverty as a wheel comprised of three layers (see Figure 1.1).[12]

The hub is the lack of material capital that creates 'unacceptable hardship' (Spicker, 2006: 240; Daly, 2018).[13] The second layer is the lack of social opportunities, manifested in the unsatisfactory fulfilment of the rights to education, housing, health, employment, personal security and welfare. While these aspects are embodied in the structural paradigm, the PAP adds the third circle, entailing the relational/symbolic aspects of poverty. These include disrespect, humiliation, shame and stigma, assault on dignity and self-esteem, Othering, diminished citizenship, and being denied the position of being knowledgeable.[14]

Figure 1.1: The poverty wheel

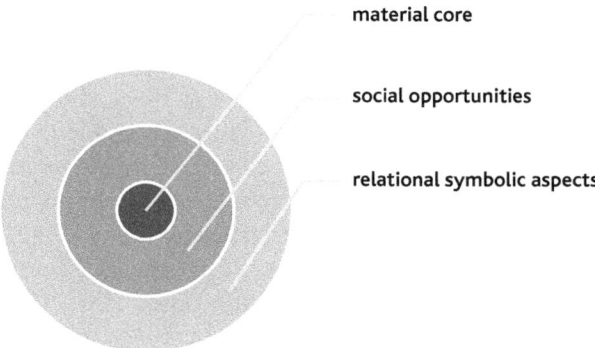

The inclusion of relational/symbolic aspects in the definition of poverty is transformational, and it has major implications for social work. Its importance lies in the rich array of interpersonal interactions that it can open up and in the political charge that they embody. The understanding that poverty is not only an issue of inequality located in the macro-sphere, but also an issue of injustice on the micro-level, sheds light on the everyday experiences of people in poverty, in which they feel the effects of power and powerlessness. These experiences, which the psychiatrist Pierce (1970) labelled 'micro-aggressions', consist of the subtle, seemingly innocuous behaviours engaged in by the non-poor, including professionals, in their interactions with people in poverty.

The following anecdote illustrates the interconnections between the three layers of the poverty wheel. Tal, a social work student, accompanied Gila to the electric company to settle Gila's debt. The clerk, seated in an open space that offered no privacy, was sympathetic and tried to help but needed her supervisor's approval to do so. She called loudly to the other side of the large, crowded office: 'Svetlana ... I need your advice, I've got a welfare case here.' Gila said nothing but Tal saw her cringing silently.

Gila's dependence on Svetlana's help in this situation prevented her from protesting against the humiliating remark by the clerk. Using the stigmatising idiom 'welfare case' is a clear example of micro-aggression and was felt as such by Gila, as the cringing manifested. The destructive impact of micro-aggression lies in the immediate pain that it evokes; however, more than solely that, it also lies in the fact that other members of society disregard it. The fact that these aggressions take place at the micro-level makes it very easy to ignore and deny them (Spicker, 1984; Chase and Walker, 2013; Walker et al, 2013; Walker and

Bantebya-Kyomuhendo, 2014). Like unnamed trauma, they become experiences that are not narrated or shared with others, are not talked of in public, and are not processed within the self (Gupta, 2015).

In addition, placing the manifestations of the symbolic dimensions of poverty in interpersonal relations at the centre of the analysis has made possible a new theorisation of welfare that recognises poor people as active social agents who resist their hardship on an everyday basis. Recent research shows that the basic experience of poor people is of resisting poverty (for example, Chamberlayne and Rustin, 1999; Narayan et al, 2000; Regev-Messalem, 2014; for a detailed account of the ways in which people resist poverty, see also Lister, 2004: 124–57). This struggle remains hidden from non-poor people as long as it is unsuccessful, and because poverty is not ultimately overcome, the illusion is created that poor people have not been trying to escape it. In contrast, recognising the resistance of service users to their situation makes them partners in efforts to combat poverty (Williams et al, 1999, cited in Lister, 2004). This is so even when their struggle takes the form of passivity or even self-harming behaviour.

To sum up, the ontological premise of the PAP sees poverty as a violation of human rights, stemming from injustice and unequal socio-economic structures that manifest both in the limited opportunities open to poor people for education, employment, health, housing and so on, and in the area of interpersonal relations through limited opportunities for recognition, honour and respect. In this ontological perspective, people in poverty are perceived to be resisting poverty in their daily lives, both in explicit and roundabout ways.

Epistemology

In contrast to the positivistic stance of the conservative and structural paradigms, the epistemic foundation of the PAP is critical-constructivist. This approach challenges the pretension of positivist epistemology to reveal objective truth or truthfully represent autonomous reality (Anastas, 2012; Parton and O'Byrne, 2000). The *constructivist* component of the PAP's epistemology allows it to focus on reality as a construct produced through social relationships and interactions. This means that knowledge is always partial and positional. One needs to include various sources of knowledge in order to get a fuller picture of reality, including life knowledge that originates in experience. The *critical* component is the one that adds a focus on power relationships and processes as the context in which reality and knowledge are constructed (Kincheloe, 2005). Thus, it is not enough to ask service users for their opinion. One has to take into account the situation and context in which the question is asked, especially the differences in social and symbolic capital that each of the parties holds.

According to this epistemology, every process of knowledge production is highly political. As such, professional knowledge aimed at knowing the Other always entails a position regarding the status quo, which it either supports or challenges (Rossiter, 1996; Ife, 2005). For instance, a professional assessment regarding service users' motivation is usually granted legitimacy and has significant power over service users' lives. Meanwhile, the service user's assessment of the social worker's motivation to help them or to understand them is not granted any legitimacy. Although the latter assessment might be valid and true, it does not count and does not have any impact on the social worker. The PAP's epistemic stance shifts the discussion from questions such as 'Is the family motivated to change?' to new questions, such as 'Who makes decisions regarding the family's motivation?' and 'What power is granted to the family to determine its own motivation?'

The PAP considers with the same seriousness knowledge regarding the concrete reality of the lack of money together with the endless obstacles that it creates *and* the socially limiting context that people in poverty face in their interpersonal encounters with the general society. The paradigm is based on a continuous effort to create a complete knowledge of poverty: how does it look exactly? What does it mean in terms of handling everyday tasks? What difficulties does it place in the way of people trying to fulfil their dreams? What does it mean in terms of interpersonal relationships and opportunities for recognition? These questions challenge the conservative paradigm that essentialises poverty and directs our attention to poverty as a historical construct given moral and cultural meaning in a specific ideological context.

The relationship between professionals and service users, regarded by those who ascribe to the positivist worldview as an obstacle to objectivist knowledge, is the starting point for the PAP's epistemology and the main arena in which professional knowledge for assessment and intervention is to be obtained (Howe, 1997, 1998; Ruch, 2005). In the spirit of Howe's (1998: 55) call for 'a framework that unites the way we understand people with the way we work with them', we term this *relationship-based knowledge*.

Relationship-based knowledge has five principles, all of which have strong links to PAP practice since the way in which practice is performed enables or prevents the development of this kind of knowledge. First, the relationship should be close and based on ongoing, stable contact. In order for social workers to understand service users' subjective experience, knowledge regarding their lives should be gathered not solely through one-on-one interactions or the superficial reports of other professionals, but rather through diverse interactions that reveal the real context of their lives (Saar-Heiman et al, 2017).

Second, and in accordance with the ontological premise, desired knowledge should be based on an understanding that poverty affects every aspect of service users' lives. This understanding should lead social workers to be interested in and to ask service users about the various concrete manifestations of their material deficit, their dealings with the social institutions that govern their daily lives and their subjective experiences regarding their lack of symbolic capital.

Third, relationship-based knowledge entails a deep sense of the perspective of people in poverty. Based on the idea of positionality, the intersectionality of poverty and other aspects of marginality (for example, gender, race, ethnicity and disability) are theorised to have created a unique perspective on society (Crenshaw, 1991). Thus, social work practice should be guided by service users' perspectives and knowledge and should be framed in accordance with this new knowledge.

Fourth, relationship-based knowledge is based on the hermeneutics of faith, which aims to restore meaning to a text, in contrast to the hermeneutics of suspicion, which attempts to decode disguised meanings (Josselson, 2004). In practice, using the hermeneutics of faith as a guide, social workers treat service users as if they say what they can in order to get help. This standpoint assumes that service users are always aware of the imbalanced power relations between them and social workers. Hence, service users might not tell the entire truth, but at any particular moment, they tell what they can in accordance with the level of trust that they have developed with their social worker and their assessment regarding the power and choice that they have in any specific encounter. The role of the social worker is thus to 'examine the various messages inherent in ... [the] text, giving "voice" in various ways to the participant(s)' (Josselson, 2004: 1).

Fifth, relationship-based knowledge does not require jargon, or alienated language, which reduces service users' subjectivity and treats them as 'cases' (Moffatt, 1999). The practice of writing psychosocial assessments should be guided by tangibility and specificity, as well as rendered in language that describes daily difficulties, in order to provide a space for a mutual, shared investigation of solutions and interventions (Rojeck et al, 1988).

The following example illustrates the subversive nature that this relationship-based knowledge can take and its effect on practice. Dana asked her social worker for material assistance in order to buy dining room furniture. When offered a certain set – the only one that she could afford with the assistance that she had received – Dana refused to take it because it had iron legs, saying that she preferred wooden ones. The social worker, who had known Dana only briefly, was tempted to interpret this reaction as proof that she was ungrateful or not as poor as she claimed. Yet, when she overcame this temptation and continued to help her find more suitable furniture, Dana revealed that her husband had been violent towards her and their children, and had hit them with pieces of furniture. Her rejection of the iron-legged table and chairs was not the 'spoiled' reaction of an ungrateful, poor woman, but rather the rational calculation of a mother protecting her children and herself. Understanding this point changed the social worker's perspective on helping Dana to purchase the wooden furniture.

Axiology

In line with the PAP's ontology, which sees poverty as a violation of rights and poor people as active agents fighting poverty, and with the epistemological notion of knowledge as developing in relationships shaped by imbalanced power, the PAP takes an axiological stance of solidarity with service users and challenging power relations. These are the leading principles of PAP practice. Since people are perceived to be resisting poverty, the position that social workers should adopt is not to motivate them, but to side with them in their resistance in order to ensure its success. To achieve this, practitioners need to overcome the Othering that is so prevalent in the professional and public discourse, and develop an ethic of solidarity. Being the extension 'of our sense of "we" to people whom we have previously thought of as "they"', solidarity is created by 'the imaginative ability to see strange people as fellow sufferers ... by increasing our sensitivity to the particular details of the pain and humiliation of other, unfamiliar sorts of people' (Rorty, 1989: 192).

The ethic of solidarity rests upon highly politicised ground since it is achieved through the acknowledgement of power differences that originate from one's history and social position. Juhila (2003) describes how in order to obtain assistance, service users must adopt the institutional identity of 'good' clients, that is, to show that they need the social worker's help and have the motivation to be helped, and to avoid questioning professional knowledge or criticising institutional policy. Engaging in behaviours that deviate from these constraints puts service users at risk of being construed as 'bad' clients, who are undeserving of professional assistance (Juhila, 2003). Moreover, as social service users, they are constantly regarded as objects of suspicion for cheating and lying in order to be entitled to benefits (Bullock, 1999; Handler and Hasenfeld, 2007; Patrick, 2016). Bureaucracy and neo-managerialism have institutionalised these attitudes and made them appear 'natural' (Handler and Hasenfeld, 2007; Cummins, 2018). In this context, achieving solidarity across power relations requires specific awareness of the effects of power (Rossiter, 2007) and Othering on professional practice. According to our paradigm, solidarity means that social workers take a stance and behave as partners of their service users in their struggle against poverty. Where the conservative paradigm aims to change service users' behaviour or attitudes, the PAP aims to change service users' conditions in society. Expressed differently, instead of representing societal attitudes by telling their service users what is wrong with their behaviour, decisions or attitudes, and what needs to be fixed in their relationships, poverty-aware social workers will represent their service users' perspectives on the social structure, social institutions and the social constructions of poverty to the society at large.

In extreme cases, the attitude of standing by service users might create ethical dilemmas regarding the stance that professionals should take vis-a-vis possible violations of the law. Should a social worker conceal the fact that service users work informally though they claim to be unemployed? What is the role of a social worker who knows that a service user who receives benefits as a single mother actually has a new spouse? These important questions merit further discussion, but for now, we might consider them as a call for social workers to utilise the endless opportunities they have to side with poor people in their Sisyphean struggles[15] with social institutions in cases that are not extreme, and to strive to maintain this position as far as possible in more challenging cases.

Importantly, taking the side of service users does not require complete agreement with their behaviour or attitudes, and, at times, social workers should tell their clients that they do not agree with them or that they think they are acting in a way that harms themselves or others. However, such statements must come from a perspective of understanding service users' pain and realising that under harsh circumstances and difficult situations, this may be the best that they can do. Paradoxically, taking the side of service users creates a space in which social workers can actually criticise them because the criticism is grounded in a relationship of trust.

Practice derived from the PAP paradigm

The PAP adopts Fraser's (2003) and Lister's (2004) articulation of the politics of redistribution and the politics of recognition&respect as two interconnected mediums through which practice is channelled. The politics of redistribution is a tool for achieving economic justice, while the politics of recognition refers to the efforts to get cultural justice. Although they might be applied separately, the PAP sees them as interconnected. As Fraser (2003, emphasis in original) says, a genuinely critical perspective must probe the hidden connections between distribution and recognition: 'It must make visible, and *criticizable*, both the cultural subtexts of nominally economic processes and the economic subtexts of nominally cultural practices.' Practice, then, should be simultaneously economic and cultural, 'albeit not necessarily in equal proportions.... It must assume both the standpoint of distribution and the standpoint of recognition, without reducing either one of these perspectives to the other' (Fraser, 2003: 63).

PAP practice connects redistribution and recognition in two ways. First, it combines methods coming from activist and community social work that focus on redistribution with those coming from relational psychoanalysis and critical social work[16] that emphasise recognition. The politics of recognition&respect in this regard is grounded in a deep understanding of the processes of Othering that shape so much of the interpersonal interactions and personal experiences of people in poverty.

By combining the two methods, the PAP is able to develop an array of practices that target social injustice as both a structural problem that takes place in external reality and an experience of the human subject in internal reality – in the personal and interpersonal spheres. Practices that deal directly with the external world vary from the active actualisation of rights and material assistance, to community development, service development and policy practice. Practices that deal directly with the internal world are based on therapeutic intervention that focuses on close relationships and dealing with issues of power and powerlessness.

Second, the PAP connects the politics of redistribution and the politics of recognition&respect through the understanding that *every* action practitioners take contains aspects of both. This means that each one of the practices mentioned earlier contains aspects of both redistribution and recognition, and constitutes intervention in the external and internal world. When PAP social workers intervene in external reality (redistribution), it is done in a way that takes into consideration the need of people to be recognised and respected, as well as the specific barriers that poverty creates for people striving for recognition. The main goal of the intervention might be to achieve a change in the external reality, but in order to advance social justice, it must also involve recognising service users' knowledge, needs, pain and resistance.

The PAP's practice of the active realisation of rights is a good example of this fusion as it is a way of actualising one's rights based on a deep understanding of the experiences of micro-aggression that form part of the obstacles that cause people to give up their rights in the first place. Similarly, the specific practice of material assistance is based on an understanding that material needs are also experienced emotionally and that their fulfilment or frustration are registered deeply within the self. This contradicts the popular distinction made between basic material needs and emotional needs (a more detailed account of these practices is to be found in Part III, 'Rights').

Combining redistribution and recognition&respect might also take another form, in which the direct goal is gaining recognition. This must be done with careful consideration of the difficulties that originate in the external world and of the role that power plays in external and internal realities. For example, a therapeutic dialogue can move from talking about emotions, dreams and experiences – contents of the internal life – to talking about issues belonging to external reality – like debts or housing – while recognising the effect of power on both. The therapeutic aspects of the intervention will not be exhausted by dealing directly with the internal world, but need to be based on the recognition that the external reality is a major source of deprivation and distress requiring a direct response as well. The dialogue can then move from discussing how to solve a concrete problem (and how to overcome power disparities along the way), to working through emotions.

The purpose of the move between the external and internal worlds is to create bridges between them. In terms of the individual human subject, these bridges are necessary in order to experience the self as a cohesive whole. In terms of social justice, these bridges manifest the political and transformative nature of the battles for both redistribution and recognition in the interpersonal realm. Through these bridges, PAP practice seeks to respond to the three layers of poverty: the material shortage; the lack of social opportunities; and the dearth of relational-symbolic capital. It seeks to overcome the material shortage and to expand the social opportunities realistically open to service users through the development of a specific practice called the 'active realisation of rights', through coordinating services, as well as through policy practice. It strives to grant recognition and to correct situations of a shortage of symbolic capital by establishing a close relationship of solidarity between social workers and service users, based on an analysis of the helping relationship as a power relationship. It intervenes in the real-life context and employs an ongoing critical reflection in order to overcome Othering (Fook and Gardner, 2007).

Neoliberal policy sacrifices poor people for economic growth, and the policy of new managerialism, with its focus on outcomes, leads to the abandonment of the ethical aspect of social work practice, the individualisation of social problems and the Othering of poor people (Featherstone, 2016). Based on an understanding of the political nature of the interpersonal encounters between social workers and service users, the PAP challenges these trends and calls for social workers to base their practice on a fiercely analytical attitude regarding social structures, ideologies and constructions. Grounded in this analysis, social workers can take a stand, adopt an approach of resisting poverty, side with poor people in their day-to-day struggles, be positional and involved, and reshape practice as a vehicle of social justice.

Notes

[1] An earlier, shortened version of this chapter was published in the *British Journal of Social Work*, 46(6): 1793–808 (2015).

[2] The term is based on the call by Davis and Wainwright (2005: 261) to social workers to develop a poverty-aware approach that includes 'detailed understanding of poverty's impacts on their clients on the individual, organizational, and social levels'.

[3] Oscar Lewis is a key figure for understanding the conservative paradigm. He grew up in poverty as the son of a family of immigrants to the US from Eastern Europe. During his youth, he was exposed to Marxist and socialist ideas, and was influenced by them. As he advanced in his academic career, he opted to devote his life to ethnographic research on poor communities for progressive aims. For years, he lived with his wife in poor neighbourhoods in urban centres and villages in Mexico, Puerto Rico and Cuba, as well as in the slums of New York, in order to describe poverty from close up. He wanted his descriptions to become evidence of the hardship and the banal cruelty of daily life in poverty and an indictment against the society that created these situations. His ethnographies were novel for their time. Indeed, his research influenced the Johnson administration's policy of a war on poverty. However, alongside the ethnographic studies, he published a short article on the culture of poverty, which transformed the concept of 'the culture of poverty' into a popular concept that connotes an individualistic discourse that blames people for their poverty (Rigdon, 1988). It is interesting how a well-intended scholar who had known poverty from personal experience found himself contributing to the conservative discourse that he objected to.

[4] Garrett (2018: 88) describes the term 'underclass' as developing from the concepts of the 'social residuum' of the 1880s, the 'social problem group' of the 1930s, the

'problem family' in the 1950s (and 1990s) and 'troubled family' of today. He does not refer to the 'culture of poverty', though I regard the links to be quite obvious.

5. The picture was first introduced by Perry (2002) in a study that examined four different types of neglect. The differences from the norm were observed with only one type of severe neglect; moreover, brain size and function recovered when these children were removed from the neglectful environment and placed in foster care. As Garrett (2018) shows, one of the examples of the picture's dominance and tempting emotive strength is to be seen in the choice of British parliament member Graham Allen (2011) to use it on the cover of his first and second Independent Reports on Early Intervention. In Israel, the picture has become very popular in the training of social workers on trauma, and is mainly used to point to the harm caused to children by neglectful poor mothers.

6. For example, see Johnson, Riis and Noble (2016), who conclude a state-of-the-art review on poverty and the developing brain published in *Pediatrics* by warning that 'attributing risk based on socio-economic resources alone may unnecessarily stigmatize families and communities whose children are thriving despite constrained resources'. They go on to say: 'On the other hand, pediatricians may serve as ideal advocates for programs and supports that provide financial benefits to poor families ... and in efforts to reduce socioeconomic disparities' (Johnson et al, 2016: 12). See also Chaudry and Wimer (2016: s25), who claim that 'Taken together, the body of the evidence does suggest that improved income and reduced poverty can lead to meaningful improvements in children's outcomes, particularly their academic and educational outcomes.'

7. In a three-part series published in the prestigious medical journal *Lancet*, McCoy et al (2017) review the evidence regarding poverty, brain development and slower early childhood development, as well as the measures to overcome it. While poverty is given a leading role in the review of the causes of impairments in brain and childhood development, it is absent in the review of recommended measures to overcome it, which focus mainly on effective early childhood development programmes.

8. Wastell and White (2012: 397) criticise the policy in the UK, concluding that 'The co-option of neuroscience has medicalised policy discourse, silencing vital moral debate and pushing practice in the direction of standardised, targeted interventions rather than simpler forms of family and community support, which can yield more sustainable results.'

9. Mullaly (2007) developed a comprehensive proposal for radical social work that he called 'structural social work'. In his book's first edition in 1993, he lays out a vision for social work that is based on critical theories and aims at social change. Mullaly's focus on oppression and dominant–subordinate relations as his analytic axis places him closer to PAP than to the structural paradigm as presented here. My aim in presenting the structural paradigm as a positivist approach, and not as a radical/critical one, is to conceptualise the dominant school of thought that has inspired community social work. Although this school of thought originates in a transformative sentiment, it has been developing as a more reformative movement over time.

10. A structural causality of poverty was associated with higher interest in working with the poor among social work students (see Weiss, 2006).

11. In a book on his experience as a psychoanalyst in a public clinic in New York, Neil Altman (2011) describes one of his colleagues, the director of a care unit in a hospital, who held a seminar called 'The Other patient' in order to learn how

to work with poor service users. The point was that the majority of the patients of this unit were living in poverty. They were 'the Other' because they did not match the ideal of the private patient. Altman uses it to show that the deceptions built into therapeutic theories with regard to the question of who is treatable allow professionals, even those with liberal political ideas, to marginalise poor people without viewing it as a political act.

[12] Lister suggests a two-layer wheel that includes the material core and the relational/symbolic aspects. The intermediate layer is my addition.

[13] Daly (2018) calls not to dismiss money and material resources too readily by pushing into broader conceptualisations of poverty, such as capability, social exclusion or deprivation.

[14] Lister mentions all the aspects listed here except the last. Since her book was published, there has been more and more attention paid to the recognition/non-recognition of knowledge as an important part of Othering and the struggle against Othering. The ATD Fourth World Movement has contributed to this (see Krumer-Nevo, 2005; Fourth World University Research Group, 2007; Gupta and Blewett, 2008).

[15] Roose, Roets and Bouverne-De Bie (2011) propose to 'imagine the social worker as a *happy Sisyphus* and as a productive social worker who embraces the irony of complexity and ambiguity as a vital element of social work practice'. They call to see the ambiguity of social work as an opportunity to stay engaged and to act reflexively in the face of complex social problems.

[16] Activist and community social work offers relevant methods of intervention at the macro-level, such as community organising, service development and policy practice. Current psychology, especially the updated version of relational psychology, and critical social work, mainly feminist and anti-oppressive social work, offer methods of intervention at the micro-level.

PART I

Transformation

This part of the book unfolds four points of view regarding the transformational character of the PAP. Similarly to other critical traditions, such as feminisms, the PAP offers a way of seeing the world. Its perspective reveals to us aspects of reality that were previously concealed. Once we adopt this perspective, we cannot avoid seeing power relations, structural injustice and Othering.

The first two chapters of Part I, 'Transformation', exemplify how this new way of seeing the world changes the ways in which social workers speak and write about service users. Chapter 2, 'How to speak critically about poverty', provides an overview of six basic principles of the paradigm and their translation into spoken professional language. Since it is based on a lecture given in 2013 to an audience of practitioners, it sounds something like a manifesto. It urges social workers to be aware of the language they use and to change it.

Chapter 3, 'How to write a critical case study', is written in a much more pedagogical-academic manner. It is based on an analysis of a case study written by a social worker for a group supervision in one of the PAP courses organised by the Ministry of Welfare and Social Services in 2016. This weighty chapter covers ideas regarding the politics of representation and exemplifies how writing according to these ideas changes the case study. Following what took place in the class, the chapter presents three versions of the same case study and offers some guidelines for the critical writing of such a text. This chapter can serve social workers who wish to gain insight into this aspect of their work and can also be used for teaching purposes; I find it very useful in my own teaching. After discussing the theoretical principles presented at the beginning of the chapter, I give my students the first version of the case study and ask them to write their own comments on it in order to help the social worker who wrote it to turn it into a critical text. Only then do we read the second and third versions together.

Chapter 4, 'How to teach poverty critically', deals explicitly with teaching. It is based on a lecture at an international academic seminar, and describes the challenge of revealing social workers' basic conservative conceptual framework and replacing it with a critical one. The chapter presents this challenge as containing both cognitive and emotional elements. I recommend this chapter for those who are involved in teaching professionals.

The concluding Chapter 5, 'Frequently asked questions about poverty and poverty-aware social work', is exactly that: a list of ten questions that often arise during the process of learning the paradigm. When they are first introduced to the PAP, students often say that they find it difficult to defend the critical perspective in their discussions on social issues with friends and family members. This chapter aims to be of assistance in this regard.

2

How to speak critically about poverty

This chapter is a version of a lecture given in 2013 at a conference entitled 'Speaking Differently about Poverty'. The conference was initiated by an Israeli organisation, Shoulder to Shoulder. The participants were mostly practitioners, joined by people from local government, philanthropic causes, the business sector, third sector organisations and the Ministry of Welfare and Social Services. With the influence of the wave of mass social protest in 2011 and the establishment of the National Committee to Combat Poverty in 2013, this conference marked the beginning of renewed interest in poverty among practitioners. The warm responses that I received were an expression that this large and diverse audience was ready to think openly about poverty.[1]

Introduction

When I was a young social worker 20 years ago, I felt that my experience and understanding of the women and men living in poverty with whom I worked was different from that of my colleagues. I felt it strongly in the language that we used when talking about service users during team meetings or when chatting in the corridor. All in all, feeling different from my colleagues was an unpleasant experience for me. I am happy that there are many more people today who talk and think similarly to me. I have been fortunate to have some of them as academic colleagues and some as fellow practitioners; others are my past and present students.

Since that time, I have been developing the Poverty-Aware Social Work Paradigm (PAP) that is currently being implemented in a fieldwork training programme for social work students at Ben-Gurion University. What I would like to present here today are six principles of the paradigm that inform the way in which we speak about poverty. Our rhetoric – the way we speak – is important because the language that we use reveals our basic, sometimes unconscious, assumptions regarding service users and regarding our own role. It denotes our social status, social class and position with regard to the subject that we are talking about. We can describe the same behaviour of a service user by saying that 'She stood up for herself' or that 'She was aggressive and demanding.' These two forms of expression display not only our basic assumptions towards her, but also our response to that woman.

The first principle is to acknowledge the knowledge of people in poverty, to view people living in poverty as having legitimate and important knowledge

This is a fundamental principle that is always relevant. It is relevant not only when their knowledge seems 'right' or 'good' to people with no direct experience with poverty, but also, and especially, in cases where this knowledge seems to outsiders to be wrong or partial, or as the kind of knowledge that has led to service users' problems. Acknowledging the 'knowledge' of people in poverty means that one has to acknowledge what people have to say about reality, as well as to understand reality through their eyes – to acknowledge their point of view and perspective. Moreover, it includes acknowledging their analysis of reality, in other words, the rationale and the theories that they are guided by. People are guided by theories, and theories exist for everybody, irrespective of one's level of education. People have theories even if they are not in the habit of explaining them to others or to themselves.

The meaning of 'knowledge' as I see it might be better understood if I compare it to the popular use of the concept of 'voice'. When I first thought about the way in which professionals treat the knowledge of people in poverty, I thought the crucial step that social workers should take is to move 'from noise to voice', meaning to stop seeing people living in poverty as creating 'noise' and begin seeing them as having a 'voice'. I thought that what people often say or the way in which they behave in their efforts to resist poverty is perceived as 'noise': an indistinct, undefined, irrelevant, repulsive and distancing cacophony. As I saw it, they hate poverty and do not accept it, but what they do, especially when they do not succeed in combating poverty, is regarded as 'noise'. As a result, it is not surprising that much of the response to their actions and behaviour was directed at restraining them and lowering their voice – 'civilising' them.

Instead, I suggested regarding them as having a voice. Based on the original use of the term by the feminist Carol Gilligan (1993) as a metaphor for the knowledge of marginalised groups, I thought that 'voice' would capture the normative essence of the perspectives of people in poverty and the interpersonal exchange of voicing and listening. However, over time, the term 'voice' has lost its original, radical force and has been abused. I realised that in the context of asymmetric power relations, it was being used to say, 'I accept that this is your voice, and I will let you have your say', in the sense of, 'I allow you to express your experience, but it is your subjective or idiosyncratic experience, and therefore, regretfully, we are unable to use it or to consider its relevance.'

Under the influence of the body of work by ATD Fourth World (1996), as well as through the ideas of Peter Beresford and his colleagues (Beresford and Turner,1997; Beresford and Wilson, 1998; Beresford et al, 1999), I realised that the concept of 'voice' needed to be changed to 'knowledge'. Thinking about people living in poverty as having *knowledge*, not only voice, reduces the fundamental gap in power relations present in professional interactions and compels us to develop new ways of listening and a new type of dialogue. When thinking with the aid of the concept of 'voice', the aim of the intervention is perceived to be assisting service users to make their voice heard. Whereas, when using the concept of 'knowledge', the implication is that service users have knowledge that contains perspective, theory, attitude and experience, just like professionals. Thus, as Bruno Tardieu (1999: 175) from ATD Fourth World phrased it: 'We discovered that the main thing was not to give the poor the chance to make their voice heard, but to open our ears. It is not about empowering the poor, but about humanizing citizens and institutions.' Thus, the professional aim is to bring about change among us – among the professionals; it is we who need to learn how to listen and to identify the knowledge of service users, as well as how to take account of it in decision-making processes.

The second principle is to recognise the pain of people living in poverty

Rosa, one of the first service users that I met as a social worker, was a woman whose child was taken away from her when he was three months old. When I got to know her, he was 16 and had spent his whole life in institutions – the best our system had to offer. However, at age 16, he had not been to school or worked at all, and his future did not look bright. She used to say:

> 'I have been a social services client for 40 years and what have I got out of it? My son is disturbed, and you did it to him. You said I was not capable of being a good mother, but it seems you did not exactly succeed with him either.'

As I said, I was a very young social worker and I thought to myself:

> 'What are you talking about? *We* did not succeed? He used to come back to us after home visits with burn marks from cigarettes, and *you* come to *us* with complaints? The very fact that you are complaining is a symptom of your problems – a sign of your external locus of control and your inability to be introspective and to change.'

However, this type of listening led nowhere. Like anybody else, she hated it when she felt blamed or attacked. Her inability to be a good mother pained her. This stemmed from a very deep place of failure. If we listen carefully, we do not hear her as somebody who has an 'external locus of control' or an 'inability to be introspective'; rather, we hear somebody speaking indirectly about her pain. She speaks about it indirectly because she is not used to people listening to her. As nobody wants to admit failure, especially a failure of motherhood, the moment I spoke to her about how much she wanted to be a good mother, how extremely difficult it was and also how hard it was for her to give him up, some of her anger dissipated. Hence, the second principle is to listen to the pain, to understand that what we perceive as people's behaviour is part of a wider emotional world. Giving recognition to the knowledge of people in poverty also involves recognising the pain connected to poverty and understanding behaviour not as autonomous, but as having emotional causes. In a way, it is about seeing service users as subjects who carry social suffering.

The third principle is that the material/concrete and the emotional are always interconnected

As opposed to Maslow, who ranked needs in hierarchical order, placing concrete needs ahead of emotional needs, what we learn from people living in poverty is just how closely linked these two kinds of needs are. To illustrate this point: people can give up basic needs if they are not given to them in the way that they want; and people can live in the street in protest at their apartment being small or cramped. The significance of this is that every statement made by professionals regarding the concrete, material world needs to take account of its emotional content. When a social worker says to a woman who comes to the office as winter approaches to request blankets that there are no blankets, she is not only leaving the woman with an unsatisfied concrete need, but also with a serious emotional insult. This is because the woman might feel that she has failed as a mother because, at that moment, she feels that she has failed in our eyes, failed in her attempt to achieve recognition – to make us see her and understand her and the gravity of her distress. Hence, dealing with concrete needs necessarily touches on emotional needs and vice versa, and this complexity should be considered in all our therapeutic interactions.

The fourth principle is that we have to recognise what poverty is and how it expresses itself in the reduction of real opportunities or real alternatives

In other words, we have to recognise everything that people have to forfeit because of their poverty, or that is caused to people by poverty. Poverty does not just cause people to forfeit money and the possibility of buying expensive things, to go on an annual family holiday, to buy good food, to go to the swimming pool during the summer holidays, or to send a child to summer camp. What people also forfeit because of their poverty is opportunities, for instance: the opportunity to be educated; the opportunity for good employment; the opportunity to walk on safe streets and not where the street lighting has been smashed and it is unpleasant to wander around in the dark; and the opportunity to choose the nursery that they want their children to attend because they can only send their children to nurseries that are subsidised by our system. These are all opportunities in the realm of the external reality.

However, the lack of opportunities is also linked to what Ruth Lister (2004) relates as the relational symbolic dimensions of poverty, in other words, the lack of opportunities to feel valued, to be seen as having knowledge, to be respected and to receive recognition. Poverty involves daily experiences of the lack of symbolic capital. This occurs, for instance, when service users take two buses to get to our office, with a baby in their arms, only to discover that we have gone on maternity leave, or that the form they are waiting for has not been signed because our team director is either sick or on holiday. There is no malicious intent, but there is a lack of awareness of the fact that poverty creates a reality in which people are dependent on others to meet their very basic needs, and this consequently creates daily opportunities for demeaning experiences.

Lee Rainwater (1970), a Harvard sociologist, argues that people who do not live in poverty tend to doubt the stories that people tell about their poverty. He claims that this is because we immediately put ourselves in their situation and say to ourselves that we could not live in that situation. It causes us cognitive dissonance: how can other people live in a situation that we could not possibly live in? Rainwater suggests that there are two ways to resolve this dissonance: first, we can say to ourselves that the stories we heard are lies or manipulations – in reality, it is not as hard as service users describe it; and, second, if we see with our own eyes that the reality really is so bad, then we resolve the cognitive dissonance by telling ourselves that service users have got used to it. Apparently, they are not like 'us', who would take it to heart or sink into depression; 'they' survive because they have developed a sort of thick skin.

These two solutions cause alienation between people with and without direct experience of poverty. If service users are liars, as the first option suggests, we deny the very fact of poverty as a horrible situation. If people in poverty have developed a thick skin, as suggested by the second option, we deny their full subjectivity and humanity. Either way, we are establishing people in poverty as Others and creating an unbridgeable gap between us.

The fifth principle is not to accept poverty and to create a practice that stems from opposition to poverty

This is a seemingly very simple statement but it is sometimes difficult to implement. The idea behind it is that poverty is a violation of human rights and social justice. It is a social phenomenon, being the result of socio-economic policy and the structure of the social security system, the job market, public housing, health services and the education system. Poverty does not exist because people have made mistakes in their lives. Rather, it is the result of unjust social structures embodied in certain people who, for various reasons such as their ethnicity, gender, (dis)ability or race, have become the disadvantaged in society.

Our practice should be based on the strong conviction that 'poverty is not alright'. As citizens and as professionals who see poverty from close up, we know that it is not right. It is not right that people do not have food to eat or cannot send their kids to after-school classes, or that they should live in an apartment over a drug den. This is all not right. It is not that the people in poverty are not right, but that the social situation is not right. Anybody who feels now that what I am saying means removing responsibility from poor people is beginning to understand why this apparently simple principle is not simple. I will get to that in a moment. In the meantime, I want you to stay with this feeling of uneasiness in the body. I want you to say out loud: 'Poverty is not alright, poverty is not logical, poverty is not just.' From here, we can connect to people or listen differently. From here, we can accept people who say: 'Poverty is not fair; it's not right for us.'

The sixth and last principle is that people living in poverty constantly resist poverty

They hate poverty. They do not accept it or justify it. Sometimes, they manage to resist it successfully, for example, when they earn enough from working legally. At other times, they resist through illegal work, or through ways that seem destructive to us, for example, when a woman gives birth in order to be entitled to an apartment, or when a young woman has sex with a man who abuses her because she has nowhere else to go. This principle makes us realise that parents who raise their children in poverty wish to be good parents. Their most common aspiration is that their children will live better lives than they have lived. For them, a good life is exactly what it was for Freud: they wish their children to be happy in work and in love.

It is important to appreciate that even in the worst circumstances, people resist poverty and hardship, and people usually know that they are making every effort to resist poverty. Yet, they are sometimes not clear about it. Therefore, it is our role to listen actively for people's resistance actions to their poverty.

Active listening means that we listen and also *say* to people that what they are doing is not an expression of their mistakes or defects. It also means we see that they are doing things to improve their situation, even when these may not be working. When we connect to people's resistance – to their desire to reduce the poverty or its effects – we are handing the responsibility back to them. My contention is that they actually take responsibility all the time. We do not need to motivate them to take responsibility, and we do not need to be afraid to tell them that what is happening to them is unjust, and not all of it is their responsibility.

It is only because their actions are sometimes unsuccessful that it appears they are not taking responsibility. Our task is not to *educate* them to take responsibility, but to help them to succeed in their resistance activities. Our task is to connect to them from a place that says: 'Poverty is not alright. It seems to me that you also think so, and you are doing things in order to improve your situation, but you are not succeeding. Let's see what we can do together to improve your situation.'

This knowledge is created through close relationships with people, through acknowledging their perspective and knowledge, and by recognising their suffering and emotional needs, as well as their reality and the way in which it limits opportunities. It is knowledge that takes the will of people to get out of poverty very seriously and recognises the acts by which they attempt to do so. In short, it is created by standing alongside them and not against them.

Therefore, how does one speak differently about poverty? First, do not say 'poor people', but 'people living in poverty'.[2] 'Poor people' is an attribute, whereas 'people in poverty' are fully human: the poverty is outside them and they can have complex relationships with it – in my view, relationships of resistance.

Second, we must not allow double standards to determine what we say. Professionals often say about people in poverty that they do not plan their time because they arrive late. However, when *we* arrive late, we say that we are 'simply multitasking and sometimes things slip'. When people in poverty do not manage something, we say that 'they do not take responsibility'. However, if we, as professionals, do not have the blanket or food to give, or the permit to supply, we do not say that we are not taking responsibility. We say that we are operating within a limited system. Therefore, I suggest that we take the contextual and compassionate interpretation that we apply to ourselves and to people we love, where we understand that a person is not omnipotent and acknowledge efforts even when they are unsuccessful, and apply it to the people that we work with, who really know what poverty is.

I want to suggest dispensing with a number of words; actually, all the words that nobody wants to hear about themselves, like saying about a woman that she is 'manipulative'. People living in poverty are not more manipulative than other people, but they have fewer opportunities, so they sometimes have to deal with reality by using whatever means they have. Their problem is not their 'manipulative conduct', but the fact that they do not have real opportunities to succeed in other ways. We need to first recognise their actions not as manipulative, but as an attempt to resist poverty. Then, we will be able to connect to what they are doing and know how to increase its effect.

I would be happy to dispense with the phrase 'from dependence to independence', which appears so frequently in the brochures of various intervention programmes. We are all dependent all the time, in one form or another. Without my parents-in-law who helped me look after my children when they were small, I would not have become a professor. I was dependent on them. We are physically and emotionally dependent on our money, our social status, our parents, our children, our work, our friends and our partners. This is not considered 'dependence' because it functions and succeeds, and is sometimes mutual. The problem for people living in poverty is not that they are more dependent, but that they do not have people on whom to be dependent in a beneficial way. They are dependent on impersonal systems that cannot take account of all their needs. Their problem is that they are dependent on social workers who cannot handle dependence because they have too big a caseload. Dependence, in itself, is not a problem. People living in poverty maintain contact with the welfare services not because they have a disturbed psychological need for dependence, but because they understand that without parents and without decent work, a regular income and a bank account, they will not really succeed – and they are right. The problem is not to educate them towards non-dependence, but to offer them opportunities to succeed independently.

A student once told me that a woman she was working with was a 'total loss', a term usually applied to a car after a bad accident. I suggest removing this from the vocabulary as well. I suggest adopting a number of alternative words: poverty is not alright. People living in poverty are not to blame for poverty. They do not like it. They are doing what they can to reduce their hardship. In order for them to succeed, they need our help. Our task is to work alongside them, to find a way to open up possibilities and opportunities for them. Instead of talking about the need to change people living in poverty, I suggest talking about closeness, and to examine to what extent we are close to our service users. I suggest talking about our commitment and involvement, about caring and solidarity. These are the words I suggest as a platform for practice.

Notes

[1] A video of the lecture in Hebrew is available at: www.youtube.com/watch?v=QO0UcMB88n4

[2] I thank my teacher, Jonah M. Rosenfeld, for teaching me this.

3

How to write a critical case study

Semadar, an experienced social worker, wrote the intervention story that forms the core of this chapter for the purpose of a professional consultation in the framework of group supervision. She read the text aloud to the group. The question on which she wanted consultation was not rhetorical, but practical: how do you deal with a family in which children are at risk, with whom all previous attempts to assist have not fared well? When I heard Semadar, I felt that the rhetoric of the text – the specific words that she chose to describe the family – revealed a difficulty in their relationship. Although there was no doubt that the children's situation was worrying, I was concerned about Semadar's difficulty in presenting the family in a way that would reveal both the subjectivity of each of its members and the complexity of the context of their life. After Semadar finished reading the text, we analysed it in the group, noting the principles of writing a critical intervention story. During the week before our next meeting, I commented on Semadar's text and she rewrote it, giving consideration to my comments.

This chapter is based on that supervision and on the later use that I made of the text for the purposes of teaching and training. The chapter includes three versions of that text: the first is the original version written by Semadar that already includes the comments I wrote to her after the first discussion; the second version is the corrected version that Semadar wrote; and the third version was written by me in light of the new information that arose in our second discussion. In addition, the chapter outlines the guidelines for writing a critical psychosocial report.

Introduction

One of the basic ideas of the PAP is simple: professionals constantly need to make an effort to recognise the subjectivity of the people they work with, to view service users as complete people and to bring this recognition to the relationship. In order to recognise service users' subjectivity, one has to also acknowledge the context of poverty in which they live. Therefore, we have subjectivity, on the one hand, and the context of poverty, on the other. Sometimes, recognising subjectivity and context seems like a simple task; however, often, it requires effort because the rules of discourse regarding poverty and the kind of power relationship that characterises the helping relationship lend themselves to reducing the humanity of service users and to ignoring their context.

Social work takes place within the fraught arena of power relations. The social worker's power stems from sources originating outside the realm of professional interaction, like their level of education, social status, class and, in many cases, ethnicity. Social constructions regarding poverty that portray people in poverty as the Other[1] also contribute to these power disparities. However, most importantly, power emanates from the professional encounter: the gap between the social worker's excess power validated by her professional role, and the service users, who are characterised by their problems and are dependent on the social worker's response to fulfil their needs.

The inherent danger in power relationships is that social workers are liable to reduce the total humanity of service users by means of prejudices, Othering and essentialism, rather than contextual interpretations. This danger is more likely to manifest itself when dealing with people in poverty because the judgemental attitudes regarding them are so dominant in the public discourse, and these go hand in hand with the professional inclination to individualise, rather than contextualise, behaviour.

For social workers, the struggle against otherness and the reduction of the humanity and subjectivity of service users needs to be an active struggle, and it should take place at all levels of professional activity, including the level of representation that is manifested in writing professional reports. The question of how to write about service users is not only practical, but also political and ethical. Hence, the representation of the other always reflects more and less conscious choices, interpretive processes, ideologies and professional and public moods. The final status of truth granted to the written text determines and fixes the representations of the described service users and increases the power of the professional.[2] Thus, the supposedly innocent wish to get *to know* the other for the purpose of help carries the potential for both emancipation and subjugation. In the form of emancipation, this process carries the potential for the other to feel understood, supported and empowered. Winnicott's empathic knowing is of this type. In its second form, it carries the potential for subjugation, when the process of knowing stems from the drive to master the other, to control and change them, in what we can call, following Foucault, a panopticon knowing.[3]

Too often, the organisational context of social work and professional jargon produce and justify the latter kind of knowledge (Rojeck et al, 1988; Howe, 1996; Moffatt, 1999; Morris et al, 2017; Grell et al,

2019). In the first kind of knowledge, social workers have a sympathetic regard for the other that, while not avoiding seeing weaknesses and difficulties, places them in a context that gives them meaning and reduces the guilt and shame associated with revealing them. In the second kind of knowledge, social workers take a supervisory approach, which creates an experience of unpleasant exposure, of nakedness involving humiliation. Representing service users, who have immanent representational vulnerability, without falling into the trap of Othering is our challenge for today.

With this aim of avoiding the trap of Othering in mind, let us read Semadar's first text on the Lev family. The comments I wrote to Semadar appear in the footnotes. When reading it, we need to ask ourselves: what do we think and feel about the people described in it? Do we feel close to them? Does the text respect them? Does it present their perspective and knowledge? If they were to read it, would they recognise themselves? What would they think and feel?

The first version: case study,[i] written by Semadar with my comments

The parents are in their late 30s. The mother[ii] – cognitively handicapped, comes from a humble, poorly resourced home. She finds it hard to keep a job, and has difficulty internalising accepted rules and norms. There is something childish and immature about her.[iii] The father[iv] – has a permanent job[v]; comes home every day at five; barely functions; hardly helps around the house.[vi]

They have three children: Moshe (seven) is a school pupil. Avraham (five and a half) is diagnosed with autism, with suspected intellectual disability. He does not talk at all; relieves himself in his pants or on

---

[i] Please insert pseudonym. It will be easier to recognise their subjectivity when they have names. Can you please entitle it 'intervention story' instead of 'case study'?
[ii] Please give her a pseudonym.
[iii] The description here focuses on her faults. Instead, we want to know her history *from her perspective* – how would she describe herself? What is her pain? (What does she find hard?) Where do you identify her resistance to poverty? (What is she trying to achieve and not succeeding? What is she good at?)
[iv] Please give him a pseudonym.
[v] It would be interesting to know what job.
[vi] Add details about the history and present of their relationship – how they met, when they married, their relationship – summarise it in just a few sentences.

the floor. His nursery reports extreme restlessness, unease and violent behaviour towards the staff and the other children. Attempts were made to use psychiatrically prescribed medical treatment that brought some temporarily relief, but currently the situation is very serious. The nursery staff suspects that the parents are not giving him the correct dose of the medication.[vii]

Lea,[viii] the daughter (four), has developmental problems.[ix] She talks only a little, and goes to a special education nursery. The nursery reports that she does not interact with the other children, that she sleeps a lot and steals food from other children's bags. Often, she has outbursts of anger and crying.[x]

The routine at home: currently, the mother is not working.[xi] She neither cleans the house nor cooks.[xii] The father complains a lot about it and, lately, they have had ongoing arguments against this background. The mother fetches the children from nursery and brings them home, where they spend the rest of the day playing with smartphones[xiii] and eating unlimited amounts of chocolates and snacks.[xiv] When it was suggested to the mother to keep the snacks and the chocolates in the cupboard so they would not be accessible to the children, she did not act on it.[xv] She seldom takes the children to the playground.[xvi] The parents have minimal interaction with the children. There is no joint play and there are no orderly meals. For about a year, Avraham suffered from a toothache that was not treated. Recently, as a result of our pressure, they started taking him to the dentist.[xvii] The parents have allowed Lea, from the age of three, to shower on her own, with no supervision at

[vii] What is the parents' attitude to the medical treatment? What was their experience with it when they gave it? Is there anything positive to say about Avraham?
[viii] You have given the three children pseudonyms, but not their parents. How do you understand it?
[ix] What problems?
[x] These phenomena raise serious questions – how do the parents and the children explain the theft of the food and how do they explain the outbursts? Do you have any assumptions about this behaviour?
[xi] For how long?
[xii] What does she like to do? How does she spend the hours when the children are at school?
[xiii] What games do they like?
[xiv] What do the parents think about it? How do they explain it?
[xv] Why? How does she explain it?
[xvi] What does the mother say about the reasons for not taking them more to the playground? How does Avraham feel at the playground? How does she feel there?
[xvii] Do the parents know a dentist who can work with children with special needs? How do the parents explain it?

all, putting her at risk of slipping in the bath. Avraham relieves himself everywhere in the house, and the parents are not sufficiently aware of the importance of cleaning up immediately after him.[xviii]

Contact with the extended family: the mother spends weekends at her parents' home,[xix] but the father and the grandmother are in conflict, and he accuses his wife of being in league with her mother. The father's parents help a lot with caring for the children. The parents do not know how to manage their income.[xx] They spend a lot on smartphones, snacks and sweets instead of buying equipment essential to the children's development.

Lately, there has been a deterioration in the couple's relationship.[xxi] The mother claims that the father does not help her with the children, and the father claims that although she does not work, she does nothing around the house. The father has left home a number of times and gone to stay with his parents.

For the last two years, the mother has been receiving parental guidance at the nursery,[xxii] but according to the social worker's report, she has not implemented any of the steps suggested to her.[xxiii]

The family was referred into my care by their previous social worker after they moved to our town. In the referral, it said that the children were grossly neglected and that the parents were not adequately equipped to deal with them in an appropriate way.[xxiv] In their previous dwelling, they received intensive treatment for six months in the framework of a special, intensive family programme but their social worker reported that they had not made any changes.[xxv] Of course, we all understand the emotional and objective difficulty of the parents to have to raise children with special needs.

Recently, there have been reports from the nursery and from neighbours to the effect that the mother has been beating the children and shouting at them. The police have come to their house twice and the mother was shocked at the police being called. She claimed she "only occasionally gives the children a little smack".

[xviii] How do you know that they are not aware?
[xix] Add briefly the history of the relationship of the mother with her parents – from childhood.
[xx] What do you mean? What is their income? Do they have debts?
[xxi] Why? What caused the deterioration? What was their relationship like until recently?
[xxii] What did they try to teach her?
[xxiii] How does she explain it? What did she think of the guidance?
[xxiv] What was the parents' request when they got to you?
[xxv] What treatment did they get? What did they think and feel about the treatment?

The family has already been in my care for six months. The parents have received parental guidance from a counsellor who specialises in working with children with special needs, and, at the same time, a family assistant tried to help them with managing the household.[xxvi] Both the parental counsellor and the assistant reported throughout that the mother was not cooperating. She does not explicitly oppose what is said to her, but, in practice, does not implement what has been decided.[xxvii] In summary, the parents are simple, kind-hearted but limited people. They are willing to improve but do not have the basic tools to implement the parental guidance that they are being given. The principal difficulty I have to cope with is: how patient and forgiving can we be with the parents when we know that there are helpless children in the picture?

Writing an intervention story critically

The aim of critical writing is 'to convey a structural and cultural understanding of service users' problems, acquaint readers/organizations with concepts of human rights ... replace negative stereotypes of service users with a holistic comprehension and encourage greater respect and less criticism and blame' (Weiss-Gal et al, 2012: 4; see also Shimei et al, 2016).

From my acquaintance with Semadar, I know that she is committed to her work and to the families with whom she works. One can see it in her attempts to reach out to this family and to recruit various carers to help. Despite this, the text is a good example of uncritical writing because it fails the two main tests of critical writing: the test of subjectivity and the test of context.

The test of subjectivity

It fails the test of subjectivity because the family members are described only through their faults, shortcomings and behavioural problems. There is no doubt that were they to read the report, they would not feel pride or respect. Their inner world – their wishes, dreams, fears, emotions and feelings – are totally absent. Their pain is not even mentioned, as if they live a life without pain. Their needs are unclear. Although we can assume that they have many needs as people and as

---

[xxvi] What did they think about it? Did they ask for it?
[xxvii] Who decides? Why does the mother not cooperate? What is the parents' attitude to the attempts to educate them?

parents, we have no idea how they define their needs. Their knowledge, including their perspective, assumptions and theories regarding the situation, do not count. Although not an absolute indication, I often find that descriptions of service users that do not use their names (aliases) tend to describe them as caricatures (in this text, 'the mother', and 'the father') and fail to describe their subjectivities.

The test of context

In addition, the text fails the test of context because it does not put the subjects in the restricting context within which they function, and that they resist. By 'context', I include different aspects of service users' outer world. In this case, the immediate context includes parenting children with special needs in conditions of poverty and exclusion. This should be understood in the broader social context of the limited social opportunities open to the family. Although Semadar says that she understands the great difficulty of parenting children with special needs, this understanding is not expressed in the description. For instance, the report mentions that the parents are not dealing with Avraham's dental problems; however, there is no mention of the obstacles involved in giving dental treatment to a young child with special needs, who has difficulty following the dentist's instructions. In addition, there is no attention to whether the parents know a dentist that they trust for this kind of treatment. The same applies to Lea; it is not clear in what circumstances and context she tends to get angry and burst into tears at the nursery. That fact that these behaviour patterns are not placed in a context leaves the impression that the behaviour is not rational, is strange and is arbitrary. This is also implied in the mother's behaviour of 'false' compliance with professionals that does not take into consideration the power hierarchy in her relationship with them, including her need for their help and her fear of their interventions.

While contextualisation aims to give a comprehensive view of the horizontal context, namely, the current context of the family, historisation gives a view of the vertical context of life. In this case, the historisation is missing. The text gives very few details regarding the history of the parents, and the information given does not help us to understand the potential for achieving change. The aim of historisation is to delineate the contours of the chronological context of the family's life and to place the behaviour in the present within it. Simply stated, it could be said that the historical context of a person's life, and mainly their childhood, is critical because it contains their experiential seed that is manifested during the course of life. Understanding this experiential seed is crucial in order to derive beneficial meaning from present situations. In the case of the Lev family, for example, the quest for historisation would lead us to ask whether the mother has worked in the past and why she stopped, or what characterised the couple's relationship before the latest deterioration.

Moreover, the history of the family is necessary in order to identify the potential for changing the present. Listening to the history is not only intended to help to *explain* the present; rather, it also aims to identify in the past the potential for an alternative development in what is called in narrative therapy 'the unique outcomes' (White and Epston, 1990).[4] Looking for the unique outcomes, that is, for occurrences in the past that contradict the situation in the present, can help us when we feel that our impression of a service user is one-sided and dominated by negative attributions. In this text, it is necessary to look for the unique outcomes of the family members, for example, times in life when the mother worked, any expression of her own will or initiative, or moments in which the parents interact with the children. The mother especially is described as being so weak that in order to see her fully, we need to look purposefully for the ways in which she resists her poverty and distress.

In general, the text is a good example of the conservative paradigm regarding poverty. In terms of ontology, it portrays the family members as objects – a totally inferior Other. The text makes liberal use of words that focus on the deficits of the parents (and the children), such as 'cognitively handicapped', 'humble' and 'limited', as well as negative phrases like 'immature', 'not cooperating', 'no orderly meals', 'neither cleans the house nor cooks' and 'not working'. Throughout the report, what stands out is the attention to what the parents and the children lack.

In terms of epistemology, it presents the professional standpoint as the only one. In fact, what the social worker and the family assistant say about the mother is presented as truth, whereas the parents' knowledge/opinion of the children and the reasons for their difficulties, as well as their perspective regarding the professional help offered to them, do not appear at all. In fact, the text does not reflect the parents' or the children's knowledge and point of view regarding their situation at all.

The axiological stance that the text reflects judges the parents, and especially the mother for her functioning as a housewife and a mother, and regards the professional's position as a combination of an educational and supervisory one. In response to this discussion, Semadar rewrote the story, as follows in the next section.

Semadar's corrected version: an intervention story with the Lev family

The parents – Ricki and Nissim – are in their late 30s, with three children, two boys (Moshe, aged seven, and Avraham, aged five and a half) and a girl (Lea, four years old). Avraham and Lea have special needs. The mother, Ricki, grew up in a home in which there was no positive model of maternal functioning. As a result, she finds it difficult to handle the daily routine: containing the children, sitting with them to play and cleaning the house. Hence, in her experience, people around her (social services, her husband, her in-laws, the therapy team and her workplace) are always criticising her and blaming her for not functioning properly. All this makes her feel incapable as a mother, as a woman and as a person. As a result, Ricki's self-confidence is very low. She has very little joy and she does not have much mental strength to cope with the difficulty of raising her challenging children.

Consequently, and in order to limit the criticism she receives from others in her environment, Ricki has built a mechanism of hiding, and does not openly present what she really thinks and feels. As she is coping alone with the difficult care at home and with the children, she does not manage to find the inner resources to internalise, implement and improve her functioning. Ricki understands that excessive access to social media and giving too many snacks can harm the children, but, on the other hand, in this way, she achieves a calmer household for everyone. On the few occasions when she tried to implement the recommendations of the parental counsellor and limit the time the children could have with a smartphone, Avraham and Lea reacted with uncontrollable outbursts of anger, which she found extremely hard to handle. This caused her to return immediately to her earlier behaviour patterns and to disregard the professional's recommendations. Sometimes, when Ricki feels that she is having a hard time with the children, she asks her husband's parents for help and frequently leaves the children there. When she argues with the children, she often regrets her actions, goes up to the children to hug them and apologises for being violent and impatient. Ricki is trying to achieve quiet, calm, joy and tranquillity in her life. She does this by occupying the children with eating snacks, looking at social media and leaving them as much as she can with close family, while spending time shopping and in cafes.

Ricki is a pleasant person, is respectful of people, appreciates being helped, is thankful and grateful, is non-judgemental, is modest, knows when to ask for help when needed, can express her feelings, would like the best for her children, and is willing to help others. She keeps close contact with her relatives and family, as well as her husband's family. She does not bear grudges. It is important for her to improve her relationship with her husband.

The father, Nissim, works as a production worker in a factory. He met Ricki seven years ago through a matchmaker. He comes home every day at five. He does almost nothing to help at home. He loves his children and tries to give them warmth and love, but raising them falls mainly on Ricki.

Their relationship has had its ups and downs. Ricki often feels that Nissim is not interested in her and does not love her. His sisters have frequently told her that because she is not careful about her personal hygiene, he does not want to have sex with her. Nissim often involves his family in his difficulties with Ricki, thus creating a coalition against her, making her feel even weaker. In addition, he blames her when her parents do something not to his liking.

The children: Moshe is seven, a school pupil. Avraham is five and a half, and has been diagnosed with autism, with a suspicion of cognitive disability. He does not talk at all, and he relieves himself in his pants or on the floor. The nursery staff report excessive restlessness, unease and violent behaviour towards the staff and other children. There have been attempts at psychiatric medical treatment that have brought some relief but the situation is currently very serious. The nursery staff suspects that the parents are not giving Avraham the correct dose of medications. It is difficult to keep him occupied during the day. He constantly asks to have the smartphone that helps to calm him. When he is calm, the whole family is calmer and is able to get on with things.

Lea, four years old, has developmental difficulties. It is not clear whether the cause is environmental or neurological. She talks a little, is withdrawn and goes to a special education nursery. The nursery staff reports that she has virtually no interaction with the other children. She sleeps a lot at the nursery, takes food from other children's bags and eats it. She constantly wants to have showers. She has outbursts of anger and crying. The parents have no explanation for it. I also do not have any theories about it, so it is worrying. Perhaps she likes water, or it is the result of the lack of boundaries at home.

The routine at home: the mother is not working and it is not clear what she does all day. Perhaps she plays on the computer. I have been told that she has been seen shopping and sitting in a cafe with the family. The parents argue against the background of the father's complaint that his wife does not do the housework. The mother fetches the children from nursery. When they get home, they spend a lot of time playing with smartphones and eating unlimited amounts of chocolates and snacks. The parents say that the children love snacks, so they give them to them to let them have a good time.

The parents have little interaction with the children. They do not play together and there are no orderly meals. For a year, Avraham suffered from a toothache that was not treated. Recently, following pressure, they started taking him for treatment. The child relieves himself everywhere in the house. The parents view this as an objective difficulty but do not express any opinion as to what is causing this (they do not look for reasons or other factors).

Contact with the extended family: unfortunately, I do not know enough about it to write anything. The mother goes to see her parents on weekends. The father has a conflict with his mother-in-law. He feels that she is constantly criticising him. He blames his wife for collaborating with her. The father's family helps a lot with dealing with the children. The father's sister cleans the house once a fortnight, and is paid for it.

The father's income is below the poverty line but they are also entitled to a Disabled Child Allowance that puts them above the poverty line. In addition, they receive subsidies for housing and nursery school. Despite this assistance, they are still unable to manage financially, and claim that they do not have money to buy clothes and toys for the children.

For the last two years, the mother has received parental guidance at Avraham's nursery to provide her with tools to cope with his difficulties. However, according to the social worker, she has not implemented any of the tools given to her. She claimed that the guidance helps her but, in practice, there has been no noticeable change indicating use of the tools given to her.

Recently, there has been a deterioration in the couple's relationship. Nissim was cross that Ricki does nothing around the house, that she neither works nor cleans and does not cook, and he has to pay his sister to clean the house. In addition, he blames her for what he considers negative vibes from her parents. Ricki argues that he does not help her with the children. Nissim has left home a number of times, for a week at a time, and gone to live with his parents. Ricki raised the possibility of divorce, saying that she had no problem with the idea: "Nissim can take Avraham and I would remain with Lea, she is a good girl."

Recently, there have been reports from the nursery and from neighbours to the effect that the mother has been beating the children and shouting at them. The police have come to their house twice and the mother was shocked at the police being called. She claimed she "only occasionally gives the children a little smack".

The family was referred to me six months ago by the social worker who worked with them before they moved to our town, with the understanding that there was gross neglect of the children and that the parents did not have the necessary tools to cope with them appropriately. Before the move to our town, they received treatment as part of an intensive care programme for six months. The coordinator there said that they had made no changes. They also had a parental counsellor, who specialises in children with special needs, and she still works with them. When we met, the parents sought help with the children. They claimed that things were difficult for them. Ricki said that she had a dream to learn confectionery (I think that this is a dream that cannot be realised at the moment because she does not even have the strength to do more basic things. Since I have known her, she has barely cooked anything and she does not bake – this dream feels detached from reality).

The parental counsellor was impatient with the parents and was not suited to the family. She claimed that the mother lied to her a lot (something that I was also exposed to). Recently, a parental counsellor who worked with them in their previous place of residence has been allocated to the family. She has also reported having great difficulty with the mother, who does not cooperate sufficiently. Recently, the counsellor has heard that the mother gave Avraham a slap or two and the child cried as a result. One of the nursery workers also reported that she saw the mother in the street hitting the girl and pulling her forcibly. Realising that the nursery worker would report the incident, the mother got anxious and said that she was fed up with our treatment and did not want anybody to come into her house. The counsellor tried to calm her and to direct the conversation towards the mother's lack of the right tools for managing the children, saying that that was why she was there and that she wanted to help her.

The parents come regularly to the meetings with me and are open with their difficulties. Recently, they shared the difficulties in their relationship with me. I helped them to start seeing a couple's therapist. They say that they are very happy with the care they receive but, in practice, I feel the mother has unspoken reservations. I do not know if they say this just to please us.

Is it good enough critical writing?

The revised version reveals important information regarding the family and its relationship with professionals that did not appear in the first version. One can see that Semadar made an effort to rectify the balance of the description away from focusing on 'negative and irrational' behaviour towards including Ricki's knowledge and positive characteristics. In the first version, Ricki was described as non-cooperative with the extensive treatment offered to her because of her cognitive weakness and her immature personality – essential characteristics that render her beyond help. This non-cooperative behaviour has a different meaning when placed in a context, specifically one of power relations. Semadar tells of her avoidance of Ricki's request to learn confectionery as it seems 'unsuitable' to her. Ricki's request to learn confectionery is crucial information because it is one of the few indications of her subjectivity – it is a reflection of her dream and evidence of her wishes. An intervention that treats her as a subject should regard this as a precious piece of information and build on it. In addition, the information that the previous parental counsellor was not suitable is also important and sheds new light on her reports. Including this information (which was, in fact, already known to Semadar when she wrote the first version) is a big step towards critical analysis. The new version also helps to reveal the gaps that exist in Semadar's knowledge regarding important aspects of the family's life, such as Ricki's history, her relationship with her family and the parents' explanations for Lea's behaviour.

Yet, some critical aspects are still missing from this version and the interpretation given to the facts is essentially conservative, and not critical. Thus, analysing this version can deepen our discussion regarding what is critical in critical writing.

In contrast to the first version, in which Ricki's behaviour was interpreted as arbitrary, in the second version, Semadar strives to understand the possible motives for Ricki's behaviour. For example, she explains Ricki's difficulty of keeping to the daily routine, to feed the children and play with them as an expression of the fact that she has 'low self-confidence, her joy is limited and she does not have a lot of mental energy'. She also mentions that Ricki 'did not have a positive model for maternal functioning'. These explanations put Ricki's behaviour in a context but still leave Ricki as an essential Other. In order for an explanation of behaviour that we recognise as a problem or difficulty to become critical and be useful in practice, it has to be very specific – *to refer to one's pain and to put it in a social context*. In our context, the low self-confidence, limited joy and mental strength, and lack of a positive model for maternal functioning are too general and do not capture Ricki's pain and social context. What is Ricki's perspective regarding her difficulties? Does she think that she has low self-confidence? What precisely was her experience with her mother? Does she regard her mothering model to be 'not positive', and in what respect? These questions are left unanswered. Moreover, it is not clear whether these are explanations that Ricki gave to her situation or psychological generalisations made by Semadar, and if the latter option is correct and those statements do not reflect Ricki's own experience, what is her experience? How does she explain her difficulties? What is her point of view?

The second aspect that masks Ricki's subjectivity is the disregard for her knowledge. One such instance is Semadar's disregard for Ricki's wish to learn confectionery. It is an ambition that Ricki explicitly shared with Semadar. In the text before us, this is almost the only direct expression of Ricki's dreams in which we can hear her internal world without the mediation of interpretation. Any intervention that could strengthen Ricki, as a parent and as a person, must devote a generous space to her dreams, encourage her to express them and relate to them seriously. However, the text does not show that Semadar validated Ricki's right to a dream such as this. Neither did Semadar hold a meaningful discussion with Ricki about this wish in which Ricki could experience Semadar as supportive and as standing by her.

Furthermore, Semadar seeks to approach Ricki's experience of failure. She writes that 'in her personal experience, all those around her constantly criticize her and blame her for not functioning properly (welfare, the husband, the husband's family, the care team, the work place). All this makes her feel that she is not a good mother, not a good woman, not a good person'. This explanation seems contextual but it disregards Ricki's social situation, mainly because Semadar ignores the fact that Ricki's feeling that she is not valued does not stem from an idiosyncratic interpretation, but refers to real facts that Semadar herself reports. As Semadar reports, Nissim blames Ricki, his sisters humiliate her and the helping professionals view her as the principal obstacle to the improvement of the children's condition. The question of whether Ricki's experience stems from her internal world or from events occurring in external reality is critical. To perceive it only as a manifestation of the inner world (clearly every experience like this has echoes in internal reality that might come to the fore explicitly during the intervention) ignores important parts of the micro-aggression and the injustices that occur in Ricki's outer world. This disregard for her reality leaves Ricki isolated and is liable to cause her to doubt her interpretation of reality.

Taking Ricki's experience of failure as a valid judgement of the external reality has far-reaching practical significance. It compels us to tell her that she is coping with an extremely difficult situation, and that we are not surprised that she is having difficulty coping with the children alone, with no help from her husband and no support from the family. After validating her experience and contextualising it, we would go on to show genuine curiosity[5] regarding her perspective on her history and on her present situation, siding with her and thinking together with her about how to change the reality. Consequently, the corrected version that Semadar wrote does take an important step in the critical direction and reveals important information that did not appear in the first version; however, it uses contextualisation and historisation in too general a manner, is shallow and fails to give a rich account of Ricki's subjectivity. The third version of the story, which I wrote, seeks to take a further step in the critical direction, according to the guidelines set out in Box 3.1.

Box 3.1 Guidelines for writing a critical psychosocial report

The service users' knowledge: what is her reality and how does she perceive it? How does she explain her situation? What are the issues that she wants to deal with and how, from her viewpoint?

The internal world: what are her principal experiences in the world? What are her feelings, needs, fantasies, dreams, fears, hopes and wishes? What makes her feel bad and what helps her to feel better?

Life history and life story: what is her history and how does she tell it? What are the principal events and relationships that influence it? What does she consider significant in her life story?

The material and concrete level: what is the service user's situation with regard to concrete, material resources? What is her situation in terms of exercising her rights? What is her health, housing and employment situation? How does she define her needs in terms of her material life?

By covering these four topics, the following questions will be addressed:

- What are her needs? (Material and emotional, in the past and in the present.)
- What is her pain? (In relation to the past and the present.)
- How does she resist poverty and hardship? (In relation to the past and the present.)

The third version: Lev family, an intervention story (written by me)

Ricki and Nissim are in their late 30s. They are the parents of three children, including two children with special needs: Moshe (age seven); Avraham (age five and a half), who suffers from autism and a moderate degree of cognitive disability, does not speak, and relieves himself everywhere; and Lea (age four), who has developmental problems and speaks only a little. I have known the parents for about six months since they were referred to me for treatment when they moved apartments, following concern about neglect of the children.

The children: the nursery reports that Avraham is restless, very anxious and violent towards the staff and children. There have been attempts to give him medical-psychiatric treatment. There seemed to be relief for some time following the treatment but, lately, there has been a deterioration and the staff at the nursery are worried that the parents are not careful enough about giving him the medication. With regard to Lea, the nursery staff reports that she does not interact with the other children, sleeps a lot during the day, takes food from other children's bags and has outbursts of anger and crying.

Recently, there have been reports from the nursery and from neighbours to the effect that the mother has been beating the children and shouting at them. The police have come to their house twice and the mother was shocked at the police being called.

The parents: Nissim works for a minimum wage as a production worker in a factory and is away from home until 5pm. When he comes home, he does not take responsibility for the children or the household. Ricki has not been working for the last few months. I do not know what work she did in the past. She fetches the children from the nursery and spends long hours with them alone. For most of the time, the children watch television or play with smartphones while eating snacks. Ricki and Nissim both have difficulty playing with the children.

The parents married about seven years ago, by arrangement. The couple's relationship is marked by Nissim blaming Ricki for not doing the housework and not caring for the children properly. Nissim's family is very involved in the lives of the couple and the children. On the one hand, Nissim's parents and his sisters assist with childcare; on the other hand, Nissim frequently involves his family in the difficulties that he has with Ricki, thus creating a power coalition against her and weakening her. Ricki feels that he does not love her and is not interested in her. His sisters have contributed to this by often saying that because she does not take sufficient care of her personal hygiene, he does not want to have sex with her. In addition, he blames her when her parents do something that is not to his liking. I do not have any details about Ricki's relationship with the parents. Nissim has left the house a number of times, for a week, and gone to live with his parents, threatening to leave Ricki.

In the town where they lived before, they received assistance in the framework of an intensive programme for families with children at risk. In this framework, they received parental guidance and a family assistant; however, according to the reports, there was no change in their situation.

When I met them for the first time, they said that they needed help with caring for the children. Also, Ricki said that she has a dream to learn confectionery but I did not assist her to realise this dream because it seemed to me to be detached from her abilities and talents. I got the impression that Ricki was a pleasant woman who is able to express her admiration for whoever helps her. She is able to express her feelings. Both parents are willing to accept any help that I offer them and they do generally cooperate, though it might be for the sake of outward appearances. They have started getting parental guidance as well as a family assistant, but these two professional women report that although Ricki agrees with their requests, she does not implement their advice. My impression is that they do not trust the helping professionals enough to say directly what they want, or to share their reservations about the treatment they get. There has been no improvement in the relationship between the parents and the children. When the parental guidance counsellor and the family assistant suggested to Ricki that she keep the sweets in the cupboard so that the children could not reach them, she tried it but the children reacted with uncontrollable outbursts of anger that Ricki could not tolerate, and the situation reverted to what it was. The parental counsellor did not provide Ricki with an alternative plan to calm the children. She was not supportive of Ricki and not patient enough. For about a year, Avraham suffered from a toothache that was not treated. I do not know why they did not take care of it, but lately, following pressure from me, they have started taking him for dental treatment.

It is clear that Ricki loves the children and wants the best for them. After arguing with them, she initiates hugging them and regrets having been hostile and impatient with them. At the same time, she struggles with having to cope with the challenge of raising them. She shares the difficulties that she has with the children and Nissim with the professionals, and she tries to follow their instructions, but their efforts to help her have not found a way to her heart yet. However, the parents persist with their attendance at meetings with me and other professionals. Lately, they have shared their relationship difficulties with me and asked for help with them.

Implications for practice

In the first version that Semadar wrote, Ricki was an object, 'the non-functioning mother'. With the change in the versions, she has become more present, a subject. Certain bits of information arise that make her human: her relationship with her parents, her professional dreams and her expectations of her relationship with Nissim. Her hardship has become clearer, and within it, her loneliness and lack of support seem to scream out. Nissim is backed up by his family and has symbolic capital by virtue of being a working man. He feels free to come and go, and to leave his family from time to time; he blames Ricki for failing as a housewife, as a woman and as a mother. Ricki is not valued by any of the family members, and not by the professionals who are supposed to treat her. She is blamed for not coping alone with the children's distress and their severe outbursts of anger. When she achieves some quiet by allowing them to play with smartphones, to watch television and to eat sweets (activities that most parents find themselves doing), she is accused of negligence and not setting limits. When she confronts them or flares up at them, she is suspected of being a danger to them. Her knowledge is not significant to anybody, nor are her wishes and struggles. When she requests help from Nissim, he disregards her, and in this, he is supported by his family and the professionals. When she expresses her wish to learn confectionery, she is ignored. It is not surprising that she does not manage to hold her own. She is not used to entering into a negotiation about her needs, or about the ways of receiving help that suit her. As she does not manage to hold her own, and because she has been made to accept that her opinion is not important, she tends to agree with the demands of others even if they do not suit her. This explains her willingness to cooperate with the parental guidance counsellor and the family assistant even when their suggestions do not suit her. However, this tactic makes the professionals see her as a 'simple' woman who 'does not internalise' their instructions.

While the final version makes Ricki more of 'a subject', it still leaves holes in the picture regarding the children and Nissim, as well as regarding Ricki herself. What are their subjectivities? What are their dreams – and fears? How do they understand their situation and what bothers them? These questions cannot be answered in this exercise of writing because of the absence of relevant knowledge regarding the family. Their context is also quite indistinct, both materially and in terms of relationships. Semadar mentioned that they have very little money to live on but she thought that this was the result of their unwise pattern of spending. Only in the second version do we learn that Nissim's income from work is below the poverty line. As already noted, their relationships with their families, especially with Ricki's family, are also described in statements that are too general, and need much more detail for there to be beneficial future intervention. The last issue that is sorely lacking from the description is the relationship of the family with the staff of the children's nursery. The teachers and other professionals at the three children's schools are very important, and their relationship with both the children and the parents is also very important. Especially important is the nursery staff's view of Ricki, which appeared to be tainted with criticism and contempt. In addition, the description lacks any reference to the power that professionals hold vis-a-vis the parents. This omission is glaring because the professionals think that they can mask their power with kindness and good will while Ricki, the 'simple woman', understands it and expressed this understanding by declaring that she does not want any more professionals at her home after the police visits.

The concluding sentence of the first version was Semadar's question, 'how patient and forgiving can we be with the parents when we know that there are helpless children in the picture?'. The answer to this question requires a detailed evaluation of the level of risk to the children, their difficulties and strengths, as well as a detailed evaluation of the parents' potential to become good-enough parents. The third version changes the focus of the worries about the children. It shifts from being about eating sweets to being about their difficulties and their own inner world: does Moshe, the eldest boy about whom we know nothing because he does not display any behavioural pathologies, get the support he needs in the school? Why does Lea cry so much, steal food and sleep so much at the nursery? What is the story behind her showering? Is it a problem at all?

The last version draws attention to the blind spots in the professionals' efforts to help Ricki, and opens new directions regarding future intervention, which is so crucial when discussing the children's risk. In order for Ricki and Nissim to become good-enough parents, they need to meet professionals who view them as complete people, who will offer them real opportunities to realise themselves and establish a helping relationship with them. The leading questions for such an intervention will be: what do Ricki and Nissim want? What do they think they need in order to become better parents? What are their dreams? What are their fears? What are the real alternatives that are open for them? In practical terms, it seems that before there can be any change in the parents' behaviour, there has to be a comparable change in the attitudes of the professionals. This will make the couple feel that the professionals are on their side, are seeing their difficulties and their need to be valued and respected, and are treating them accordingly.

Notes

1. I use 'Other' with a capital 'O' to refer to the social construction of the other as inferior, and 'other' with a small 'o' to refer to another person.
2. What is called 'the crisis of representation' occurred in the middle of the 1980s simultaneously in anthropology and feminism. In anthropology, it started with the publication of *Writing culture: The poetics and politics of ethnography* (Cliford and Marcus, 1986), and in feminism, it was the publication of the anthology *This bridge called my back* (Moraga and Anzaldua, 1983).
3. A panopticon is a circular building with cells arranged around a central well, from which the people inside the building could be observed by a single watchman at all times. Michel Foucault, in his *Discipline and Punish* (1995), used the idea of the panopticon as a metaphor for a power mechanism that modern societies use to discipline, observe and normalise their citizens.
4. Michael White and David Epston, the founders of narrative therapy, used the concept of 'unique outcomes' to refer to areas of experience that went undamaged by the problem. The therapist seeks to identify the unique outcomes in order to make them part of the self and to increase their influence on the present.
5. Netta Ofer-Ziv, an Israeli psychologist, coined this concept, which integrates Kohut's concept of empathic attunement and Daniel Hughes's writing on curiosity as a source of confidence.

4

How to teach poverty critically

Training is an important component of the PAP. Ever since the Ministry of Welfare and Social Services adopted the paradigm, I and my team of excellent graduate students have developed dozens of courses on the PAP for different audiences – from practitioners in various roles, to managers and directors of social services departments and supervisors at the ministry. This chapter builds on this experience. It is based on a lecture that was presented at an international seminar on the PAP in June 2018 at Ben-Gurion University.

The first and most challenging course that I taught during the year that the Ministry of Welfare and Social Services seconded me from the university was a course that trained social workers to work in new programmes that targeted families whose children were considered to be at risk. It was a very intensive course, as well as the first to integrate the PAP and the topic of children at risk. I felt like I was being watched by my colleagues from the ministry, who anxiously wanted – and needed – the new programmes and training to succeed. The social workers in the class did not know one another. They came from all over the country, did not like travelling to the course and did not like the idea of someone from academia offering them the knowledge they needed for practice. They were also doubtful about the relevance of learning about poverty to their practice with parents who abuse and neglect their children.

The first day of the course dealt with the questions of what poverty is and why it is relevant for social work practice. I started with an introductory exercise in which I asked everyone to tell the group about a memory that had to do with poverty – it could be an ongoing encounter, personal or family experience, or even a one-time encounter with a stranger, even with a beggar. The stories that arise are always moving, and I see them as a repository of poverty themes, containing both the content of what poverty is and emotions that reveal the positions that people take vis-a-vis poverty. On the board, I wrote the name of the narrator, a few words on the main subject of their story and the dominant emotion that they described. In this way, in the first lesson, we were already collecting a wide variety of events, attitudes and feelings that reveal the complexities of poverty that we would address as the course continued.

After that, I taught the students how poverty is measured and I showed them a great deal of data on poverty in Israel and internationally, for comparison. My aim in showing these data is not only to make them more knowledgeable, but to continue increasing their awareness of their hidden attitudes and prejudices that we touched on in the first lesson. The data made poverty visible and enabled us to begin questioning certain conservative premises regarding poverty. I wanted the students to face what poverty is: poor housing conditions; a lack of educational opportunities; and the exact amount of state cash benefits, especially the income support benefit.

Usually, after the students begin to realise how awful poverty is, and how structural it is, I see in their eyes the passing thought 'So why don't people go out to work in order to improve their situation?' Then, I present data showing that work on its own does not free people from poverty (NII, 2018). My goal at this stage is to establish the foundations of structural or critical positions on poverty and policy.

From my experience, I know that during the third lesson, the students try to refute the data showing that poverty is a policy issue by individualising it. They talk from their own experience about people in poverty who lie, who abuse their children, who reject the opportunities given to them for education or employment, and who buy their children a new smartphone when they do not have enough for food or other basic necessities.

At this stage, the challenge of teaching becomes crucial: how do we connect the behaviour of individuals with structural explanations? The discussion of this issue is always an important moment in the course. My aim in the discussion is to dispel the fundamental notion that poverty is a product of people's pathology, and to get the students to think about how to translate the data on poverty that we have just learnt into an understanding of the behaviour of individual people.

Afterwards, I devote three lessons to the three paradigms: the conservative, the structural and, finally, the PAP. We use these three paradigms as analytic tools that help us to understand the everyday behaviour of people in poverty.

In this specific course, these lessons were a secondary theme to the issue of connecting poverty and children at risk. When discussing these issues, my aim is to motivate the social workers to recognise the full extent of the service users' subjectivities and to connect a macro- with a micro-systemic analysis and practice with the interpersonal and intrapersonal.

After we talked about the conservative and the structural paradigms, in the middle of learning what the PAP is, one of the social worker-students, Hana, an experienced social worker in her 50s and a woman with a great deal of presence, suddenly stood up in the middle of the class and said angrily: "I'm fed up with this brainwashing. You're doing brainwashing here. I'm sick of all this poverty." Then, she took her bag and left the classroom.

What will happen with the course, with Hana (the social worker who left) and with the group? Generally, I have two reactions to situations in which I feel attacked: my initial reaction is to resist. I said to myself: 'Why does she call it brainwashing? If we taught them cognitive behavioural therapy for several lessons, would she also call it brainwashing? No. So why does she call learning about poverty brainwashing? There's no brainwashing.' I felt that I had to repel the attack. However, after a few minutes, I took a deep breath and I asked myself: 'Why did she really call what we're doing brainwashing? Why did she experience it as such?'

My conclusion was that Hana was right. She might have put it in a way that was unpleasant for me at the time, but she expressed something that is true. Other people call PAP training 'a conversion': they say that they were converted to the PAP. A different way of saying this, which I prefer, is to call it 'a language': people say that the PAP is a whole new language. Brainwashing, conversion or a language – they all refer to the same thing: PAP training, the logic behind the choice of exercises, the order of lectures, and their content and language are intended to cause a paradigmatic change in the learners: to move them from conservative ways of thinking and language to critical ones.

The biggest challenge in PAP pedagogy is how to deconstruct the hegemonic perceptions of poverty. In this context, teaching PAP is a challenge similar to the challenges that one faces when teaching other critical approaches, like feminism. There are many ways to teach critical approaches. However, we all know that a critical approach or a critical theory is not knowledge; it is life, it is praxis. It is a kind of *habitus* that people wear. How do you teach it and what does this *habitus* include? The critical *habitus*? I would suggest five elements:

1. Making room for vulnerability, pain, anger and guilt

Einat Vager-Atias, who has worked with me for many years, once said that I should have warned her that her entire position in life was going to change. That she was going to be a lot more angry, sometimes more vulnerable. That she was going to see things in reality that she would have preferred not to see: injustice, inequality, pain. If these are the facets of reality that PAP training asks the students to face, then the training should support this process of learning to see more, becoming angrier and more vulnerable. Seeing more can also arouse guilt, especially when experienced practitioners are introduced to the PAP. 'How did I act or think like that?' and 'How did I ignore crucial aspects of the service users' lives?' they frequently ask. PAP pedagogy has to help practitioners to deal with these strong emotions and to give space for working through these experiences.

2. Allowing oneself to be an outsider

Being critical means agreeing to be an outsider, at least in the conservative professional communities that dominate the state's social services. This is especially difficult for practitioners who were used to being insiders. Since PAP training seeks to make practitioners 'wear glasses' that help them recognise the invisible subtext of inequality, which is never obvious and whose existence others deny, it means agreeing to be unusual. There is no course in which this point does not arise. Young students and senior social workers alike tell me that after learning the PAP, they feel like outsiders in their teams, with their friends and even in their families. At the dinner table, they find themselves arguing about topics that they had not argued about before. In his study, Timor-Shlevin (2019) documented social workers who talk about concealing from their colleagues what they do in accordance with the PAP because they want to protect themselves from attack. In a sense, they agree to be outsiders (otherwise they would not implement PAP practice) but they want to prevent others from treating them as such. In other situations, social workers have talked painfully of giving up on what they think in order to protect themselves. Only two weeks ago, I was told by a social worker who worked at a boarding school for ten years about a professional meeting that she attended that included the father of a girl who is a pupil at the school. The social worker, Edit, said at the meeting that the father's parenting difficulties were connected to the fact that he worked all night, every night, and since he did not have a place to live, he lived in a friend's warehouse. All the staff members immediately attacked her, saying that instead of helping them to explain to the father that he should take responsibility for his parenting, she was defending him. They wanted him to start parenthood counselling. She was stunned by this response and felt defeated. She told me that after the meeting, the father called her and told her that he felt that he was not being listened to. She said that she thought he dared to share this with her because he thought that she felt the same way. What will she do with this experience? Will she fall back into line? Or, will she see it as an opportunity to reposition herself in relation to her role, in relation to the profession and in relation to this father and his daughter? What does she need from me to succeed in this repositioning?

3. Transforming knowledge and attitudes into practice

Teaching the PAP includes teaching both theory and skills. The success of this pedagogy is not measured in teaching evaluations or the students' grade-point averages. Success is measured in the teacher's ability to accompany the practitioners in a way that once they are alone with a service user who irritates them, hurts them, discourages them or frightens them, and they search for the words with which to respond to them, they will find them in the vocabulary of the PAP. This is a huge challenge: how do we influence them to open something within themselves that produces this language in real time? This means that after they have agreed to identify the inequality and the injustice, and they agree to take the side of service users, they also know what to do about it and have the skills to do so. The fact that we have increasing numbers of documented PAP interventions today is, of course, a very significant tool in this regard.

4. Remembering the radical baggage

One of the things that I least like to hear is that I teach 'empathy' or the 'strengths perspective'. I hardly use these words in my teaching, but people sometimes translate the PAP into concepts that they already know. Do not get me wrong, the humane tradition that brought 'empathy' and 'strengths' to the world is not alien to the PAP, and, in fact, it is part and parcel of the PAP. However, the terms do not play a central role in PAP pedagogy because they are apolitical and they strengthen language and practice that focuses on individual solutions to poverty (Roose et al, 2014). Instead of 'strengths', the PAP uses 'resistance to poverty'; instead of 'empathy', the PAP uses 'solidarity' and 'standing alongside'. The PAP is critical because it is based on ongoing deconstruction, that is, the undermining of hegemonic concepts, and then reconstruction, that is, the rebuilding of a critical paradigm (Fook and Gardner, 2007).

However, it is sometimes very difficult for people to understand this approach. Recently, I received an invitation from one social welfare service to give a lecture on the PAP. In the email, they wrote: 'It is important to us that the lecture deals with the experience of the person who lives in poverty, its impact on her functioning, her perception of crises, her abilities in this context, and less on the social struggle.' The overemphasis on 'functioning' and behaviour reveals the conservative stance that is explicitly manifested in the concluding words. They invited me to teach them the opposite of what I teach. How should we explain that the 'social' components and 'struggle' are the cornerstones of the paradigm – that this is the very basic position from which the 'experiences' and 'perceptions' are understood?

5. Making a change without abusing power

The last challenge is how to make this shift to the PAP approach while avoiding abusing the power that lies in our hands. How do we position the PAP as a very clear agenda, on the one hand, and as an agenda that does not preclude anyone or invalidate other ways of thinking, on the other? Of course, it does not always work. When it works, it is the result of being very close to the experiences of the professionals, yet it forces them to conceptualise their knowledge, that is, to place it in dialogue with the critical knowledge of the paradigm.

In the last part of the lecture, based on my experience, I will try to formulate in a few words how to deal with these challenges. First is addressing the experiences of the practitioner-learners and conceptualising them as knowledge. This is achieved by inviting practitioners to share stories about their 'stomach aches': personal or professional matters that cause them pain, where they are unsure, that bother them, or that stick in their memories. These experiences are important because they represent the need for change, and make it a personal need. Combining these with cognitive learning about poverty and about paradigm leaps starts critical reflectivity and the deconstruction of dominant conceptions. Building on these principles, every PAP course goes on to make the critical reconstruction through an ongoing mutual focus on experiences, knowledge and moral stances.

Second is presenting the paradigm as an analytic tool. The paradigmatic structure – in distinction from just an arbitrary collection of arguments – enables thinking about its premises as analytic tools and using questions like 'What is the phenomenon under discussion?', 'How do we know it?' and 'Wherein lies the 'good' in this case?' in order to analyse complex situations and to plan practice. In other words, knowing the paradigm is not about reciting its principles, but about using them to understand direct practice, policy, procedures and regulations better, and to start imagining alternatives to them.

Third is using the group. In order to learn and to practise the PAP, one needs support. It is impossible, or at least not effective, to be critical alone. Thus, forming the class into a group, in fact, a support group, contributes to this process. It is important for two reasons: (1) it is necessary for maintaining reflexive processes because it is very difficult to engage in reflection alone and it is helpful if there is someone to ask you questions that stimulate reflection; and (2) it helps one to cope with the experience of being an outsider. The group becomes important when it acts as a sort of sisterhood and when it includes both ample humour and seriousness.

Fourth is the importance of dialogue. In order to connect ideas, ethics and experience, dialogue is the best medium. Like other critical pedagogies (Freire, 1970), PAP pedagogy uses dialogues much more than frontal teaching. The dialogue enables the integration of ideas into the self and the linking of theory and practice. The difficulty in conducting this dialogue is how to turn it into a convincing argument that does not invalidate the other person's point of view. This is a very delicate and challenging task, especially when students advocate conservative arguments. The goal of the response in this case would be to continue the dialogue, to offer other points of view and to say explicitly and through the structure of the lesson that our goal is not to decide what is right, but to open a space to examine possibilities.

Fifth is a critical construction of the course. The dialogic medium elicits many stories that the students bring from their experience. As I said, we sometimes call them 'stories of stomach aches'[1] and they are important because they embody the need for change. These stories play a central role in class and we deal with them through ongoing deconstruction and reconstruction. Deconstruction focuses on invalidating existing concepts and then reconstruction focuses on the rebuilding of a critical paradigm. The pace changes but this structure, aimed at eliciting rich narratives of professional experience, forcing the students to deconstruct hegemonic ideas and then to reconstruct new ones, accompanying the students through this process, reassuring them, and suggesting another way, always exists.

Last is the use of language. It is very clear during the course which words are 'in' and which are 'out'. Many words that were not previously part of the students' professional language have become part of it. For example, 'micro-aggression', 'symbolic capital', 'intervention in the real-life context', 'lack of opportunities', 'point of view', 'relationship-based knowledge', 'standing alongside service users', 'real alternatives' and 'recognition' are the words and terms that the course is based on. Students become very aware of their use of language. They laugh about it at first, but in cases where it succeeds, their language changes, both in speaking about service users and in writing social reports.

I would like to end on an optimistic note regarding the contribution of PAP pedagogy. This came from a study that examined the perspectives of 235 service users on the social work treatment that they receive in the framework of social services departments. Based on quantitative measures and qualitative interviews with service users, Brand-Levy and Malul (2019) found significant differences in the levels of satisfaction with the relationship with the social worker between service users whose social workers had undergone PAP training and service users whose social workers had not. This was found to be stable at two points of time, even when the service users did not participate in a special programme and so were not entitled to a special budget and their social worker had the regular huge caseload. Rising satisfaction does not mean that service users moved out of poverty, but it does have a significant meaning as to the chances to work with them collaboratively. Finally, there is one more optimistic note: Hana, the social worker who left the room resentfully, came back the following week. She was a very forceful and assertive practitioner; hence, she became a dynamic advocate of the PAP.

Note

[1] I thank Menny Malka for suggesting this phrase.

5

Frequently asked questions about poverty and poverty-aware social work

After some time of acquaintance with the PAP, social workers often confront me with some questions: why do people in poverty not work? How can their budgetary priorities be changed? What explanation do we have for the difference between those who manage to extricate themselves from poverty and those who do not? What is the difference between providing fish to people in poverty and teaching them to fish? Other people tell me that they are confronted by similar questions when arguing in favour of people in poverty with friends or family. This chapter collects the questions that are frequently raised and answers them.[1]

Some people say that an intervention programme should be based on providing hooks and not fish, because fish provide only a temporary answer whereas hooks provide tools for ongoing change. Is this so?

Social workers like to distinguish between hooks and fish, and are proud of the hooks that they supply because 'fish' reminds them of charity, which is not in line with professional ethics and is not considered professional activity. Moreover, the distinction between 'hooks' and 'fish' echoes the distinction between psychosocial treatment and material assistance. This distinction has two outcomes: first, it causes material assistance and psychosocial treatment to be seen as two different things; and, second, it confers a higher status on treatment, leaving material assistance as less legitimate. However, in the PAP, material assistance and treatment are much the same: *fish can become hooks and hooks can become fish since material and emotional needs are closely interwoven.* This is a matter not of conditioning material assistance on emotional treatment, but on seeing them as interconnected. The need for a basic material response carries with it powerful emotions, and the form that the response takes should take account of the material and the emotional needs together. It is clear to us that when a mother breastfeeds her baby, she is providing the baby with an answer to both a material and an emotional need at the same time. She feeds the baby's stomach and heart. It is also clear to us that if she only gives the baby milk or only a warm hug, the baby will fail to thrive. The question as to whether a material response can also provide emotional needs *depends on the way in which the professional person views the connection between the needs and delivers the responses.* Material assistance can feed the soul if it is provided with a deep recognition of the humanity of service users and with respect for both their material and emotional needs, and their ability to choose. In other words, it should be based on solidarity, and should express an attitude of standing by service users in their struggle to improve their lives.

If only people were willing to work, they would manage to get out of poverty. Right?

We would like to think that employment is the ultimate solution to poverty, but that is sadly not the case. In Israel today, more than half of the families who live in poverty are working families, yet their income is below the poverty line (NII, 2018). A single mother with one child lives in poverty even if she works full time for a minimum wage. The income of a couple with two children who work 1.5 full-time jobs on a minimum wage is also below the poverty line (NII, 2018).

To understand this, we must consider the characteristics of the job market, or, more precisely, the lower end of the employment market. In fact, what people forget when recommending work as the major vehicle to overcome poverty is that the jobs open to most people in poverty are at this lower end of the employment market, characterised by low wages, instability and a lack of tenure and career development options.

Another major obstacle on the way to overcoming poverty through work is the paradoxical relationship between work and support. We are used to thinking that work increases the social support that people have but, in fact, one needs a lot of support in order to work. For example, most jobs at the lower end of the employment market pay hourly, and not monthly, wages. Every hour of absence from work, due to a meeting with the child's teacher or a visit to the doctor, means that the wage decreases. Moreover, working entails expenses such as childcare, travel and clothing. Integration into the job market that will extricate a family from poverty requires a lot of formal and informal support; when that is non-existent, breaking free from poverty by working is very hard.

Finally, when we say that people in poverty should work in order to overcome poverty, we assume that they have never worked or that they do not want to work. Research teaches us that people are motivated to work, and that most of them move through their lives between periods of formal work, informal work, illegal work and no work according to the real alternatives open to them (see, for example, Blank, 1989; Prins and Schafft, 2009; Achdut and Stier, 2020). The issue, then, is not how to change or motivate the people; rather, it is how can we offer real alternatives for people to work in such a way that will extricate them from poverty?

Is it true that people live in poverty because they do not plan their budget properly and their priorities are misguided?

Poverty is, first of all, a severe material shortage – a very small budget. It is not a culture or a particular family characteristic. When we talk about priorities and budget planning, we assume that there are sufficient funds and if used wisely, the families' needs will be met and they can break free from poverty. However, the truth is that poverty means that people and families live on a budget that does not suffice, even for the most basic expenses. The poverty line standard per capita is low but it does not tell the whole story. It is important to remember that many people live on a much lower income than the poverty line. In fact, the average income of people in poverty in Israel is 30 per cent below the poverty line (NII, 2018).

We tend to think that if people who have a low income did not spend money on dying their hair or on cigarettes, it would make a significant difference to their financial situation. However, for the most part, the truth is that even if they did not spend money on these things, they could not extricate themselves from poverty in the wider sense of the word: they could not improve their housing or health situation; and they could not enhance their children's educational opportunities. People in poverty generally plan their budget, no less than anyone else; they simply live off too low a budget.

Thinking that poverty is about priorities allows the people not living in poverty to feel that they are immune to poverty, that is, that it will not happen to them because they can manage their money wisely. However, this perception obscures the fact that when there is no money, there is no money.

People in poverty tend to be dependent. Do you not think that social workers must avoid encouraging dependence among their clients?

It is important to distinguish between 'dependence' in the sense of reliance and dependence as a character trait. People in poverty *rely* on social workers long-term because they are constantly dealing with multiple, acute needs and serious obstacles, and because they do not have other support systems. That does not mean that they are dependent or that they like relying on the social worker for years. Clinical experience shows that people maintain a relationship with the welfare system because they have no choice (Krumer-Nevo et al, 2006).

We can also adopt another perspective on dependence: a developmental one. 'Dependence' is a vital phase in standard development before we become independent. Theories of psychological development from Bowlby (1969, 1973) onwards teach us that people who have had a good experience of basic security in their early childhood will have a better transition to independence. The problem is that people in poverty have often not experienced beneficial dependence and opportunities to reduce their reliance on welfare. If we think of it this way, the ability to experience dependence in the framework of a supportive and caring relationship is essential to enabling growth and development. Thus, our experience in social services departments shows that when people are offered a close relationship and an adequate response to their needs, they do not develop continued dependence, but rather develop a sense of capability and desire for independence.

People become poor because they made bad choices. Right?

A bad choice can only be made if one is faced with a *real* choice, that is, a good choice. However, because the concept 'free choice' is so prevalent in our neoliberal era, it is no wonder we think that people become poor because they have made bad choices. They are accused of making bad choices in choosing their partner, in having too many children too early in life, in not working and in not acquiring a profession.

However, do we always have a free choice? Contemporary welfare theories claim that in order to understand what choice *is* in circumstances of poverty, it must be placed in a context, which means examining what the real alternatives were from which people had to choose (Lister, 2004). Did they really have the option to choose a path that would lead to a better outcome, or did they have to choose between two unsatisfactory options? The nuances are important.

I do not mean to say that people do not have choice at all, but that professionals have a moral duty to acknowledge the real alternatives that people have when facing a choice. For instance, a woman has to choose either to go to work or to receive an income support benefit. The only job that she can get is cleaning offices at night, but there is no institutional arrangement for her children at night. Is this an option of going to work or not a real alternative? If she does not work, she will not be able to support her children and pay her debts, and she is liable to be considered lazy or a parasite. If she works, she will have to find a different arrangement for her children every day, and she might find herself with no arrangement one day. Poverty means limited real alternatives. I call choices made in this context 'impossible choices' because either choice leads to a dead end.

Does poverty-aware social work free people of their responsibility for their situation?

I am asked this question often. No, I do not think it frees people from their responsibility for their situation. On the contrary, in order to understand the situation, we must distinguish between responsibility for the development of a problem and responsibility for *contending with* the problem. The standard professional discourse connects the two as if in order to make a change, people must acknowledge their role in creating the problem. Therefore, social workers think that they must help people in poverty acknowledge their problematic behaviour or the mistakes that they have supposedly made that led to their poverty. When service users refuse to do so, they are perceived as not taking responsibility for their situation. However, the truth is that structural failures in the employment market and in education, health and housing systems play a major role in shaping life situations that lead to poverty. Usually, no one assumes responsibility for these structural failures and their effect on daily life, not even the professionals: the employer does not assume responsibility for not offering better or better-paid jobs; the school principal does not apologise to the parents and students for the fact that in their school, the percentage of students entitled to a graduation certificate is very low; and the public housing authority does not assume responsibility for the fact that one apartment in the building is a drug den. Also, social workers have a hard time saying to their clients that the world is unjust, unfair and non-egalitarian. However, this type of discourse, in which social workers discuss with service users the structural failures that they face, is vital. Without it, service users' experience of injustice is not recognised. Moreover, they feel blamed for circumstances that are beyond their control. Paradoxically, if social workers acknowledge that parts of the situation are beyond the control of service users, it frees them from guilt and shame, and connects them with their strengths.

If structural aspects have such a crucial impact on poverty, how are we to understand that in the same neighbourhood, some families succeed in raising children that come out of poverty and some do not?

Indeed, parents have a significant impact on children's lives, but the fact that there are differences between families should not lead to blaming parents whose children do not manage to break away from poverty because we must remember that parenting skills are determined within a context and are affected by it. For example, the birth of a child with a disability or the disease of a family member can have an enormous impact on a family's ability to cope, even for a family that coped fairly well until then. The family's support system has a major impact as well. The personal, familial and social elements, as well as the interaction among them, shape the way in which the children grow up. It is important to adopt a complex perception that identifies the power and impact of the structural elements, without dismissing people's option to resist this power, on the one hand, and without blaming the people whose attempts to resist fail, on the other.

'It would not happen to me.' Is this statement true?

It is convenient for us to think that poor people brought poverty on themselves due to their personal or familial pathologies – that it would not happen to us! The truth is that the factors whereby people are forced into poverty are related to normative crises such as the disease of a breadwinner or of a family member, the birth of a child, divorce, or unemployment (McKernan and Ratcliffe, 2002; Rigg and Sefton, 2006). When these normative crises occur in families whose financial and social existence is very fragile, they become decisive. People who are not poor tell themselves 'It would not happen to me' because the feeling that poverty is random and can happen to anyone is very threatening. It means that we do not have the control that we would like to think we have, and that the world is an unsafe and unjust place.

The problem with 'it would not happen to me' is the distinction that it creates between people in poverty and the rest of society. Thinking that there is a fundamental difference between people in poverty and the rest of society is dangerous. It is almost the original sin in regard to poverty since it leads to Othering, exclusion and stigmas. These, in turn, allow professionals to ignore and deny the reality of poverty, and it distances them from service users. In fact, precisely because thinking about poverty is so emotionally threatening, it makes the awareness of these feelings crucial for social workers.

The active exercising of rights that is advocated in the PAP means that people in poverty should be supported in every step of their negotiations with administrative authorities. If they do so, how will they learn to solve their bureaucratic problems on their own?

This question brings us back to the issue of dependence. The point is that the PAP regards service users not as having a problem of dependence, but rather as having a problem of their social and symbolic capital. On their way to actualising their rights with administrative authorities, they must overcome many obstacles related to: their level of education; their unfamiliarity with the bureaucratic language; and the fact that they are often met with micro-aggression, disrespect and negative stigmas that make it very hard for them to get what they need.

The PAP version of active exercising of rights entails doing what is needed in order to realise rights. If service users need to be accompanied to administrative authorities because they do not feel confident enough or because they do not succeed when they go alone, then it is very reasonable that somebody they trust should accompany them. This is often the only way for service users to solve their bureaucratic problems and, no less important, be treated fairly. Our experience shows that problems that people have tried to deal with on their own for months and even years, to no avail, were solved as a result of the determined involvement of a social worker. The involvement led not only to a concrete solution, but also to the strengthening of the relationship and the empowerment of the service user.

Nevertheless, it is important to remember that actual accompaniment is not always required. When service users feel that social workers are willing to accompany them "to the wolves", as one woman once phrased it, they feel empowered and they can choose what kind of help they really need. Often, they choose to have their social worker prepare them for their meetings with administrative officials, and not actually accompany them. Whatever the form of accompaniment, it must be decided on jointly with service users, based on the recognition that there might be a genuine need for such accompaniment and that it is not about the person being weak or incapable, but rather about the weaknesses of the system.

People busy with basic survival and struggling to provide for their primary existential needs are not available for the therapeutic process. True?

The answer to this question depends on our perception of what a therapeutic process means. Poverty-aware social work is therapeutic by nature. However, in order to understand it, one must distinguish between more conservative psychodynamic approaches where external reality has no autonomous status and is always perceived as an expression of internal reality, and contemporary psychodynamic approaches. The latter are found in feminist treatment or relational psychology, where there is room for both external and internal reality – a conception that undermines conventional hierarchical therapeutic relationships.

The therapeutic act takes place, to a large extent, in the professionals' willingness to listen and respond to the emotional needs of the clients, which are constantly manifested. It is crucial to identify the emotional content that accompanies talk about concrete matters, seemingly unrelated to emotion, and once it is identified, to know how to respond so that both the concrete and the emotional aspects are addressed.

What determines whether it is therapy or not is not only what the client brings, but rather the way in which the professional responds to the client's needs. People struggling daily to provide basic needs also constantly experience the need to be loved, to be appreciated and to be seen as worthy human beings just like any other person. The ongoing situation of reliance on others to provide for basic needs only exacerbates those emotional needs since the emotional and material needs are always entwined. They cannot and must not be disentangled. This means that material assistance must go hand in hand with consideration of the human needs for belonging, security and appreciation. Unlike Maslow's pyramid that placed material and emotional needs in a hierarchical order, in the PAP, we perceive all needs to be interconnected, existing together and manifesting together. We seek to create a therapeutic relationship that responds in an integrated manner to all these needs.

Note
[1] A shorter version of the chapter appears as a YouTube film.

PART II

Recognition

The second part of the book is devoted to one angle of the practice of the paradigm: placing relationships at the centre. Close relationships are central in PAP practice. However, is it possible to establish close relationships when we understand that these relationships are contaminated by power? Since processes of Othering go hand in hand with the power relations that constitute the encounters between social workers and service users, relationships are political. In light of this situation, this part of the book aims to work through power and overcome popular notions regarding poverty and professional socialisation that join together to direct the attention of social workers to diagnosis and pathologisation.

The four chapters in this part of the book borrow from current psychoanalytic theories on the concept of 'recognition'. Chapter 6, 'Poverty, recognition, therapy', presents the concept of 'recognition' and links it to poverty and therapy. Based on a review of works by philosophers and psychoanalysts, the chapter argues that recognition is a basic component of the therapeutic relationship that enables the psychological experience of one's subjectivity. The chapter argues that in order to give recognition to service users living in poverty, social workers should acknowledge those aspects of service users' inner worlds: their needs and knowledge; the emotional pain caused by poverty; and their ways of resisting poverty. Acknowledging all of these enables full recognition and makes it possible to see the full humanity of service users, as well as to establish close relationships with them.

The recognition of these three areas is further detailed and exemplified in the next three chapters. Chapter 7, 'On needs and knowledge: Sarit's story', exemplifies the recognition of the needs and knowledge of people in poverty through the story of Sarit. Sarit was one of my interviewees during my doctoral research, and her story has accompanied me for many years. I analysed it using the concept of recognition for the purpose of this book.

Chapter 8, 'On emotional pain', presents excerpts from women's testimonies on emotional pain in their lives. Pain is an embodied phenomenon. Thus, in order to recognise service users' pain, social workers must adopt their perspectives. Unlike pathology, which is determined by the social worker with or without the approval of service users, pain can only be defined and determined by service users. Hence, the recognition of pain requires close and trustful relationships.

Chapter 9, 'On minor movements of resistance', closely examines the efforts that people make to resist poverty. Much has been written on the agency of people in poverty and the various strategies that they use to overcome it. This chapter focuses on the manifestations of these efforts in the encounters with social workers, including situations in which social workers feel that they have been manipulated or abused by service users. This analysis will, I hope, assist social workers in maintaining close relationships under very difficult circumstances.

6

Poverty, recognition, therapy

In a supervision meeting, Liat presented her work with a single mother, who had approached her at a time of crisis when the woman's landlord asked her to vacate her apartment. Liat met regularly with the woman over a period of about 18 months, during which time she helped her to find another apartment and to process the ongoing experience of eviction, isolation and alienation that had accompanied her throughout her life, and was aggravated by the landlord's decision. Their sessions together helped the woman to gradually regain her trust in the world and to temper the aggressive behaviour that she had been using to protect herself for years. Although I viewed this as therapeutic work, the social worker summed up her presentation by saying: "This was not therapy because we did not focus on the woman's childhood, but dealt with the emotions that arose concerning her daily hardships." The question is, therefore, what is therapy? Does it reside in what the service user brings? What is the connection between concrete assistance, for instance, helping to find an apartment, and emotional change processes? What are the curative elements in intervention? This chapter deals with these questions.

Introduction

My main argument is that in order to deal effectively with people living in poverty, that is, to become relevant to them, social workers need to develop a poverty-aware therapy stance. This stance is based on a combination of practices aimed at making a change in the external world and practices dealing with the inner world, with an emphasis on the various roles that power plays in both. The concept of 'recognition' was developed in the 1990s by philosophers of critical theory, especially Axel Honneth and Nancy Fraser, and simultaneously in relational and intersubjective psychology in the work of Stephen Mitchell, Lewis Aaron and Jessica Benjamin, and it is a key concept in this context.

My contention is that the existence or non-existence of a therapeutic stance depends on whether or not there is a relationship of recognition, and it is this stance that creates the therapy and not the specific content dealt with by the social worker and the service user. In other words, therapeutic situations can occur even in everyday situations, when using simple language and when talking about matters connected to concrete reality. It is widely accepted in social work that neither the external nor the internal reality is autonomous since every occurrence in external reality is registered in the inner world. The question is: how do we link the two realms of reality and respond to both of them at the same time?

The principal feature of the PAP's therapeutic stance is recognising the way in which social power relations determine service users' external and internal worlds, as well as helping relationships (Schofield, 1998). In saying 'recognising', I mean recognising the content linked to both the external reality and the internal reality. As the concept of 'recognition' carries political weight, it is well suited to act as a bridge between the internal and external worlds. Paraphrasing Benjamin (1988: 21), we can say that without the relational and interpersonal concept of recognition, the material reality becomes one-dimensional, for it is only against the background of the mental and interpersonal experiences that the external world is thrown into high relief, that is, presented in its full vitality.

It is interesting that the work of the philosophers Honneth and, to a lesser extent, Fraser has gained interest in social work and stimulated writing about practice (Garrett, 2010; Webb, 2010; Davies et al, 2014; Rossiter, 2014; Houston, 2015; Boone et al, 2018, 2019), while current psychoanalytic writing about recognition has for some reason not penetrated the therapeutic discourse in social work. It has not even entered the discourse on relationship-based social work (Borden, 2000; Howe, 1995; Ruch, 1995, 1998, 2005, 2018; Schofield, 1998), with which it shares basic principles, such as the focus on subjectivity, the importance of the professional's self and the understanding that the helping relationship is both real and a transference relationship (Tosone, 2004; Clarke et al, 2008; Segal, 2013).

What is recognition? How does it shape the therapeutic relationship? What exactly do we seek to recognise in the PAP? These are the questions that we will deal with here. As I have said, the concept of 'recognition' has both psychological and philosophical origins. Its psychological roots are to be found in early neo-Freudian approaches, which were critical of the centrality of drives and of the inner mental world of Freud's theory, replacing them with the interpersonal sphere and with emotional needs, specifically the human need for relationships with others. These approaches start with ego theories, object relations theory and attachment theory, and go on to self psychology and the latest theory of intersubjectivity (Mitchell and Aron, 1999; Clarke et al, 2008). These theories are very different from one another but they share the perception that interpretation alone is not the curative factor in therapy. They suggest instead that the therapeutic relationship and the therapeutic intention are essential for achieving change. In addition to their caring and empathetic qualities, these relationships should be based on giving recognition. Benjamin (1988: 15–16, ellipsis in original), a leading feminist intersubjective psychoanalyst, says that 'To recognize is to affirm, validate, acknowledge, know, accept, understand, empathize, take in, tolerate, appreciate, see, identify with, find familiar … love.'

Kohut viewed the empathic matrix as the unique context from and in which the human self is conceived and exists. The child is dependent on their mother's recognition in order to exist, that is, to become psychologically alive. However, the need for recognition is not particular to childhood or to the mother–child relationship; it is a permanent component of human experience that continues throughout life. Benjamin (1988) compares it to the need of a plant for sunlight that provides it with the energy it needs for its existence. She refers to recognition as the confirmation of others which tells us that we have created meaning, that we influenced and that we showed intention.[1]

> A person comes to feel that 'I am the doer who does, I am the author of my acts' by being with another person who recognises their acts, their feelings, their intentions, their existence and their independence. Recognition is the essential response, the constant companion of assertion. The subject declares, 'I am, I do,' and then waits for the response, 'You are, you have done.' Recognition is thus reflexive: it includes not only the other's confirming response, but also how we find ourselves in that response. (Benjamin, 1988: 21).

With a writer's sensitivity, Erri De Luca (2002: 45), in his book *God's Mountain*, describes a moment of receiving recognition in the words of the novel's hero, a 13-year-old boy[2]:

> In the dark Maria comes up to the washbasins.... She told the landlord she's had enough. He took it badly and threatened eviction. Maria's parents owe him back rent. Maria spat at his feet and left. She plucked up her courage. Just became a woman and already she knows disgust. I've had it with this game, she said, of him calling her princess, dressing her in the clothes of his dead wife, putting precious things on her, and then touching her and asking her to

> touch him back. Now she doesn't want it anymore because I'm here. I'm here. It makes me feel important. Till now my being around or not didn't make a bit of difference. Maria says that I'm here. Before you know it, I'll realize that I'm here, too. I wonder whether I couldn't have realized this by myself. I guess not. I guess it takes another person to tell you.

For the young speaker, Maria's words about his existence are, at the same time, an announcement that he exists and a pre-echo of his existence, establishing him as a subject aware of himself. Maria's words change his feeling about himself since the experience of the self is dependent on the echo that precedes it and confirms it, both present before it and continually accompanying it. Being granted recognition from a significant other prepares the ground for a self-recognition that is expressed as belief in oneself, in self-respect and in self-esteem.

A person's ability to be helped is also learnt and exists within a relationship of recognition. When a person needs help and receives it, in addition to the concrete help, the human subject also receives recognition of the hardship as real, and recognition of deserving to be cared for. In this way, recognition contributes to the subject's self-experience of having value. Moreover, giving recognition can rehabilitate a damaged self. Recognition helps the subject to bear the mental pain that they may be defending against ineffectively.

The critical theory philosophers of Honneth and Fraser have made an important contribution to our understanding of the links between recognition and social justice, perceiving giving recognition as having an ethical dimension (Brunner, 2008). According to Honneth (2007: 71), people possess intuitive images of justice:

> The normative core of such notions of justice is always constituted by expectations of respect for one's own dignity, honor or integrity … the normative presupposition of all communicative action is to be seen in the acquisition of social recognition: subjects encounter each other within the parameters of the reciprocal expectation that they be given recognition as moral persons and for their social achievements … moral injustice is at hand whenever, contrary to their expectations, human subjects are denied the recognition they feel they deserve. I would like to refer to such moral experiences as feelings of social disrespect.

At the same time, directing continuous misrecognition to individuals on the grounds of their group affiliation may lead to social pathologies, which can be manifested in four main ways (Zurn, 2015, cited in Houston and Montgomery, 2017: 182).[3] First, *invisibilisation* involves ignoring the presence of the other, making them non-existent in a social sense. Otherwise, it can be manifested by disdainful disregard, paternalism or tokenistic partnership with service users, as, for example, when parents are invited to a case conference at the child protection services but their presence, voice and knowledge are fundamentally ignored. Second, *instrumental rationalisation* is the privileging of means–end rationality over all other forms of reasoning. It is manifested in focusing on 'the most expedient, cost-effective way of achieving a predefined end but does not deliberate on the *value* of that end ... [it] is a driving force in modern capitalism and fuels the proliferation of bureaucracy, technology and rational-choice economics for solving problems in modern-day life' (Houston and Montgomery, 2017: 188). In social work, instrumental rationalisation is expressed in inordinate attention to the 'means' instead of the 'ends' of social work interventions and in over-bureaucracy (procedures, checklists and audit criteria) replacing relationships. Third, *reification* means the objectifying of the subject, ignoring their subjective world, emotions, knowledge and intentions. In social work, reification shows itself when procedures come before responses that are human-centred or when social workers reify service users in order to protect themselves from feeling their pain. Finally, fourth, *organised self-realisation* is the current cultural trend that forces people into a process of individual self-improvement and realisation. In social work, it can be seen in the case of involuntary service users who are forced to identify the internal causes of their behaviour in order to achieve change.

These forms of negating recognition can induce shame, anger or alienation from others and from the self (Honneth, 2001; Frost and Hoggett, 2008; Frost, 2016). Together, they become experiences of non-existence in the psychological and social sense. As the experience of social recognition is a condition of identity development, misrecognition is necessarily accompanied by a feeling of the threat of losing the self and of a deep, intimidating severance from society. When a person's sense of existence is endangered, when they feel that they are not noticed, they might take active steps to cause other people to notice them. These efforts can be expressed in a range of behaviours, from normative behaviour, through protest and rebellion, to self-destructive behaviour (Honneth, 2001).[4]

Recognition and the political

The interpersonal character of the concepts of 'recognition' and 'relationship' makes them vulnerable to a neoliberal application that neuters their political meaning. There are two risks in this regard. First, recognition might take the place of the politics of redistribution. This can happen when distributive injustice problems are treated by recognition only, while ignoring their material aspects and the necessary redistributive steps that should be taken. Fraser (1995) argues with Honneth exactly on this point. She claims that while 'recognition' is an effective tool for coping with issues of cultural injustice, as, for example, with LGBTQ (lesbian, gay, bisexual, trans and queer*) people, it can be used in order to mask economic injustice, such as poverty. She calls for an examination into the interconnectedness between the economic and the cultural spheres of life in order to face the complexities of social problems. Webb (2010) claims that such an integrated conception of justice, which is based on the examination of both cultural *and* economic discrimination, should direct social work practice and theory in order for the profession to create a just society.

Second, Garrett (2010: 1527) warns critical social workers about the adoption of recognition theory because, 'being a diverse field, with numerous internal debates and disagreements ... [it] tends to neglect or under-theorize the role of the state'. Social workers who are employed by the state are limited in their ability to recognise the marginalised and the oppressed because recognition of that sort requires recognition of the oppression itself.

Consequently, practice that aims to deal with poverty from a social justice standpoint needs to take these two risks very seriously. Here, Fraser's distinction between distributive and cultural injustice is crucial in order to understand poverty as a lack of both material resources and of social opportunities (which requires remedy in the form of redistribution), as well as a lack of symbolic resources (which requires a remedy in the form of recognition and the struggle against Othering). Thus, as I will elaborate later, the PAP promotes Lister's (2004: 186–9) call to constitute the politics of poverty by combining the politics of redistribution and the politics of recognition&respect (Gupta et al, 2017).

I found an interesting observation relating to Garrett's warning in the current psychoanalytic literature on the state as it is experienced by the oppressed. Neil Altman (2011), a psychoanalyst who bases his theoretical work on his practice in public child psychiatry clinics in New York, expands the use of psychoanalytical tools to understand the power of the state, and suggests viewing public services as an intra-psychic representation of society and the establishment, experienced as powerful, strong, harmful, discriminating and excluding, while, at the same time, having the potential to be beneficial. Service users experience welfare services as being powerful and professionals as being able to provide the services essential to them and, in so doing, at least partially to correct the injustice and vulnerability that they have experienced throughout their lives. However, the expectation of correction is dashed because of the poverty of social services and the helplessness of the professionals. This situation traps the professionals and the service users in a world of bad objects, in which the service users attempt to receive recognition while the professionals respond as the repulsive or punitive object of the sort familiar to the service users. This experience arises whenever service users request help and social workers do not grant them the visibility and recognition that they need. What, then, should be done in order for professionals to become new and good-enough objects?

Some writing on social work takes a similar approach. Niemi (2015) refers to the failure of social workers to care as signifying the state's ultimate failure to care. The result of this failure is service users' experience of psychological and social outcasting. Ruch (2005) calls for relationship-based practice to integrate ideas from the anti-oppressive and empowerment approaches with psychodynamically derived ideas. Tosone (2004) proposes to broaden relational social work to include intra-psychic and interpersonal, as well as intra- and inter-systemic, dimensions. To be exact, one needs to consider relational social work not only in terms of internal and actualised object relations, but also in terms of the individual's internalisation of, and interface with, the macro-systems of the larger society, that is, cultural, economic and political institutions and structures. Succinctly defined, relational social work is the practice of using the therapeutic relationship as the principal vehicle to effect change in the client's systemic functioning, referring to the inherent interconnection of the intra-psychic, interpersonal and larger community systems (Tosone, 2004: 481).

Recognition and poverty-aware social work

What does recognition look like? What aspects of the human subject and their life reality are we seeking to recognise? How does recognition manifest itself?

In the PAP, recognition encompasses 'affirming, validating, acknowledging, knowing, accepting, understanding, empathizing'

(Benjamin, 1988: 15–16), both of one's material reality and of one's particular subjectivity. It manifests itself in interest in the external world, with its material and social facets, and in the internal world, including meanings, emotions, desires, fears and dreams. The interest that we are talking about is not only intellectual, but a sincere interest that involves taking a stance on the subject matter and siding with service users.

Recognising poverty as a material phenomenon

Taking an interest in the concrete reality of a person's life is not a technical matter. What it boils down to is, in effect, confronting the manifestations of distributive injustice on the micro-level. Rather than avoiding the mundane details of a service user's poverty, I suggest delving into them, and seeing them as an opportunity for a therapeutic encounter. It is an opportunity for recognising a person's immediate and social context, as well as their inner life – their pain, hopes and agency. Thus, it is an opportunity for the social worker to oppose injustice. For the service user, the struggle to obtain an answer to material needs is an opportunity to gain recognition; for the social worker, it is an opportunity to offer it.

The act of recognition, in which the social worker makes it clear that they *see* the injustice that poverty creates, has a major impact on the subjectivity of the service user and on the helping relationship. It validates the human subject's experience and makes them feel that they are not alone. The responses that the PAP offers in this regard – a flexible budget, the active exercising of rights and policy practice – become important tools. The range of responses to needs – from the immediate need for a flexible budget, through the longer process of the active exercising of rights, to structural change through policy practice – become tools of solidarity. They serve to encourage the social worker to recognise service users' struggles to achieve material goals and to join them in this struggle.

Recognising poverty as a symbolic/relational phenomenon

The very fact of taking an interest in the person's experience of external reality has an impact on their inner world. Furthermore, validating the human subject's experiences should be seen in the context of the many instances where it is often ignored or judged. It needs to be remembered that people living in poverty are used to situations where they describe the injustice that they endure and are then required to examine what *their* part was in the injustice and what *they* can do to prevent or change it. Responses of this sort delegitimise their story and invalidate their experiences.

In this situation, putting the experiences of injustice into words and including them in a narrative that is shared with social workers who represent the establishment contributes to one's self-experience. It contributes to the experience of autonomy and self-control within a context in which service users have only limited control. In fact, this narrating of their experiences and responses to material needs is what gives the relationship its therapeutic value, similar to the comforting touch and smile of the mother that accompany her feeding of her baby.

Narrating the experiences of struggle to achieve material goals can be utilised by the social worker, who, after succeeding with exercising rights, asks the service user how they feel about the fact that, together, they managed to achieve what was impossible for them to achieve by themselves. Merely asking the question frames the situation as unfair and unjust, and invites the service user to reflect on it. When social workers express interest in service users' opinions regarding their situation and emotions, it brings home the fact that poverty is not taken for granted, and encourages the service users to analyse their situation and position themselves as knowledgeable. Simply being able to talk about experiences of social suffering that are not spoken about in other contexts allows the experiences to be given meaning and become an integral part of the inner world.

By recognising instances of injustice in real lives, social workers are able to fully recognise service users' knowledge: their needs, their pain and their resistance to their poverty. Each of these four components – knowledge, needs, pain and resistance – will receive comprehensive consideration in the following chapters. Very briefly, I can say here that relating to service users' *knowledge* is a radical step that social workers take to overcome Othering since it reminds them that people in poverty are more, not less, familiar with the reality than the social workers themselves. By taking an interest in service users' *needs*, they immediately transcend interest in their material life reality and are able to stand by them in their struggle against poverty. Relating to the *pain* exposes the emotional aspect of the experience (Frost and Hoggett, 2008), and relating to their acts of *resistance* to hardship makes it possible to identify their stance in relation to it, their strengths and the active dimension of their lives.

I will conclude this section with a few words on a subject that deserves more than a few words. I am often asked whether recognising injustice in the external world means *solving* it. This question is posed by social workers who suddenly feel the weight of responsibility that the recognition of poverty as a violation of rights places on them. They feel that recognition alone is insufficient for addressing distributive injustice and fear that despite all their efforts, they will not necessarily bring about change in the external reality. For example, they will not be able to help the service user to move to a better apartment, or will not manage to find a suitable workplace or an educational framework. I like this question because it is a sign of a deep understanding of the complexity of the required responses. In fact, the desired position is for social workers to try to provide both: recognition and redistribution. I hope social workers *never* forget to shape their practice in ways that enable them to give recognition. At the same time, I hope social workers are always careful not to turn recognition into a token pursuit, and do not employ it at the expense of the struggle to obtain material resources in the external reality.

By way of response to this question, I explain that responding to material needs can take place without giving recognition, as in the instance of the clerk at the electricity company who allowed the service user a reduction of her debt but referred to her out loud as a 'welfare case'. One might think that this was preferable to a situation in which the clerk both remained aloof and refused the service user a reduction. However, I cannot avoid thinking about the damage that these words have on the self-experience of the service user and of her experience of the relationship with the state. As we know, severing the links between the material and the emotional or between the external and the inner is always damaging. This brings me to my final point. A true recognition of people in poverty should always lead to seeing injustice; thus, its importance cannot be minimised. Recognition is the oxygen of the experience of the self and the existence of interpersonal relationships in a democratic society. Therefore, giving recognition is a call to social workers to be agents of democracy.

Notes

[1] Benjamin and the whole intersubjective school's understanding of recognition is that it is a fundamentally reciprocal mutual phenomenon (even as the mother 'creates' the baby psychologically by her recognition, she is created as a mother by the recognition of her baby). This important, mutual element is less relevant to the analysis that I am proposing here, basically due to the emphatic imbalance of power governing the relationship between social workers and people in poverty. Nonetheless, the intersubjective, mutualist perspective has interesting potential for development in the future.

[2] I thank Batya Shoshani for drawing my attention to this citation and its discussion in the Hebrew edition of Heinz Kohut, *How does analysis cure* (Kulka, 2005).

[3] Houston and Montgomery (2017) offer examples for each one of these mechanisms in social work practice. They chose these four mechanisms from Honneth's

    discussion of a larger list of social pathologies since they regard them as most relevant for the social work profession.
4   Honneth claims that social struggles often arise following the systematic negation of recognition. Experiences of recognition negation or of giving distorted recognition, that is, contempt, which can be expressed as exclusion, humiliation, insult, ignoring, disdain, oppression or discrimination that the members of one group display towards the members of another group, create immediate emotional responses among the members of the group that experienced them, and can manifest as behaviour that disturbs the existing social order. Houston (2015) criticises Honneth on this point, claiming that the negation of recognition actually makes social organisation more difficult (on the constraints on getting organised, see also Lister, 2004: 149–56).

7

On needs and knowledge: Sarit's story

Sarit's story, taken from my PhD dissertation, was published in a Hebrew book entitled Women in poverty: Life stories: Gender, pain, resistance *in 2006. Over the years, the story has been widely used for teaching on numerous programmes. Originally, I used it in order to explain the concept of intersectionality and its contribution to the understanding of poor women's lives. Although the intersectional perspective is very important as it stands, in this chapter, I present a new analysis that focuses on Sarit's knowledge and her needs.*

Introduction

This chapter is dedicated to the recognition of service users' knowledge and needs. I will first say a few words about the two concepts and then illustrate them using the story of Sarit, whom I interviewed in the framework of a life-story study.

Knowledge

As a young feminist, I initially preferred the term 'voice' to 'knowledge'. As opposed to the objective, generalised 'knowledge' disconnected from the knower, I wanted to celebrate the subjective, personal and located 'voice'. Later, influenced by British scholars such as Peter Beresford (Beresford and Turner, 1997; Beresford and Wilson, 1998; Beresford et al, 1999; Beresford, 2000, 2001; Beresford and Croft, 2004) and activists such as ATD Fourth World (Tardieu, 1999; Rosenfeld and Tardieu, 2000),[1] I was alerted to the importance of thinking of service users as having *knowledge* as a central component of social work practice.

One incident with a senior official of the Ministry of Welfare and Social Services also contributed to this shift in my thinking from 'voice' to 'knowledge'. She was a member of a steering committee of a conference that I organised in 2002 in the framework of participatory action research. At this conference, people with direct experience of poverty were asked to present position papers on the education, housing and welfare social systems, written after a long process of discussions with groups of people coping with poverty all over Israel (Krumer-Nevo, 2009). The conference consisted of three sessions, each devoted to discussing one social system. Each of the sessions opened with the position paper, followed by the responses of stakeholders from the relevant field, including representatives of the various governmental ministries.

The position papers summarised the shared knowledge of the groups about the participants' experiences with the social systems, their attitudes regarding them and their message to the relevant minister. The encounter with the senior official of the Ministry of Welfare and Social Services took place at a meeting of the steering committee in which we discussed the form the presentations of the position papers by the activists at the conference would take. She said: "I want the activists to say, 'motherfucker'. I don't want them just to say what they think using nice words. I want them to be authentic." She wanted what she perceived as the authentic 'voice' of people in poverty, that is, an emotional, uncontrolled expression of frustration and anger.

What made this well-intentioned social worker think that 'motherfucker' is more authentic than being knowledgeable? Why did she prefer this form of presentation for delivering the participants' intimate knowledge about the social systems? Was this their preferred way of presenting themselves at an academic conference?

Her formulation of what was 'authentic' convinced me how important it was to insist on talking about people in poverty as having *knowledge*. I understood how slippery the slope might become if we did not insist on taking very seriously the fact that people in poverty have knowledge. In this context, knowledge is what people know about their private lives, about their goals and motivations, about the context of their lives, and about society and its institutions. It also includes their thinking processes: their perspectives, interpretations, meanings, hypotheses, theories and analyses (Beresford, 2000). This knowledge is unique because it stems from their marginal societal position. In fact, it is this marginal position that gives them access to information that allows them to develop a perspective that others, who are positioned closer to power, lack (Crenshaw, 1989).

The knowledge of people in poverty is often ignored – both what they say and their right to say it. In some cases, they themselves contribute to the dominant perception that they do not know, or that what they know is less valid or less worthy compared to what others know. They might explain this by saying that they have had only very little formal education, that they do not use 'proper language' or that they do not feel comfortable enough to express themselves.

This should not conceal the fact that they always do have knowledge and that recognising this knowledge is crucial for any process of help.

Too often, professionals deny the knowledge of people in poverty. In a way, this denial is 'built into' the helping encounter because, ostensibly, this is an encounter between someone who needs help in order to know how to go about things, and one who is an expert and 'knows'. Moreover, this approach to the encounter makes professionals believe that what service users think and know is the cause of their hardship: 'If they knew better and behaved better, their situation would have been better.' It is especially hard to recognise as 'knowledge' what people say about their seemingly non-adaptive or irrational behaviours, particularly because the professional ear is attuned to judging what people say and to exposing pathologies or mistaken perspectives. Thus, social workers are preoccupied with providing service users with new and corrected knowledge and changing their perspectives. In acting like this they are imitating what the Brazilian critical educator Paulo Freire (1970, 2006 [1970]) describes as the banking model of knowledge. This model is based on the assumption that the student/service user is an empty vessel and education flows in a one-way direction, from the knowledgeable professional to the unknowledgeable student. In fact, *critical* education is based on acknowledging that knowledge exists on both sides – in teacher and in student – and the practice derived from it is the art of dialogue. For social workers, a meaningful dialogue is the result of a sincere interest in the experiences, thoughts and frameworks of interpretation of service users. In the context of a dialogue of this sort, a process of self-understanding can develop and, as we shall see later, both partners are enabled to voice their opinions (Saar-Heiman and Krumer-Nevo, 2019).

Needs

The concept of needs, at least according to Abraham Maslow's influential work, is a central concept in psychology. Maslow, one of the founders of humanistic psychology, criticised the focus on psychopathology and instead focused his work on motivation and needs as positive aspects of psychological development. He was interested in human potential and the developmental path that people travel to fulfil that potential. Although he was interested in psychological processes, he did not ignore physical needs, and in his famous 'hierarchy of needs', he tried to integrate physical needs, such as the need for food and shelter, with emotional needs, such as the need for love, esteem and self-actualisation. However, it is precisely this effort to integrate physical and emotional needs in a single hierarchical model, according to which one had to fulfil basic needs in order to experience higher needs, that drew criticism. The critique focused on the hierarchical model, pointing out the many human situations in which people who do not fulfil their basic needs still experience what Maslow considered 'higher needs'.[2]

I found this critique to be crucial when trying to think about poverty with Maslow's concepts in mind. In fact, Maslow's model contributes to the dehumanising discourse regarding people in poverty because, according to the model, the fact that people in poverty do not meet their basic needs implies that they cannot experience higher-level needs, and this make them less human. Knowing so many people living in poverty, I knew this not to be true. Physical needs are not experienced independently of other needs. On the contrary, they always involve very strong emotional experiences, as well as emotional vulnerability. The need for food or other basic necessities always entails questions of personal identity or self-esteem such as 'Am I a good provider?' or 'Am I a good mother?', as well as questions regarding the relationship with others, such as 'What does the social worker think of me?' and 'Does she appreciate me in this situation in which she knows I cannot meet my own basic needs?'

Here, I am getting to the crux of this talk: once we accept that basic, physical and emotional needs always coexist, then any intervention, even if focused solely on finding shelter or food, is potentially therapeutic when it responds to both kinds of need. If social workers understand that the process of providing basic needs and the little talks that are part of it are opportunities for giving recognition, empathetic interest and respect for the emotional experiences of service users, these encounters can become positive experiences in themselves and the cornerstones for change and the further development of a therapeutic relationship. We also need to bear in mind that the situation of dependence on others to provide for one's basic needs makes the human subject extremely vulnerable. In the context of welfare, this vulnerability is intensified because service users are often dependent on social workers whom they do not trust, and by whom they do not feel trusted.

Given this situation, the most effective way to recognise and to show respect for the emotional experiences of service users is by acknowledging their knowledge. When professionals relate to service users as having essential knowledge about their needs, theories regarding the reasons for their circumstances (which might vary from personal to societal) and ideas about how to fulfil those needs, service users experience a recognition of their full humanity that is so important, and yet so rare, in their lives.

Sarit

Sarit is 22 years old and a mother of three young children, ranging in age from two-and-a-half years to two months old. She is separated from her husband and lives in a rented, three-room apartment with her children. She has difficulty paying the rent, though she gets a housing subsidy from the public housing authority and an income support benefit from the NII. In high school, she studied hairdressing but dropped out at the age of 16 prior to completing her studies. Her file at the social services department indicates that she requested assistance with paying municipality taxes, help reconnecting to the water supply company subsequent to disconnection resulting from a debt and assistance in writing to the Housing Authority requesting their continued rental subsidy in order to avoid eviction.

I received her address from the social services department. They do not maintain close contact with her and she is considered to be 'uncooperative' since she tends not to show up to set meetings. Nonetheless, when I called her, she said, "No problem, we can meet at my place since I'm at home with the baby." She is on the fourth floor of the building, which has a neglected garden with a small bench. There is no elevator. The staircase seems cared for and the postboxes are not broken. The lights work. I knock on the door and Sarit opens it. The house is spotless. There is a large window in the living room overlooking the main street through which one can see the sky. The serene mood of the early morning is only broken by the rumble of faraway busses and birds chirping. The living room is extremely small and simply furnished, with a large sofa next to a smaller one, a table and television. On the floor next to the sofa stands a baby seat with the sleeping baby, and a baby monitoring system. Sarit explains that the baby was born with medical problems that cause breathing difficulties. She underwent a course in first aid and cardiopulmonary resuscitation (CPR), and she explains that the monitoring system coupled with her first aid knowledge had, indeed, saved the baby's life. Later, she proudly shows me the bedrooms: one in which she sleeps and a second – the children's room – which is spotless, neat and overflowing with teddy bears, dolls and toys. Sarit talks and smokes incessantly. Her story stands in stark contrast to the spotless apartment, the orderliness and organisation to which I am witness. What follows in Box 7.1 is a transcript of Sarit's answer to my initial request that she tell her life story. She related the difficult life events uninterrupted, without any intervention on my part. Her story reveals parts of her history, her knowledge and her needs.

Box 7.1 Sarit's story

'When I was four years old, two more siblings were born…. I was four and my sister was two, and another sister was three months old, and my father died. We lived with my grandmother. Then, my grandmother fought with my mother. She told my mother that she needn't bother coming back and blamed her for everything all the time. My mother moved away but not too far from where she was living before. All the time, my grandma used to come and snoop, because he [Sarit's father] was her only son. My mother's sister lived with us, took care of us, and my mother worked three jobs a day and we rarely saw her at home, and the situation was grave. I remember that we barely ate meat and things like that. She used to buy rice and other inexpensive items and maybe, once a month, we ate meat. It was really hard.

When I was ten years old, my mother met someone and married him and that was that. She had more children from him – a girl and three boys. In the meantime, I didn't get along with my stepfather. We fought constantly and … he used to throw me out of the house, and I used to go to my grandmother and I lived with her. When she fought with me, I ran off to my aunt's house. I didn't have anywhere to live, I used to go from place to place, and at 17, I met someone and went to live with him, at his parents' home. At 18 we married … that was that. We were pregnant as soon as we married, I got pregnant, I had a miscarriage, and afterwards, after unsuccessfully trying for a year, I got pregnant again. During this pregnancy, we already had problems … we didn't get along, a big mess. We fought a lot and that's it … we left his parents' house and rented an apartment. We didn't have any money. We had lots of financial problems and they evicted us from the apartment.

Then, we didn't have anywhere to live so we had to go back to his parents. They fought with us and threw me out. I went to sleep two days in the … forest here because it was a [public] holiday … and I didn't have anywhere to sleep and I wanted to go to a social worker but the offices were closed because of the holiday…. I came to the social worker after the holiday and I told her that I had nowhere to live and that I was pregnant and my pregnancy was high risk so they put me up for a couple of nights in a hotel. She said that "Until they find you housing", and I went. Afterwards, she gave me a place in a hostel, I didn't want to go and I didn't go there. In the end, I looked for a rental and she paid the first month's rent. Then, I became a client in the social services department there and ... they helped me, they often paid my rent because I also couldn't work because of the high-risk pregnancy.

Later, my daughter was born and the father renewed our relationship. We lived together again and I had a social work student who actually helped me a lot. She brought us back and bought things for the child – a bed and all sorts of things ... we were together again. After the oldest one was born, three months later, I was pregnant again and the problems started again. We weren't getting along and everything ... we moved outside the city, rented some cheap place ... there it's cheaper. But, again, everything turned into a big mess and he left again. ... and ... I was pregnant again ... high risk, can't work, I couldn't even get out of bed. I used to get up because I didn't have any choice ... and there ... we were....

I already put in papers to the National Insurance Institute [to receive income support] so they would help me because I couldn't work and there was no one to support me. I had nothing. They gave me welfare, and put my older daughter into daycare, from the morning until four – and this way, I could manage. All this help didn't help me. I sometimes didn't have anything to feed her with. She used to eat lunch at the daycare and everything, but, let's say ... sometimes, I would be without even a pudding to give her, without milk for the night. I don't know, like, I was in a real tough situation. I told the social worker this couldn't go on that I have to pay rent and everything, and to live like this ... now, I'm going to have another baby and ... how will I pay rent and support two children?

Then, at the birth, when I was in the labour room ... my husband came with his mother because I kept in touch with his mother and she told him, and he came and was with me for the birth. He said to me "If you want help, then come live near me, at my parents." He said to me: "If you want help with the kids, and sometimes money, here and there, help caring for them when you need or something, then come here", his mother was close and also said, "Come live here." I told him: "You pay the rent and I will come." He said: "I'll pay the difference between the rent that you pay outside the city."

Then I came to live here. He signed the contract when I was in the hospital. And I came directly from the hospital. He moved my things, did everything and that's all. Since then, we have some sort of relationship ... he doesn't live here and isn't into the marriage or anything. He just helps me with the kids and he knows that these are his kids and he is responsible for them. He doesn't work and doesn't support us. He is lazy ... can't keep a job, nothing, and then there is chaos and I don't want my kids growing up the way I did, with fights and everything. I fought plenty with my stepfather and there was a big mess at home.... I don't want my kids to grow up the way I did. I say: "The best is to be alone. I can do whatever I want and I'll take care of them the way I want."

I went to the Housing Authority with both kids and said: "I am sitting here until you provide me with housing." I sat there until the evening. Before they closed, they brought me a social worker. She told me: "Go home, don't worry, it'll be ok" because at the end of the month, the landlord was supposed to evict me … and I didn't have anywhere to go. She said: "Don't worry, go home and we'll help you with housing and everything." I went home and the next day when I called, they told me: "There is nobody like that in our social workers, we don't know who or what you are talking about." They just gave me any name and wrote it down on a paper. I went to the social services department and started crying and fighting with them. I told them: "I have nowhere to live, if he kicks me out of the apartment and you don't help me, I am coming to live here in your office." The social worker said: "Look, I'll pay your rent this month but get yourself together." I said: "I can't get myself together; I have got problems and all. I can't pay the rent." Then she said to me: "Put in a request to the Housing Authority – everything in writing, so they'll help you with the rent, they only help if there are at least three children."

Then I got pregnant purposely and now I have a third baby. I went back to the Housing Authority and told them: "Now I have three kids and I want subsidised housing." They said: "No, it's a big mess and even if you'll get it, the process will take a year or two." Once again, I went to social services and told her: "What kind of country is this??? I have to get pregnant so I can get an apartment? I brought another child to suffer in this world for an apartment, and in the end, I get nothing? What kind of country is this?" In the end, I put in an application for a rental subsidy … and they approved it. Now, I want to once again apply for an apartment outside of the city because outside of the city is not such a problem to get an apartment and … when I got the money, I had to pay all the months that I didn't pay him….

I went through a lot in my life … first of all, when I was young, I was rejected, I had no home, I used to go live in all sorts of houses. I used to drink a lot, I was really addicted, I couldn't stop, I drank every day until one day that I drank much too much and…. I had a friend whose parents didn't let her go out with her boyfriend, so I used to go with him and then call her and then he would go with her somewhere. Then one day, I went with him, the same day that I drank a lot and then I called her and said to her: "Come, Nir wants you and all." She said: "My parents won't let me come." So we left and … we sat in the car and talked. We were, like, really, I knew him since we were young … really I had introduced them … we began drinking and all, and … I don't know how, I fell

On needs and knowledge

asleep and didn't remember anything. In the morning when I woke up, I found myself in his house and ... he raped me and all. I left, I filed a complaint with the police and he threatened to kill me and all, so I withdrew the complaint and that's it. Since then, I am left with a lot of trauma from that situation. I don't trust anyone. I don't like friends, I don't have any friends.'

As Sarit said, she was the eldest daughter in her family. The relationship between her parents was strained. When she was four years old, her father suddenly died, and her mother worked long hours, "three jobs", in order to support her children. When Sarit was ten years old, her mother remarried and gave birth to four more children. The stepfather used to beat Sarit. Her mother did not protect them. Sarit explains that her mother was afraid of her husband:

Sarit: 'And I used to call my mother and beg that she help me, crying on the telephone. She said: "I want to help you but if I do, he'll fight with me and beat me and everything will be a big mess" ... he used to beat us all the time, lock us in the room, take out a belt and beat the hell out of us. She also used to beat us.'
Me: 'How did you manage?'
Sarit: 'This was when I was already grown up, I was already in high school and I wasn't home much ... wherever they agreed to take me in, I stayed, I didn't have anywhere to sleep, I used to go sleep at different friends' houses, whoever, I don't even know what I did, I am really lucky that I wasn't a druggie, this would have been ... if I hung out with bad friends ... I would be a druggie. [A moment of silence.] I was really lucky that I only got involved with alcohol and not drugs, I thank God for that. [A long silence.]'

Sarit dared to file a police complaint against her stepfather. For this action, she was kicked out of the house and found herself wandering the streets. Nonetheless, having a family of her own became a goal that gave her some sense of direction. At the age of 18, she got married. She immediately became pregnant but this first pregnancy ended in a miscarriage. Later in the interview, she went back to tell me the full story of this miscarriage, which was the result of her husband's beating:

> 'He used to beat me, shove my head into a mirror, he broke the mirror, one day he broke my forehead here ... he used

to bring his friends over and they sat here all night playing cards. [A short silence.] I used to fight with him and say why is he making such a big mess and stuff like that … he slapped me or punched me, I don't remember exactly, I fainted, I remember suddenly waking up, I opened my eyes and I see him standing over me and kicking me, while I am out … kicked me in the stomach, and at night … I went to the bathroom and saw that I was bleeding.'

After the miscarriage she had their three children. Due to her problematic relationship with her husband and his parents, she decided to separate from him. I met her in this situation. She is raising the children by herself but she occasionally relies on her husband's help.

Adopting a conservative paradigm one could regard Sarit's behavioural and emotional difficulties as an autonomous phenomenon, separate from context. An analysis of this sort would highlight her difficulties with authority figures, her tendency to run away, her suspicion of helping professionals and her tendency to self-destruction. Instead, I suggest seeing her as a woman who is knowledgeable about her needs and about the limitations of the real opportunities that are available to her; a woman who struggles against poverty and economic distress, memories of the past, depression and an abusive husband, as well as against an established and organised social structure that is much stronger than she is. She struggles using the particular powers she has and despite certain weaknesses, which are a part of her. In order to understand Sarit's knowledge and needs, we have to listen carefully to her story, and adopt her perspective. This entails putting her behaviour in the context of her personal history, as well as the social context in which she struggles. From her perspective, the major difficulty that she is facing is a lack of housing.

The need for stable housing is a motif that runs through her life, from the past to the present. Not having stable housing influences her whole life and is the core of her distress and her decisions. Since adolescence, she has been tossed from one place to another, 'wandering' in a desperate search for a place to live. She tells me that during that time she tried to commit suicide twice. The street introduced her to its dangers: she was raped and started to abuse alcohol.

The need for a place of her own is also at the core of her choices: the person who became her husband is the person who offered her some housing – in his parents' place. His family have also experienced economic distress but own property. However, the shed in his parents' home intensified the power that he had over her, and he took advantage of it to control her. The physical violence against her is an indication of his control over her.

If she had had her own place to live, she would have been able to distance herself from her stepfather and later from her abusive husband and his parents, and to start a new life. She cares for her children well and also assumes her role as an older sister for her younger sister and brother, whose situations, she says, are similar to, if not worse than, her own. Caring for three very young children without stable housing makes it extremely difficult for her to build an independent future, find good work, advance and improve her financial situation.

The concrete and immediate consequence of her leaving her husband is her return to the situation in which she does not have a home. Since it is clear that he will not agree to leave the place where they live, she must get up and go. In order to do this, she needs alternative housing, planned in advance before she leaves. She has plenty of experience in this field. She had already tried living in the forest, a hostel, a hotel and an apartment with a housing authority subsidy. She, rightfully, no longer trusts the bureaucratic system responsible for providing housing solutions, which is slow, impersonal and inflexible.

Her attempts to be free of her husband's control and to become independent express both higher-level needs and basic ones. She tries to meet these needs by applying for a housing subsidy to reside outside of the city where he and his parents live. However, if she distances herself, she will be entirely alone. He is the only person who can help her and he conditions his help on her living near his mother. As she is left with no choice, she agrees. However, later on, she views this decision as a mistake: "I also made another mistake when I came here … that I listened to him and I said, 'Ok, I'll come live here'…. What does he help me? He gives me 500 shekels for child support that he would have given me there as well?" She wants to divorce him, to get away, forever. However, he plays with her and conditions his giving her a divorce on her continuing to live near him:

> 'He doesn't want to give me a divorce. He says to me: "If you don't move away, I'll give you a divorce and everything will be ok." He wants me to stay here, stuck to his ass and his mother's ass, and I don't want to. I said to him: "I don't care, I am not signing, and we can stay this way until you want to divorce. You'll lock me up here? You can't lock me up." He said: "I want her to live near me so it'll be convenient for me to visit my kids every day." And near him, I can't, why is this also such a mess, he and his mother are totally

> in my life and she is not an easy woman, she is very difficult [a short silence] ... now, if they'll let me [the request to live outside the city], I am out of here. I also have no intention of telling them where I am, they are always threatening me: "If you move away, I'll find you and be careful cause I'll kill you." I ... I don't want to tell him where I live or anything, I didn't even tell him that I put in this request. [A short silence.] I don't want to have any contact with him or with his mother.'

What we learn from Sarit is that she is reflective about her life, thinking afresh about her past decisions. In addition, we learn how determined she is in her search for a stable housing situation, and how lonely and desperate she can be.

Treating Sarit as knowledgeable does not mean approving of everything that she says. A woman who became an activist in the fight against poverty once told me that she felt that people were patronising her when they agreed with everything she said. She started to feel that people were treating her as equally knowledgeable only when they questioned her thoughts and argued with her, in a dialogical way, without abusing their power. In the interview with Sarit, asking her a 'hard question' that challenged her perspective gave her an opportunity to explain her theory about life. It started with a question about the source of her strengths:

> 'God gave me these children, and now I live only for them. [A short silence.] This is what gives me the strength, makes me want to go on and ... go to work, and take care of them. At least I have someone to take care of, and now it's not someone having to take care of me, it's me having to take care for someone, and I won't make the same mistake as those who took care of me, I ... I will be the exact opposite of what my mom was in *everything*. Whatever she is, I'm her opposite.... Don't want to be like her at all, nothing, in everything I'll be the opposite of her. [A short silence.]...
>
> That I have these children, that I love and like to be with them, that's already something good, that's already good for me, it's not like I'm here now and the situation is bad ... like I was once. I'm in a much better situation cause I'm on my own, no one's beating and no one's telling me what to do, and I have a place to be and someone to care for and everything, just what ... I need is a place to put my

life together a little more, that I'd be a little better off, that I don't need to be dependent on their dad or his mom or I don't know what. [A short silence.] That I'd be just me, and my children and my siblings.

I also see myself as my mother, because she was, after all, with three children and alone, and I'm the same, with three kids, so that's why I'm saying, I don't want ever in my life that my kids feel what I felt, *ever in my life* I don't want. I will do everything for my children. *Everything*. There's nothing that I won't do for them, that they never lack anything. *Never* will I quarrel with them, and if they have a stepfather, I promise it will be someone who loves them, not like my … stepfather. [Short silence.]'

With this answer, Sarit revealed both her awareness of the similarity between her and her mother's situation, and her struggle to avoid repeating her mother's behaviour. I wanted to understand more about it:

Me: 'And what do you think you need to do so that your children's lives are not like yours?'
Sarit: 'I need to … first of all, to go out to work, to provide for them … but mind you … if I get into a situation that I'm working and it doesn't help, the wages from my work, I am capable of going out to steal too, and I don't know what I won't do, but they will lack nothing, *nothing* will I let them lack, because this country, what does it help me any? If it was helping me, it would give me an apartment.'
Me: 'And what do you think they need in order to grow up well and happy?'
Sarit: 'Everything they want.'
Me: 'Whatever they want?'
Sarit: 'Whatever they want. Everything, everything, even if it's unnecessary things, whatever they want I'll give them. [Short silence.] I know that … my eldest girl, now she can talk, every time she says to me, "Mommy, chocolate, Mommy this, Mommy that", I know it ruins their teeth and I know it's not healthy, but I give her *everything*, the whole day she's on sweets, *the whole day*.'
Me: 'Really?'
Sarit: 'So that she doesn't even have this feeling in her heart, that I'll tell her "No, I can't give you." I don't want her to be

told what I used to be told.... I grew up on this word, "No, I don't have", and "No, I can't give you".... "Mommy, buy me a shirt", I was going with torn clothes and we were wearing torn shoes to school, everyone laughed at us.'

This dialogue explains Sarit's basic motivation in life. She wants the present with her children to correct her past. She wants them to grow up differently from her. The way in which she weaves threads between past and present in this regard is common, and is not connected directly to poverty in any way. Her choices, which I may not approve of and may even seem ineffective or destructive to me, are logical within the complex context of her needs and the real alternatives available to meet them. The way in which she presents her choices does not seem shallow or superficial, or lacking awareness or unintelligent. On the contrary, she presents her knowledge and worldview very clearly. Listening to the way in which she presents her perspective, one hears that she understands the costs of her choices. She understands that giving her daughter sweets without limits is problematic but she still does it. I challenge her at this point:

Me: 'You know, I understand what you are saying and how much you don't want them to hear these words, "No, I can't give you", but still ... I'll ask you a *hard question*: you know that when she eats chocolate and sweets the whole day, it's bad for her teeth, or when you say "I'm prepared to go to steal so that they lack nothing", you know it will harm *them* too. If you steal and go to jail, that's not good for them, or if you get into trouble, it's not good for them, who will take care of them? And if their teeth are ruined, it's not ... it's just trouble for years and years.'

Sarit: 'I know you're right but it hurts me, it hurts, even if ... she'll say "Give me chocolate", and I'll get her some, and then she'll say again, "Give me chocolate", no, I can't, I don't want to say to her "No" or "I don't want to give you." Sometimes I say "You can't have that" and ... she cries, I only see her cry, I'll go and get her all the chocolate there is.... Why, when I was little, I would see kids hanging around with sweets, and I would be dying for some sweets. Once a year, they'd buy me. I don't want them to be like me, I want it just the other way around, that other kids are jealous of them, that's what I want, the opposite of what I was. As I was jealous of other kids, so I want other kids to be jealous of them. That they wear the most beautiful clothes, that they are the neatest, the cleanest that I can.... Look here, I could now pay my rent for four months ahead and get rid of this and have nothing to worry about, but no, I said, "I'll buy her a TV, I'll buy her a video so that she can watch cartoons every day, that she can enjoy herself, that she doesn't feel she doesn't have it." *Everything*, no, not just TV, say TV's OK, she needs it, but also video. I said, "Forget about it, I'll spoil her." Everything, whatever she wants, I'll buy her.'

In her answer, Sarit again weaves the present and the past in a compelling way. Although they challenge her, she does not reject the questions, but uses them to reflect more deeply on herself. The concept of 'ghosts in the nursery' is relevant here. Selma Fraiberg, a social worker and a psychoanalyst, coined it to describe negative emotional experiences from childhood that appear as 'ghosts' years later when people become parents (Fraiberg et al, 1975). The ghosts represent the repetition of the past in the present: the repetition in the relationship with their children of traumatic experiences that they, the parents, had had in the past. These 'ghosts' are re-enacted whenever the emotional pain and scarring connected with the traumatic experiences from the past have been erased or repressed: 'Memory for the events of childhood abuse, tyranny, and desertion was available in explicit and chilling detail. *What was not remembered was the associated affective experience*' (Fraiberg et al, 1975: 419, emphasis in original). For Sarit, what might be seen as 'a difficulty to set limits for her children' is not a mere behavioural problem, but a struggle to avoid a repetition of her experience as a child who felt betrayed by her mother, who did not recognise her needs. What she needs, then, is someone who will respond to her needs and will help her to work through her past traumatic experiences.

Will Sarit succeed in providing her children with everything they need without complications? I do not know. I fear that this road may lead her and them to ruin. In my mind, I can see: the social worker's criticism of her video purchases, classifying Sarit as 'someone who doesn't know how to budget'; the lack of willingness to continue providing her with a housing subsidy (because she has not proven herself as deserving of this assistance); her desperation and aggressiveness; her objection to receiving help; the court appointment of a Youth Justice Social Worker who will be responsible for looking after the children's best interests; and the increasing aggressiveness of both Sarit and the system. However, I cannot see her as someone who needs to learn budget management. I also cannot see her as someone who will go into conventional therapy because although I think she could benefit from therapy, I do not see her fitting into the conventional setting of therapy that differentiates material needs and emotional ones.

The 'hard question' gave her an opportunity to explain the depth of her needs and motivations, and to connect her concrete behaviour with issues of identity and emotional needs:

> 'I married young.... I needed someone to raise me.... I didn't understand anything about life, he used to do as he wished and I didn't understand a thing, nothing.... I gave him freedom to do as he liked. If it would be now, with the brain I have today ... I wouldn't have given him the opportunity to lift up a hand to me or do anything bad ... straight away I would have thrown him out and wouldn't have stayed with him.'

At 22, Sarit looks back and views her choices from the age of 18 as "childish". The process of maturation that she has been through during the past four years has been a sobering process, shifting her from the romantic notion that her salvation would come in the form of a husband or partner.

For me, meeting Sarit prompted intense emotions. I saw a very young woman, 22 years old, almost a teenager, in need of protection, support and partnering. Yet, she looked much older. I saw her agency and resistance in the face of her distress. I also saw the danger that she is in. I saw how blind she was to her weaknesses and to the effect of not setting limits for her young daughters. I saw her difficulty in seeing that she is "alone – alone" and the likelihood that she will not succeed in achieving the goals that she has set for herself. I also thought about the challenges that she presents to the social workers treating her. I feared the downward spiralling of her relationship with the welfare authorities. I was very fearful of this possibility because she deserves excellent care, the care that she has never received, not from her mother or from society; the sort of devotion that she has for her children. If she were to experience a caring relationship in which both her emotional and material needs were provided for, she would be able to develop and get ahead. I was afraid that if she was not offered this level of care, she would fail – she would find herself in the arms of another abusive man, or taking care of more children than she is able to care for, or turning to alcohol, depression or perhaps suicide. I was afraid that her knowledge would not be acknowledged. It was very likely that her lack of confidence, fear of pain and dependence, suspicion that closeness would once again cause her to be used, abused and abandoned, and accompanying feelings would be seen as 'defiance' and a 'lack of will to cooperate'. Her intense desire to protect her children, coupled with her sense of urgency – considerations derived from a realistic assessment of the conditions in which she functions and the psychological sense of that awful loneliness – may well be viewed simply as 'aggression'. My overall fear was that under the difficult conditions that exist in the social services, Sarit would not receive the treatment that she deserved.

Notes

[1] ATD Fourth World: All Together in Dignity was founded by Joseph Wresinski as an international movement to fight poverty, see: www.atd-fourthworld.org/

[2] Maslow argued with the critique that according to his model, the basic needs are isolable or independent of other motivations. Trying to qualify his claim regarding their status in the model, he actually reaffirmed it: 'It should be pointed out again that any of the physiological needs and the consummatory behavior involved with them serve as channels for all sorts of other needs as well. That is to say, the person who thinks he is hungry may actually be seeking more for comfort, or dependence, than for vitamins and proteins. Conversely, it is possible to satisfy the hunger need in part by other activities such as drinking water or smoking cigarettes. In other words, relatively isolable as these physiological needs are, they are not completely so.

Undoubtedly, these physiological needs are the most pre-potent of all needs. What this means specifically is, that in the human being who is missing everything in life in an extreme fashion, it is most likely that the major motivation would be the physiological needs *rather than any others*. *A person who is lacking food, safety, love, and esteem would most probably hunger for food more strongly than for anything else*' (Maslow, 1943: 373, emphasis added).

8

On emotional pain

When I started walking through the streets of poor neighbourhoods, I remember thinking to myself that the names used for these neighbourhoods – such as 'slums', 'ghettos' and 'projects', which carry connotations of crime, violence and neglect – do not really fit them. What I saw in them was their vulnerability, as expressed in the broken light near the stairwell and the neglected areas around the structures that were supposed to be gardens. It was also expressed in the predominance of mental health services and services for people with disabilities that more affluent neighbourhoods did not want in their backyard, and the absence of banks or other 'respectable' public services. What would happen if instead of calling these neighbourhoods 'slums', we called them 'areas of suffering' or 'zones of pain'? Would it be a less accurate or less valid way to describe these neighbourhoods? I do not think that the residents of the neighbourhoods would like any of these names. However, the idea intrigued me and made me think about the unconscious process of denying the pain that accompanies poverty.

Introduction

The anthropologist Nancy Scheper-Hughes (1992: xii) describes the field of research as a place of pain:

> [Participant observation] has a way of drawing the ethnographer into spaces of human life where she or he might really prefer not to go at all and once there doesn't know how to go about getting out except through writing, which draws others there as well, making them party to the act of witnessing.

The researcher would prefer not to be in the 'field'. As they are already there, they are forced to write. Writing is the ultimate fulfilment of the commitment to act as a witness. It serves as an escape, both because it is a way to process meaningfully what the researcher has seen and experienced, and because it is a means of communication. Through writing, the researcher not only works through their pain, but also transforms it into shared knowledge, changing it from a personal wound into a social problem.

Social work operates daily in places of pain. We are exposed to human pain on an almost unbearable level. Even if social workers had unlimited resources at their disposal, enabling them to allocate them at their professional discretion, coping with the pain would still be difficult and require organisational and personal support. However, as the resources are always limited, supervision is scarce and societal support for the work of social workers is always questionable, the pain is intensified and the possibility of coping with it is diminished. The pain is so deep that there is no space or time to deal with it, either in the daily routine of work or through conference presentations or publication in journals. Yet, if social workers did not allow themselves to feel the pain of others, the profession would become uninteresting and insignificant. It would become a profession of 'social bureaucrats' who dispense meagre resources according to criteria of need and neediness.

In order to deal with pain, professionals need to understand and accept that this is an important part of the profession, and that the required resources must be allocated to it. For this to happen, social workers need time when working with service users. They also need support through supervision and knowledge regarding its importance in service users' lives, as well as in their encounters with social workers, and methods of practice that will enable social workers to feel competent when dealing with pain.

There are three reasons for recognising the pain in service users' lives. First, it characterises much of the daily experiences of people in poverty. Pain might result from: abandonment, humiliation, oppression, aggression or micro-aggression; the lack of opportunities to fulfil oneself; needing to rely on others in order to meet basic needs; failing at school; internalising that 'one like you should say "thank you"'; or the struggle against similar assertions. Moreover, professionals often overlook the link between material and emotional needs. They mistakenly think that a request for material need is only 'concrete' or 'technical', and fail to understand that each such request is also emotional and is loaded with relational meaning. Feeling pain because of the difficult life circumstances associated with poverty is considered so trivial that it becomes part of being human.

The second reason for the importance of recognising pain is that it is very rarely acknowledged. People in poverty do not have many opportunities to talk about their broken hearts; nobody really wants to hear about it. The third reason that makes recognising pain important is that it shows that service users are full subjects, and distances them from being reduced to caricatures of pathology. Thus, recognising pain is a first and necessary step in deepening the relationship between social workers and service users, and making it therapeutic in nature. In this chapter, I would like to shed some light on the subject of pain in the life stories of women service users.

Interviewing Tammy

At her request, I interviewed Tammy[1] late on a Saturday evening in her home. Her husband, who was recovering from drug addiction, was serving a prison sentence at that time, so she was at home alone with the children. When we arranged the time of the interview, she asked me to come late in the evening "so that the children are asleep and we have quiet". However, what actually happened was that we sat and talked in the small living room while right next to us, Guy, who is about six months old, sat in his bouncer, and Lee, Tammy's daughter – an active, alert, inquisitive and intelligent four year old – bustled about the whole time. Lee would not go to sleep despite Tammy's requests, demands and threats. She sat and listened to us or played nearby, or tried to attract our attention. She played with my tape recorder, asked questions, brought a book for me to read to her and told me stories. It seemed that Tammy has had little opportunity to talk and tell about her life. She has a real story to tell and she drifts easily into memories. She openly tells of her adolescence and early 20s, of her addiction to drugs, about what she did to finance the drugs, and about her then boyfriend, who died in prison. After he died, she felt that she needed to fight for her life, and she gave herself up to the police in order to be sent to prison and participate in a rehabilitation programme. In prison, she recovered from drug addiction, and in the framework of the recovery programme, she met the man who became the father of her children.

In the meantime, the baby fell asleep but Lee continued to play near us and listened occasionally. Tammy ignored her, absorbed in her story. By the time we had finished, it was already nearly midnight. Tammy asked me to give her a ride to the nearby gas station to buy cigarettes. Lee asked her to bring her sweets. We left, leaving the four-year-old girl in the house awake and her baby brother asleep. From the road on the way to the car, I turned and saw Lee standing by the window looking at us with a look that to me seemed sad and worried. Tammy bought cigarettes and sweets and I drove her back home. The journey there and back took just a few minutes.

What are the main points to emerge from the interview with Tammy? I was alerted to the most troubling aspect of the interview by a pain in my gut, which I felt on my way home. The experience that came across through the words and the stories is of a life that has experienced a lot of pain. I felt it clearly, vividly, in my gut. The source of the pain that I felt was a combination of listening to Tammy's story and recognising the fragility of her mothering, in that she did not prevent Lee from listening to the disturbing things that she was telling me, and in the pain of the young girl staring at us, with what looked to me like dread. These feelings accompanied me as I read the transcript of the interview and saw Lee's mumblings that were recorded on the tape, which were a direct response to what she had heard and understood. In both Tammy's story and in Lee's life, there is pain. I was witness to that pain and I felt it powerfully at the time and for a few days afterwards. Once the sharp pain passed, what remained was a feeling of responsibility towards them. The desire to write, to document, to draw conclusions and mainly to share with others rose immediately. More than anything, I wanted to share with others my feeling of responsibility.

In cases such as this, professional responsibility is often perceived too narrowly as responsibility for the best interests of the child. The parents are perceived as the cause of their children's trauma, either by direct or indirect action. However, the automatic blame placed on the parents ignores society's failure to take responsibility for both Tammy's and her children's pain (Featherstone and Gupta, 2018), as well as the parents' subjectivities and the social context in which they operate. In order to gain a better understanding of the responsibilities of both the parents and society, we need to examine in greater detail what these are comprised of. Specifically, I want to examine the place of pain in the lives of people in poverty.

The question of pain already arose during the initial phone conversations that I had with my interviewees, in which I invited them to meet me for an interview. I would tell them that my study involves life stories, saying, "I would like to hear about your life, as if it's a story." To my surprise, the women who refused to be interviewed explained that talking about their life "can reawaken the pain". These telephone calls could have sounded absurd because in order to explain to me their unwillingness to meet for an interview, they told me, on the phone, intimate and painful details about their lives. Take Aliza, for example, who refused to be interviewed by explaining:

> 'Have I got a story to tell you.... I have had a lot of problems in life, nobody helped, I am telling you the truth. I did everything alone. They did not help me at the Baby Health Clinic nor at the welfare office. I won't say I have not had

hard times; I also tried to commit suicide, but I raised my children alone, with all the problems.'

The historian Hayden White (1981: 2) says that 'The absence of narrative capacity or a refusal of narrative indicates an absence or refusal of meaning itself.' However, these women were not refusing to tell their stories because of ignorance or denial of the significance of the pain and suffering. Indeed, as some of the women said, the pain does not stop for a moment; it accompanies them when they are alone or at night. They refuse to articulate the words of the story because they refuse to grant it existence by means of the storytelling process. They also refused to make the story exist because they recognise its significance, not because they deny it. They consciously use the refusal to tell the story as a defence against the feeling of re-experiencing the significance because the significance of the story is, for them, the actuality of suffering. The interesting point is that these women refuse to tell their stories because they are acutely conscious of the impact that these stories can have on their emotional state.

In the interviews themselves, the issue of pain arose directly, either clearly in words or in tears, and sometimes with great intensity. This pain is barely described in social work literature, and is certainly not described in the conservative paradigm, and not even in the structural paradigm. For a long time, I too related to it as non-existent, or as a 'natural' given, apparently insignificant. However, it is important to state openly that these women have, throughout their lives, been contending with suffering and pain, and they continue to suffer and feel pain. They do not 'get used to it'; their senses are not dulled. It took a long time for me to realise that the women I interviewed live with the pain and try to share it with me and certainly with others.

What surprised and shocked me was how frequently I heard from the women that they were "depressed", and that they had suicidal thoughts in the past and were having them in the present as they experience the pain of their youth or adulthood almost daily, routinely; it is never-ending. Their sharing of their pain did not come as a response to my request. I did not direct them to talk about their feelings at all. Throughout the interviews, I did not ask explicitly: "So, how did you feel?" Rather, I tried to dispense with my professional and therapeutic skills because I wanted to hear their narrative in a form that was not necessarily psychological. When I asked a question in order to get further information, I tried to ask 'anthropological' questions, directed at the real world. These were questions like: "So, what did you do? Who helped you?" When

I felt that there was something particularly difficult in the story, I said: "It's hard, it's very hard." I considered this type of response necessary in certain cases when I felt that if I ignored the woman's difficulties, it would seem as if I were not paying attention to her or not listening to her.

Although I did not direct the women to express emotions, I heard the following things from them:

Rina

Rina: 'Of course I have a lot of pain, it's all the time, it doesn't pass, it doesn't pass. I also don't sleep at night because I often take sleeping pills if I can't fall asleep.'

Me: 'And what pains you most?'

Rina: 'What pains me most is that nobody helped me at first, to give me some initial support. If they would have helped me a little at the beginning with the kids, if they would have said to me, "life is like this or this", instead of saying "adoption" and things like that straight away. I did not deserve it.... I was a woman who knows how to raise children and does not spare the children anything, and gets up at night and work, and gives them the food they need, so [they should have helped me and not taken the children for adoption]. I say this, tell the social workers to get it into their heads ... I always helped myself to get up; every time I fell down I got up again. There were also situations where I tried to commit suicide.'

Me: 'Really?'

Rina: 'Yes, when I discovered that he [her husband] was mentally ill. Do I need to get beaten all the time? Even when I was young I tried to commit suicide, when I was still with my parents.'

Bracha

Bracha: 'Alone, also alone, you have nobody to be with ... and to tell the truth, why have I got the dog? I'll tell you the truth why I have the dog. You won't believe me ... I used to talk to the dog. I am serious.'

Me: 'Yes, I know, yes.'

Bracha: 'Suddenly, you, you've got nothing to do, so you remember the family, you remember the ... all sorts of things that make you already ... so I used to speak to the dog, I'd take him for a walk, I went downstairs with him, I'm telling you really, as if I'm talking to a person ... so that's also how time passes.'

Tammy

Tammy: 'It's the result of *lots* of things together and it's *enough* already, I got to a situation that if ... I'm telling you really and truly, if I had not landed in prison I would have committed suicide.'

Me: 'You would have committed suicide?'

Tammy: 'Yes, I would have committed suicide. I made attempts with the drug. There were suicide attempts all the time. But I really would have committed suicide, that's it, like ... things I had were so, so hard, and then again I like move everything aside, and ... focus, like I push all my difficulties aside, like *I* don't interest me, the children and the house interest me more, all the time. And then, at some other time, it suddenly comes up again ... these are the difficulties in my life that I go through. Look, if I were a normative woman, who never went through that scene of prison and stuff, maybe I would have broken quickly. Me, perhaps because I am strong, what I mean is everything I went through, how do you say it? We survived pharaoh; we'll get through this. But that is not the whole story. I try to console myself but it doesn't work. I absolutely do not want to see myself in the coming years, never. I feel waste, feel emptiness and waste and everything else. It really upsets me because I know I'm capable of more.'

Dina

Dina: 'Did I get divorced to be a servant in a family? Things aren't good *for me* either; *I've got* problems of my own. I'm joking and talking, but inside me, I feel that my children do not get love, and they want things and *I don't have* with what to buy for them, and it's good, I am lucky they understand ... then I also have illnesses, I also have depression and I've got complications from ... imaginings, I'm asleep at night and I'm thinking about all sorts of things when I get up. I wait for the morning, afraid to sleep and not.... I take

	life … [quietly], although I feel difficult right inside me, I don't let anyone feel it. [Long silence.] I manage with it somehow [short silence]. We have to say "Thank God." Even if you can't manage you have to say "Thank God." Nothing can be done, it's not easy for us [short silence]. I hope all will be well, that's it.'
Me:	'And if you could change something in your past? It's impossible because the past has already passed, but if you could … say, when you are lying in bed and thinking about your life, and I don't know if this happens to you sometimes.'
Dina:	'I think a lot and suddenly a tear falls, and suddenly I start imagining how I used to be and what happened to me and … sometimes things like this come to me, sometimes I hear songs and start crying suddenly.'
Me:	'Because it reminds you of something.'
Dina:	'Yes, yes.'
Me:	'Can you tell me just one thing like that that you remember, one story like that that happened?'
Dina:	'The feeling that I grew up without parents and how I was, and I remember … my childhood, that I went from this family to that family, and things were *bad* for me in life, things were *really* bad for me from life, also because I got sick where I was staying, and I was also a servant and I worked and I worked outside home from childhood. It's not as if I had 12 years of schooling, which would have given me some standard in life or … let's say there are people who do actually suffer but they go to study, and get sorted in life. But I am nothing. Nothing. All the time I am quite down, I don't feel like every other woman that goes to work and earns money and does things. I manage with what I get and I say "Thank God."'

Sigal

'Listen, what can I say? Sometimes I … I laugh with pain. Believe me, no, not because things are good or … from pain I, I, how do you say it? I laugh to get away from reality. But inside myself? I am empty and I.… What can I tell you? Sometimes I lose hope, although I know I shouldn't. And that's it [sighs] … I've got nothing, there is nobody I can tell, you understand? So, when I speak to my mother, and my mother is sad, no better than me, so I say, "How much can I tell my mother" because I really have no choice, but I say "Her pain is my pain." And afterwards I connect my pain to hers, and you know where that's going.'

Sarit

'With the first pregnancy when I had that whole mess, I also wanted to commit suicide, but I said: "Me, commit suicide? I've got a baby inside me. Commit suicide? I'll kill another child with me?" It's enough. I saw that when I was unmarried, when I was a girl, life was very difficult and when I got married, life was very difficult. Why? Why do I have to go on living like this?'

Eti

Me: 'You said that you broke contact with your daughter from the first marriage [Eti agreed that the girl could be placed in the custody of her father in return for a divorce].'

Eti: 'Yes. I don't want to talk about it; it's a long story. Before we got divorced, he said to me, "I'll divorce you if you give me the girl" ... so, in short, what can I tell you. It was very hard for me; I was depressed. On Shabbat, it's terrible to be alone. I've got nobody, I'm at home. [Crying.]'

Me: 'It's hard on Shabbat because you really want to see the family on Shabbat, and you want someone to welcome you, eat with you, together.'

Eti: '[Crying] ... I think it's always been hard for me. I have never had it easy [cries].'

Odelia

'I try to keep myself busy all the time and not think about things that remind me of the past, that would make me go into myself and think what I have actually gone through.... I always, always I dress smartly. Nobody knows my situation.... "How are things Odelia? You always look good." "Thank you." I like getting compliments like this from people. Nobody needs to know what's going on with me, and I have this desire to study, and to study all the time ... the ambition to progress, to progress, and not go backwards. Actually, everything goes forwards. To go with the flow, to get up and say "That's it. You have to do something to change your life to what it never was actually, not to remain in the same circle."... After I got divorced, I began to cry. For about a week, I shut myself off, I was so scared ... today also I ... am strong but not strong enough to cope with the ... if, God forbid, if I collapse into the crisis of my distress or something ... sometimes, my son wants something special, and you say to him, "No, you can't", then you feel a very severe pain, very.'

Rivka

'Sometimes, I remember all those things from the past. I want to shout a thousand times [laughs].... A person sometimes remembers [long silence].... Thanks to the children, we get through everything [long silence].... I'm sick of everything. I've suffered from a young age, from the age of 12, always suffering. [Long silence.] Because of them, thanks to them [the children], I go on with my life. Why should they also be miserable? If something happens to me, they will be adopted, poor them.'

Rita

'But our relationship [with her husband who is recovering from drug addiction] has changed. It's not like it was in the past. Until a year ago, I fell into a crisis. A crisis of anxiety attacks and depression. I'm still in treatment, even now. During the crisis, I discovered I want to give myself more, to go out to work, to make a career, to study.... But I feel helplessness, I'm afraid of getting divorced, afraid to start a new life. I don't know if it's worth it. I just want the children to be well. I find it hard. When you struggle, it's hard. When you are weak, it's even more frightening.'

Idit

Idit: 'It's a nightmare I will never forget. Really, these are things, like very painful things, that I will never ever forget ... it's a very difficult childhood; nearly all my childhood [short silence], my past with men.... I don't know, it's

	also extremely difficult. In addition, I cope alone with the income and expenses of the house and … all those things that I find very hard to cope with.'
Me:	'Tell me, what makes you happy?'
Idit:	'That I have got the children, firstly. That is my joy and … I try not to think about everything I have been telling you now, what I have been through and what happened to me and what … is happening to me. I sort of get through it. Do you know something? I have friends, they see me at clubs, they see me at entertainment places, what joy I dance and dance with, you know, there's nothing like it, nobody … anybody who sees me will not realise what I have been through, but, actually, those close to me know the whole story.… They say: "Idit, that's why we are crazy about you, that's you like … with all the pain, with all you have been through, with all that, you're always joyful. You do *not* show your pain." This was said even at the time he took the child away from me, I tell you for about six months, I didn't eat a thing.'
Me:	'Really?'
Idit:	'I did not eat a thing. I just cried and cried, holding a photo of my son and crying and crying. I didn't want anybody to contact me. I didn't go out, nothing, I couldn't, you know what it's like. I was depressed, totally. What? I got to a situation where I said if I did not have this child to care for I would commit suicide.'
Me:	'Yes?'
Idit:	'I'd say to my friends, "If there is somebody looking after him now, somebody to take good care of him, I'm going." I don't want to live my life at all. I got to this situation … and … that's it [long silence].… I take them [the children] out the whole summer, that's it but what good is it to me? What? Like, emptiness, like … there's nothing like it. I have this emptiness when the oldest child is not with me, when the second child is without his father. You understand? [Long silence.]'

Simcha

Simcha:	'I always wanted my life to become a story, to make a book about my life.'

Me:	'Where did that idea come from?'
Simcha:	'From the suffering.... It's a pain that cannot be described; it calms me and makes me sad. My pain is for my daughter and for me. Maybe I should not have gone back to her father.... I want to meet somebody. I can't meet anybody. They want a healthy women who can have sex. Now I don't have the strength for sex. *Then* I could have built my future. Now it's best with the grandchild. The joy in my heart is from the grandchild [she holds a photo of him, hugs it and says: "you are my life"] ... it's a little sad. Can we stop [the interview] for a moment so that my head doesn't ache?'

Dalit

'In the first year, about a year, 14 months, it was hard for me to leave my parents, to get used to married life, situations where I had no money, I didn't have money to feed the child but when he was big, eight months old, I started to get used to this being life.'

This is a very long section of quotation, both 'dense' and depressing. I have no hesitation in presenting it here because I want to convey something of what I felt listening to them. To be sure, meeting these women and hearing what they had to say was harder than reading about it – and, of course, experiencing what they experienced, like the women did, is infinitely harder than hearing about it. I have included the quotations because I want to share them with others so that they feel responsible, with me, to work for change.

Elizabeth Spelman (1997: 88), a feminist philosopher, says that 'Interpretive battles about the meaning of the pain of a person or a group reflect larger political battles for the right to establish meaning.' When I read what the women said about their pain, I cannot avoid asking: what sort of political battle leads to a situation that leaves no room in the professional literature for the suffering of women living for years in poverty and profound social hardship? Why the taboo of silence regarding this suffering? Why does society choose not to recognise its existence?

Although the quotations from the interviews refer to suffering that is apparently a private, personal experience, I have presented them in order to make a social statement. My intention in doing so was not to evoke pity. Indeed, the women do not seek pity; they fear pity. As they said, they conceal the pain so as not to arouse pity. My intention was to reveal the suffering experienced by the women as clear evidence of the existence of a serious social problem, to raise public awareness and to advocate taking responsibility for working for change.

The suffering of these women is not recognised as 'legitimate' suffering. While they are still girls or young women and can be regarded as victims, they are perceived as 'sufferers' and are afforded sympathy. This does not apply once they become mothers. At that moment, even if motherhood arrives when they are still young girls, their suffering becomes marginal, until it disappears completely. From the time they become mothers, they no longer deserve caring and benevolence, but demand supervision. In the eyes of society, the women go from being 'victims' to being 'victimisers', and concern is directed at their children. With this shift in concern, the mothers are neglected. How do we explain the blindness of professionals to the pain of women in poverty? It is unlikely that professionals who are in contact with women in profound, continuous distress are not aware of how severe their suffering is. The explanation must lie in the fact that the discourse relating to them does not recognise their suffering; therefore, it is easy to ignore it.

In the quotations presented here, the women themselves explained how they conceal their pain: Idit tells how her friends praise her for not showing how she has to cope with difficulties; Rita says that to be weak is frightening; Rivka and Sigal explain that they get over the pain with the help of childcare; Bracha talks to her dog; Odelia says that she gets dressed up and puts on make-up because "Nobody needs to know what is going on with me"; and Dina says that "Although I feel life to be hard inside me, I don't let them feel it." None of them are proud of their pain and they do not flaunt it. They conceal it so as not to be seen in their weakness. The relations between society and these women is a reciprocal relationship of concealing the pain. The women do not reveal the pain and society, both through the professional practice it offers and by means of the academic discourse it conducts on poverty, ignores it.

Professional practice avoids relating to pain and does not recognise it, for various reasons, including the absence of appropriate organisational support (Stevenson, 1992). However, in research as well, pain is hardly presented, and quantitative research methods, which recognise only measurable variables, facilitate repressing and ignoring it. When examining phenomena from an objective, external standpoint, based principally on behaviour and measuring variation, it is difficult to recognise an abstract element like pain. A further reason for its avoidance in research is linked to pain being perceived to belong to the private sphere, to individual experience, referring only to the individual experiencing it. We are not used to thinking about a social group living in poverty as a collective that shares pain, which, as well as being individual, has public aspects common to all members of the group.

The fact that every one of the women described herself in the interview, on her own initiative, as a bearer of pain raises questions about the nature and source of pain as a common experience. Its origins lie in the helplessness, frustration, shame and humiliation entailed in poverty. They also lie in the negligible amount of freedom for positive, strong self-definition. I suggest that collective pain should also be seen as an expression of the fact that the women's stories are not recognised in the social discourse and are not perceived to have validity. The societal marginality in which the women are located is also expressed in their stories not belonging to the generally accepted canon of social stories. As a result, they suffer from the nightmarish situation of both non-recognition and insignificance. Their stories are not recognised as a cultural option, and they are thus unable to get either a response to or an interpretation of their experiences. Their difficulties, their coping, their pain, their successes and their expectations are not arranged in a narrative that is thought to deserve respect or appreciation. Hence, they are less visible to their environment and also to themselves.

Note

[1] All the names in this chapter were chosen as pseudonyms by the participants.

9

On minor movements of resistance

The recognition of the resistance to poverty complements the recognition of needs, knowledge and pain. Recognising the resistance of people to their poverty encapsulates the tense relationship between people and their context. It presents people as having agency and as active in their struggle against poverty, and, at the same time, it presents their limiting, constraining living context. When the relationship between the two elements – the people and their context – is viewed through the lens of 'resistance', it can be seen to be marked by deep discomfort. Without minimising the effect of hardship and trauma on people's psychological life, my claim is that they do not accept poverty, do not idealise it and do not take it for granted; instead, they fight against it on a daily basis. Focusing on these efforts is a source of hope for social workers, and fruitful ground for building trust and partnership. Once we accept that people resist their poverty and hardship, the role of social workers is not to motivate them to change, but to identify their struggle and help them to make it a success. This chapter conceptualises and exemplifies 'resistance' and deals with the way in which it differs from other concepts such as 'strengths' and 'agency', as well as from the use of 'resistance' in psychoanalysis.

Introduction

In psychoanalysis, resistance is a psychic configuration of defence against insight. It describes various behaviours of avoiding raising unconscious material to the conscious level. Unconsciously, the subject avoids revealing impulses, emotions or memories that threaten psychic equilibrium. Resistance is evident in all uncooperative behaviour in treatment, whether in the refusal to accept an interpretation, the non-attendance of sessions, silence or repetitive talk, or coming late to or cancelling sessions. In this context, resistance is a manifestation of being stuck, stagnation, refusal to develop or an attempt to prevent development.

In critical thinking, resistance carries fundamentally different meanings. It does not describe a failure 'to do the right thing'. Rather, it is an active effort by the subordinated to struggle with and to oppose domination. Thus, it acquires political significance. In the PAP, resistance is the struggle of people against poverty and hardship.

It may be expressed openly, having a normative significance, but can also be covert and even be manifested in destructive behaviour. It may not necessarily be an action since it can be an avoidance of action or thoughts and emotions that are not expressed in action. What makes it resistance is that it is an expression of an unwillingness to accept hardship.

Resistance and the strengths perspective

Many of the social work professionals to whom I present the concept of resistance interpret it as a synonym for 'strengths'. Often, they declare that they appreciate the strengths perspective and find it useful in their practice. However, when they assess the suitability of specific families to a particular intervention programme, they say, 'For this programme, we need families with strengths', as if there are families without strengths – as if the strengths perspective is valid only for certain families.

The concept of resistance is, indeed, similar to 'strengths' but also different from it. Saleebey (1996) developed the strengths perspective based on his critique of the individualistic approach that stresses problems and pathology, which he regarded to be a dangerous and harmful dogma. According to the strengths perspective, all people possess strengths and social workers should recognise them and focus on them. The difficulties of individuals must be tested using a holistic approach that locates personal difficulties in the context of what people know and what they are able to do: 'All must be seen in the light of their capacities, talents, competencies, possibilities, visions, values and hopes, however dashed and distorted they may have become through circumstance, oppression and trauma' (Saleebey, 1996: 297). Moreover, the focus on strengths also aims to challenge the inherent power imbalance in the helping relationship because it emphasises that the social worker should start where the service users are, as well as the latter's capability of self-determination regarding their problems and ways to overcome them.

Saleebey recognised the difficulties confronting social workers when they need to recognise strengths. First, the logic of the helping professions seems to fit a focus on problems and their diagnosis as a basis for action. Second, the organisational setting reinforces the diagnostic perspective. However, Saleebey wanted social workers to look at what is possible rather than at pathology: 'In the lexicon of strengths it is as wrong to deny the possible as it is to deny the problem' (Saleebey, 1996: 297).

Despite its original critical approach, the strengths perspective failed to produce a paradigmatic shift in social work. The compatibility between the concept of strengths and the neoliberal version of personal responsibility enabled social work practitioners to appropriate the strengths perspective for neoliberal aims. As Roose, Roets and Schiettecat (2014: 13), who analysed strengths-focused intervention with families in the child welfare and protection system, conclude:

> Social workers walk a tightrope between responsibilizing and governing families. Strengths-oriented social work risks reinforcing a process of individualization; rather than focusing on power as the dominant structure in society, power might serve the social regulation of individuals and families…. In the latter respect, government of the social domain refers to ways in which inherently structural and social issues have been problematized in terms of rendering individuals manageable within the territory of the social…. Hence, implementing a strengths perspective requires a practical and reflexive rigor … more specifically with regard to the conceptual foundations and the political nature of a strengths-oriented practice.

One might argue that the similarity between the focus on individual strengths and the fundamental notions of neoliberal ideology is what led to the popularity of the strengths perspective. The perspective that Saleebey sought to promote, according to which everybody has strengths, 'even if they are dashed and distorted', has not percolated into the depths of the helping professions and has not influenced their perception of aid and helping relationships. The recognition of power as a major factor that shapes both the helping relationship and the realities of life for service users remains hidden and under-conceptualised. Instead, 'strengths' were used only to describe constructive behaviour or normative personal abilities. Moreover, the consideration of 'strengths' became yet another diagnostic item, which was also a trend that Saleebey opposed.

Resistance and agency

The term 'agency' is a more political term than 'strengths'. It has gained prominence in the academic field, mainly among feminist and radical circles. In many respects, 'resistance' is close to the concept of agency. Ruth Lister (2004) uses 'agency' to describe the active part of a person, based on perceiving the person as an individual, with a goal, able to make a certain level of choices and operating creatively. She argues that:

> In the complex interplay of agency and structure, many researchers, rightly, emphasize the constraints and lack of choice faced by people in poverty and their sense of having no control over their lives. Yet, despite the constricted nature of the agency people in poverty can exercise, 'even the material conditions and life experiences of most of the poor are not so constrained in every sense that they are not capable of making decisions about how to cope with their situation' (Leisering and Leibfried, 1999: 40). (Lister, 2004: 132–3)

Similarly, in his analysis of theories in the sociology of education, Giroux (1983: 259), the radical educator, argues that in reproduction theories, the overemphasis of the idea of domination and the ways in which neoliberal governmentality regulates social life and reproduces social inequalities fails to provide the necessary insights regarding the many ways in which teachers, students and other human agents resist structural domination: 'By downplaying the importance of human agency and the notion of resistance, reproduction theories offer little hope for challenging and changing the repressive features of schooling.'

The concept of agency introduces the age-old debate between the power of the social structure in shaping the life of the individual, their behaviour and even their inner world, and the power of the individual (agent) themselves to shape their life.[1] Instead of taking one side in this debate, Lister (2004) notes the decisive importance of locating the agency of people living in poverty within the context of a social structure. According to this stance, both people's agency and the social structure have enormous power. People have power to choose, desire, set goals and direct their paths, and the structure has power either to enable or restrict people. The relationship between people and the structure is mutually influential.

Poverty creates many interconnected limitations and barriers, in part, because of material shortage, in part, because of the scarcity of social opportunities (to education, health, housing, employment and welfare) and, in part, because of the shortage of symbolic capital (manifested in stigma, Othering, disrespect and misrecognition). These barriers limit opportunities. This is not to say that people do not choose, but rather that the real alternatives open to them to fulfil their wishes and realise their choices are limited. Placing agency in context therefore facilitates the recognition of both the subjective complexity of people and their, more or less successful, attempts to resist poverty.

Lister (2004) suggests a taxonomy of types of agency along two axes: on one axis, it moves between everyday and strategic agency; on the other axis, it moves between personal and political/citizenship agency. Where the two axes meet, four types of agency are created. The first type of agency is the *getting out* type, which includes behaviour in the personal and strategic sphere, that is to say, behaviour by the individual in order to achieve the strategic goal of getting out of poverty, for example, integrating into the labour market or acquiring an education. This type of agency is the easiest to identify because it relates to normative, goal-oriented behaviour that is explicitly directed towards extricating oneself from poverty.

The second type of agency is *getting organised*. It expresses itself as strategic and political activities aimed at reducing the poverty not only of the individual, but also of the social group, for example, by means of collective self-help, political activity, civil involvement or social protest. The social activists who are involved in this type of agency usually have some degree of political consciousness. Since they exercise their agency in the public sphere, it is usually recognised as such.

The third and fourth types of agency are harder to identify. The third type is *getting by*, which is found in the personal, everyday sphere. It refers to everything that people routinely do to cope with poverty and to make a living, for example, by means of pooling resources, reducing expenditure to the minimum and managing the stress involved in juggling a small budget. This type of agency is often misrecognised. Its everyday, low-profile character often makes it appear 'obvious' or as mere 'survival', thus reducing the mental and physical effort that people invest in order to get by, and detracting from its significance as a type of resistance.

The fourth type of agency is *getting (back) at*, which is located in the everyday and in the political sphere. This is the most complex type of agency to identify and the hardest to understand or to give recognition to. The individual uses this type of agency to achieve personal goals while simultaneously expressing opposition to, and struggle against, the power imbalance and those in power who represent it. Agency of the 'getting (back) at' type can express itself in undeclared work, confronting the welfare authorities by means of a violation of regulations and laws, manipulation, lying, using resources received from the welfare system for other purposes, and concealing information. In contrast to agency of the 'getting organised' type, which has a more institutional character, and whose social criticism is more overt, agency of the 'getting (back) at' type has a covert and informal character. Its aim is not political change, but change on the symbolic, relational level. It is linked to the feeling of 'no more', where people mark their own boundaries and fight for their autonomy and dignity. Sometimes, this type of agency can lead to immediate and concrete gains, for example, as when a person makes a threat and manages to get what they want; at the same time, it achieves a feeling of control and the 'correction' of a previously inferior position. However, it often leads to losses, for example, when a social worker lodges a complaint with the police against a service user as a response to their threats. However, even in cases where the behaviour leads to losing concrete gains, it creates symbolic satisfaction, linked to the feeling of 'I stood up for what I wanted' or 'I also have boundaries, and I am not prepared to be quiet any longer.'

There are three reasons that make the concept of agency and the taxonomy that Lister suggests useful for social workers. The first reason is that by offering different types of agency, social workers can develop a more holistic and detailed picture of the various possibilities to exercise one's agency and to resist poverty and hardship.

The second reason is that the concept of 'agency' also includes non-normative behaviour. Whereas the concept of 'strengths' is generally perceived as representing behaviour or characteristics that fall under what is socially acceptable, the concept of 'agency' enables social workers to interpret non-normative or non-hegemonic behaviour not as pathology, but rather as opposition to an unjust social structure. Bearing this interpretation in mind, social workers can feel empathy towards behaviour that was previously perceived by them as neither understandable nor acceptable.

The third reason is that the origins of the concept of 'agency' in sociological theory (Fuchs, 2007) protect it from easy appropriation by the psychological and individual lexicon.[2] The sociological baggage of the concept prevents us from seeing the agent as a free and independent individual; instead, we see them as an individual who struggles against the social and political context, which restricts the possibilities and the real alternatives available to them.

These three reasons make the concept of agency particularly relevant to the PAP. The starting point of poverty-aware social work is that people always possess agency. In other words, they are always active and they routinely oppose poverty and hardship. By saying that people are active, we are rejecting the perception of them as passive figures whose humanity and subjectivity are shaped by poverty in a total way, and we point out the mode of opposition or rejection that people display towards poverty. They do not accept it, like it or want it.

In the event of their resistance succeeding and they are, indeed, extricated from poverty, it is easy for the public and for social workers to identify their behaviour as resistance. However, people resist poverty and hardship even when they do not manage to defeat it or reduce it, whether because they chose ineffective means of resistance or due to insurmountable structural barriers. In these cases, their resistance is not recognised, and it is perceived as problematic. Our aim as social workers is to recognise and understand expressions of resistance, major or minor, successful or unsuccessful, and normative or non-normative.

Recognition of people's resistance is important not only from a theoretical or moral standpoint, but also as a practice. It enables the social worker to stand by their service users in their struggle against poverty and in their attempts to reduce its effects. In fact, it allows social workers to shift from a position of standing *against* people in an attempt to change them, to a position of standing by them in order to change the reality that they are living in. The social worker can stand by the service users more easily and effectively when they have formed a clear impression of their resistance. Moreover, the very recognition of the resistance by the social worker can facilitate the self-understanding and reflection of service users.

Standing by service users requires social workers to become experts at recognising displays of resistance at the micro-level in order to join them. These displays can sometimes be transitory or momentary – at times, not even consolidated as behaviours at all, existing only at the level of dreams, attitudes and aspirations. Therefore, in order to recognise resistance, we must understand that we work in an arena dominated by power relations and a hegemonic discourse that induce us to see people in poverty as Others. Recognising agency in this context requires an ongoing critical reflection in order to navigate and resist hegemonic interpretations and to offer a critical one.

Recognising resistance is easier when a close relationship exists between social workers and service users. That is to say, in addition to critical reflection, what is needed is an emotional stance of closeness to service users – an attitude of standing by that enables understanding of their perspectives, the living context in which they operate and the various ways in which their resistance is manifested.

Therefore, the concept of resistance includes the concept of agency and adds a dimension to it that concerns Lister to a lesser degree. While 'agency' relates specifically to active, goal-oriented activity, the concept of 'resistance' encompasses less declarative actions, as well as thoughts, dreams, desires or petty behaviours – everything a person does in private or in the world to express their humanity, subjectivity and singularity in the face of hardship, and in order to preserve value and dignity.

The next two examples describe the two types of resistance that are harder to recognise. The first exemplifies agency of the *getting by* type and the second the *getting (back) at* type of agency.

Emil is visiting his wife: getting by

In a supervision session, Avi, a social worker, spoke about Emil, an older man, "a chronic case" known to the social services department for many years. One day, Emil came to see Avi to ask for money to pay for a bus ticket in order to visit his wife, who was hospitalised in a mental health hospital in a nearby city. Avi said that he felt helpless and was furious at the man, who seemed to him at that moment to be the prototype of the 'bad client' (Urek, 2005): dependent, being unable to take care of his basic needs on his own; and a service user who clearly did not understand the social worker's role. Emil's request sounded totally absurd to Avi since the social services department lacked discretionary funds, particularly for buying small items such as bus tickets: "With the years of experience that Emil had with the social welfare department, he should have known not to come and waste my time with such a request."

When Avi told the story, it sounded like a straightforward case. Emil definitely wanted something from Avi (otherwise he would not have bothered to come) but his request seemed out of context. It seemed as if he came with a request that he knew would be rejected. It was hard to make Avi stand by Emil. However, during the discussion, while describing Emil in more detail, Avi recalled that he had come to him carrying plastic bags filled with little presents he wanted to bring to his wife: some soap, shampoo and candies. It appeared that these were donations from local shops and private people in the town that Emil had collected shortly before approaching Avi so as not to visit his wife empty-handed. He approached Avi because he could not ask the bus driver to let him travel for free and he needed help with this final task.

This information cast Emil in a different light. It changed him from dependent to independent, from a person who did not take care of himself to a person caring for his wife, and from someone unable to understand the social worker's role to one giving the social worker the opportunity to acknowledge his efforts and small achievements, and to become a partner on his journey to his wife.

By adhering to the hegemonic discourse, we would have been ignoring the man's request, or perhaps would have begun to see changing his attitude as a goal of our intervention. Recognising his agency and resistance shifts our position entirely, makes his request totally rational and leads us to stand by him. This modified stance also makes it possible for a new dialogue to take place between Avi and Emil. When we face the naked reality of poverty, the lack of money is not masked by a 'lack of motivation' or a 'lack of understanding of the social worker's role'. In fact, it enables us to recognise the difficulties and challenges facing people who are trying to live a decent life in the context of poverty. Only after we acknowledge the way in which poverty is manifested in real life will we be able to recognise people's resistance, and then use words in the dialogue with them to name their efforts, to stand by them in order to magnify those efforts and, hopefully, to turn them into successes. If he had recognised Emil's agency, Avi would have been able to say:

> 'I'm happy you came to me for help with this one. It's amazing what you have already managed to arrange for your wife. How can we get the money for the bus ticket? You know that we don't have any budget for this kind of request, but we won't let you leave this office without arranging something. Let's think of creative ways to raise this money now.'

After helping the man get to his wife, we might exercise policy practice, with or without him, in order to set up a small, flexible budget at the social services departments for precisely this kind of on-the-spot humanitarian need.

Dana is giving birth: getting (back) at

Dana is a 25-year-old mother of a girl aged seven. Her parents emigrated from Ethiopia when she was a young girl and she grew up in boarding schools. She got pregnant with her daughter when she was 18, about to finish the last year of school. She did not realise that she was pregnant until she began to have severe stomach pains that turned out to be labour contractions. After the birth, she gave her baby daughter to her mother, who took care of her with the help of other family members. In the meantime, Dana almost severed her relationship with the family, moving from the small town where she was living to Tel Aviv and visiting them only rarely.

Seven years later, Dana was pregnant again. When she arrived at the hospital to go into labour, the social services department was notified and the day after the birth, Shirley, a social worker, came to see her in order to assess her parenting ability. Shirley asked Dana about her older daughter, and Dana said that she had raised her daughter with her mother's help throughout that time. Shirley empathetically asked to talk with Dana's mother. Dana gave her the telephone number and over the telephone, Dana's mother confirmed what Dana had said. A short while later, Shirley realised that Dana had tricked her. The number she gave her belonged to a friend, who talked with the social worker pretending to be Dana's mother.

Shirley felt deceived and could not regard what Dana did as an expression of her strengths or of any agency. When she was asked explicitly if Dana expressed any strengths in the situation, she could only point to Dana's lying to her as a "negative strength", normally associated with criminality. However, the framework of resistance allows us to see Dana's point of view. What she did was grounded in her analysis of the relationship with the social worker as a power relation, and her fear of her. She was understandably terrified that the social worker would take the baby from her, and tried to resist.

This understanding does not mean that Shirley should have ignored her concern about Dana's ability to mother the baby. However, it should have affected her opinion of Dana and enabled a new reading of what she considered an 'empathetic request' to talk with Dana's mother. Shirley said that she asked Dana to talk with her mother 'empathetically', but, in fact, Dana, who had never met this social worker before, understood this request more as an act of power and surveillance than of empathy. If Shirley had wanted to give Dana a chance to show her abilities as a mother – or perhaps to promote these abilities – she should have been very honest and clear with her while, at the same time, showing Dana that she stood by her. If Shirley had understood power as a major element in their relationship, she would not have been surprised if Dana did not trust her. After all, Dana does not know her, and does not know if she is trustworthy. Only by understanding Dana's behaviour in the given circumstances as necessary and rational would the social worker be able to begin the long process of building a helping relationship with her.

These are two prototypes of the difficulty of recognising resistance. Emil's story illustrates the difficulty of recognising resistance when what stands out is behaviour that appears to be passive and dependent. At first sight, it seems that there is no resistance at all in Emil's story. Dana's story demonstrates the difficulty of recognising resistance when what stands out is the manipulation of social workers and children in situations of risk. In this case, although it is clear that Dana is an active agent, her behaviour is perceived as having only negative significance.

To summarise what we can learn from these examples, in order to be able to use the resistance concept in poverty-aware social work, social workers should develop two skills:

1. the skill to recognise the service user's subjectivity, that is, their inner world – their desires, dreams, needs, knowledge and pain; and
2. the skill to locate the service user's behaviour, thoughts and feelings within the context of the real alternatives in their immediate environment and within the context of a power relationship.

In order to recognise the service user's subjectivity, one needs to remember that overt behaviour does not necessarily reveal everything. It is very easy to extrapolate from the service user's dominant behaviour to their inner world. It is easy to assume that Emil is passive and has a limited understanding of reality, or that Dana is dishonest. However, recognition of the service user's subjectivity entails shifting one's gaze from the dominant behaviour to areas of behaviour, feelings or thoughts that appear marginal at that time.

In order to locate the service user's behaviour, thoughts and feelings within the context of the power relations and real alternatives open to them, the social worker has to recognise the reality of life of the service user and take note of the material needs on which the behaviour, emotions and thoughts are based. In addition, it is extremely important to examine through critical reflection what role power plays in the helping relationship. These perceptions require the social worker to face poverty, not only in its overwhelming brutality, but also in its smallest details. They demand taking an interest in the source of the candy in the plastic bag or in the question of what other realistic opportunities are open to Emil in order to raise the small sum needed for the bus journey. They demand taking an interest in the myriad details of the reality of Dana's life that caused her to give up mothering her first daughter, and the context of her second birth.

The aim of the contextualisation is to allow the social worker to respond to the service user in a way that permits them to see the logic in their behaviour alongside its cost. Certain questions can help: what is the financial context in which the behaviour takes place? (Can the service user obtain the same things in a different way?) What is the balance of power in which the behaviour occurs? (Could the service user have told the social worker what she really needs and expect to get an answer?) What is the service user telling the social worker about their relationship by means of this behaviour? (What degree of trust does the service user feel? Do they feel that they are worthy of receiving what they need?)

Sometimes, when I present these ideas to experienced social workers, they say that if they regarded every type of behaviour, even manipulation, cheating or violent behaviour, as a manifestation of resistance to poverty, they would not be able to set limits for the service users and would not be able to confront them with the need to change. That is not my intention. I am not suggesting that the social workers should agree with or permit all types of behaviour. Nor do I think that the social workers should consent to the service users being violent towards them or abusive and neglectful towards their children. My contention is that their passivity is not as total as it sometimes seems, and that their manipulation or violence is often a thin veil of behaviour that conceals despair and a lack of recognition. The social worker's aim is to create a good-enough relationship based on recognition as a central principle of social justice.

Notes

[1] There is more on the structure–agency debate in Lister (2004: 126–7).
[2] Perhaps this is the reason why, in Israel, 'agency' is regarded as a purely academic concept and has not managed to percolate into the professional discourse of social work and be adopted by practitioners.

PART III

Rights

While Part II of the book focused on social workers' recognition of the subjectivities of service users as one of the central components of the helping relationship, Part III focuses on the second component: the recognition of the external world and material aspects of poverty. This recognition provides the basis for rights-based practice. Seeing rights-based practice as a necessary complement to relationship-based practice is an organising principle of the PAP. Intervention in the material aspects of poverty and improving them are achieved through four strategies: the active realisation of rights, material assistance, community work and policy practice. This part of the book focuses on the practice of the active realisation of rights and material assistance.

The first chapter of this part (Chapter 10) is titled 'What is active in the active exercising of rights?' and serves as a theoretical and conceptual introduction to the following three chapters. In addition, it describes the guidelines for the new role of Rights Exercising Social Workers, which was developed with the adoption of the PAP by the Ministry of Welfare and Social Services. Loyal to the PAP's commitment to seeing the emotional and material worlds of service users as interconnected, this chapter also explains how rights-based practice can become therapeutic.

Chapter 11, 'Material help and a flexible budget', addresses the material assistance provided in all PAP programmes. Throughout the history of social work, there has been a complex relationship between responses to emotional needs and responses to material needs. In the PAP, the internal and external realms are perceived as connected, so practice should seek to simultaneously respond to both. This chapter presents a case study in order to explore the need for material assistance in working with people in poverty. In addition, based on experience in using material assistance in PAP programmes, its characteristics – immediacy and flexibility – are discussed.

Chapter 12, 'Active rights exercising: advanced', focuses on the difficult issue of working with service users under circumstances where there are no legal rights that they can actualise. This might happen when service users do not have citizenship, or when a certain need of citizens is not covered by law. The chapter calls upon social workers to ask themselves what their role is in these situations and gives examples of what social workers can do under such circumstances.

Chapter 13, 'In the face of social injustice: a panel', brings to life the voices of an activist, students and social workers who participated in a panel that took place at Ben-Gurion University in 2015. The chapter – a transcription of the panel discussion – reveals the participants' personal experiences with the practice of the active actualisation of rights, their attitudes towards it, the characteristics needed to conduct this kind of practice and the pros and cons of it.

10

What is active in the active exercising of rights?

Since poverty is conceptualised in the PAP as a violation of rights, the exercising of rights has become an important focus of practice. In the MAPA programme, we developed this practice in two forms: first, we fostered the exercising of rights as a therapeutic process for caseworkers; and, second, we created the new and unique role of a Rights Exercising Social Worker, whose prime tasks are promoting the exercising of rights and engaging in policy practice. I say 'new' because this role had not existed in Israel before. After the National Committee to Combat Poverty in Israel recommended the opening of rights centres in 2014, the Ministry of Welfare and Social Services adopted the idea of having Rights Exercising Social Workers, and by 2016, about half of the social services departments in the country employed designated social workers in this role. This chapter briefly describes the background to the development of the active exercising of rights as a concept, and focuses on its guidelines for the practice of both caseworkers and Rights Exercising Social Workers. In addition, it presents the close link between the exercising of rights, policy practice and therapeutic processes.

Introduction

> The authority's obligation to treat the individual fairly should be expressed, firstly, by respecting her. In other words, if a regular person is bound to respect the other's humanity, all the more so the administrative authority, due to its responsibility for her peace and wellbeing. Moreover, the norm of respect for the citizen is especially important in the modern, bureaucratic state, which is wont to relate to the individual as a 'number' or 'case', as opposed to treating her as a human being worthy of individual attention. (Barak-Erez,[1] 2003: 223)

The protection of rights has been an integral part of social work since its inception as a profession at the end of the 19th century. Advocacy activity was carried out by the mothers of the profession, Jane Adams and Mary Richmond (Dalrymple and Boylan, 2013). The advocacy for social justice carried out by members of the Settlement House Movement is well recognised by the social work profession. The Settlement House Movement emerged at the end of the 19th century in the UK and the US, and reached its peak during the 1920s. It was innovative by virtue of its community orientation, which viewed the social structure as the main cause of deprivation and poverty. The volunteers at the Settlement Houses initiated wide-ranging cultural activities, established services for the benefit of the community and conducted a range of advocacy activities (Adams, 1920; Lissak, 1989). For example, at Hull House, established by Jane Adams in Chicago in 1889, Adams and the other volunteers conducted research that served to advance policy (Santiago, 1972). Already in 1924, Eileen Younghusband, who was involved with the Settlement Houses in England, laid the foundations for systematic advocacy and the establishment of a civil rights centre; at the same time, she introduced these principles of action into training programmes for social workers at the London School of Economics (Dalrymple and Boylan, 2013).

Less well known is that pioneering advocacy practices existed not only in the Settlement House Movement, but also in the Charity Organization Society, the birthplace of casework (Dalrymple and Boylan, 2013). For instance, Dalrymple and Boylan describe the work of Mary Stuart, who was appointed as a medical social worker at the Royal Free Hospital in 1895. Her job was to ensure that people who could afford to pay for treatment were not abusing the medical system, which was intended for people living in poverty. While the medical system viewed Stuart's task as protecting the system from fraud, she time and again found that the people coming to the hospital were, indeed, poor and sick, often with chronic illnesses. Her status at the hospital led to her findings becoming accepted, and the need for advocacy for people living in poverty, which opposed the prevailing perception according to which they got sick in order to avoid work, was also recognised.

Over time, a distinction arose between case and cause advocacy. Case advocacy had been carried out by caseworkers and focused on changing the individual's situation, whereas cause advocacy had been carried out by community workers and social activists in order to further policy change (Dibbets and Eijkman, 2018). As the profession developed and became institutionalised, the ties of case advocacy to social change weakened and cause advocacy came to be identified with the struggle for social justice (Dalrymple and Boylan, 2013).

There are various reasons for the abandonment of the commitment to social change by caseworkers: the pressure and heavy caseload that characterise their work limit their capacity to deal with macro-practice on the systemic level (Kam, 2014: 733); they do not see themselves as agents of social change; and they fail to identify social problems as such and instead tend to perceive the problems of individuals as stemming from individual causes (Hawkins et al, 2001). Moreover, the fact that most social workers work in services supervised by the state traps them in a conflict of interests when they want to rebel against social problems on behalf of their service users (Cloward and Fox Piven, 1975; Schram and Silverman, 2012; Reisch and Andrews, 2014).

However, the identification of practices aimed at advancing social justice with social change only on the macro-level leaves the majority of social workers' and service users' interactions and experiences – those that occur in the interpersonal sphere – outside the field of interest of those committed to social justice.[2] The PAP seeks to fill this void and to suggest *active rights exercising* as a social justice-oriented operational mode that is applicable in the interpersonal sphere as well as on the macro-level. In fact, the poverty-aware social worker views the interpersonal sphere as being not just an appropriate area for work on rights and social justice, but a crucial one, and is constantly seeking ways to give the practice of exercising individual rights a political character.

The aim of this chapter is to describe, both theoretically and practically, the concept of the active rights exercising and its place in the PAP. We are fortunate to have the experience gained in the MAPA programme, where the practice of exercising rights was developed, as well as the experience of the rights centres that have been operating in affiliation with the social services departments all over Israel.

Poverty and rights exercising

In order for individual activities to have political weight, they need to be understood in the context of power relations. This requires an examination of the relationship between poverty and the (non-) exercising of rights.[3] The task is complex because, paradoxically, poverty creates both an acute need for realising rights and daunting barriers to doing so. According to research undertaken by the New Policy Institute for the Joseph Rowntree Foundation, almost a third of eligible people in the UK in 2009/10 were not claiming the means-tested benefits that they were entitled to. Take-up rates for most income-related benefits declined in the decade to 2009/10 (Aldridge et al, 2012, cited in Finn and Goodship, 2014). Data from three European countries (Austria, Germany and Finland) show that at least half of those households eligible for social assistance did not claim it (Fuchs, 2009, cited in Finn and Goodship, 2014). In the US, Indicators of Welfare Dependence (cited in Finn and Goodship, 2014) reported to Congress that in an average month in 2009, only 32.3 per cent of families eligible for Temporary Assistance for Needy Families (TANF), 64.6 per cent of households eligible for Supplemental Security Income (SSI) and 72.2 per cent of adults eligible for the Supplemental Nutrition Assistance Program (SNAP) were estimated to have enrolled and received benefits. In Israel, according to the annual report of the NII (2017), in 2016, only 48–64 per cent of the people who were eligible for Income Support received it. Qualitative research conducted among diners at a soup kitchen in Tel Aviv found that 73 per cent of them did not receive any social security benefits. When they were assisted to make their claims, 88 per cent of the claims were accepted (Levine, 2009).

It is important to remember the specific nature of the non-take-up of rights for people in poverty. Peleg (2013) enumerates three characteristics: first, they need the assistance provided through benefits and services for long periods of time; second, the nature of the relevant rights concerns their most basic needs, hence a situation of non-exercising creates severe shortages and crisis situations; and, third, the cumulative character of rights, namely, the simultaneous dependence on a number of benefits or services provided by various authorities, makes people in poverty extremely vulnerable. Moreover, this kind of dependence on state services for the provision of basic needs creates a high intensity of contact with the authorities and enables its representatives to carry out daily surveillance at the micro-level of the lives of citizens. Taken together, these features of the non-take-up of rights create a general sense of alienation in dealings with state officials based on experiences of constant vulnerability, existential anxiety, insecurity, inability to protect privacy for fear of investigations and the constant fear of parental rights being limited or cancelled (Peleg, 2013).

Much has been written about the reasons for non-take-up. For our purposes, let us differentiate between two main types of non-take-up of rights.[4] The first type – primary non-take-up – relates to not claiming, that is, a person who is eligible for a benefit or service but does not claim it, for example, because they do not know about it, and as a result do not receive it. The second type – secondary non-take-up – is the situation where the individual is eligible for a benefit or service and claimed it but for various reasons has not received it. This type is directly linked to the workings of administrations, and to the specific way in which they handle claims and claimants. The factors that affect non-take-up of this type might be, for example, the clerks' humiliating and degrading behaviour, or giving insufficient information and advice.

Poverty creates added vulnerability for these types of non-exercising of rights in various ways. People might not claim their rights because they are not aware of the benefits of services or have incorrect knowledge about them, or because of various barriers: geographical, language, social and psychological (Elbashan, 2003). The stigma that is often connected to receiving benefits and services intended for people living in poverty is another reason that causes people to refrain from claiming their rights (Finn and Goodship, 2014). Empirical evidence shows that for benefits and services that involve a means test, the levels of non-exercising are particularly high (Van-Oorschot, 1998).

Poverty creates added vulnerability for secondary non-exercising as well, as entailed in the way in which the clerical level, that is, 'street-level bureaucrats' (Lipsky, 1980), deal with service users. The obstacles that street-level bureaucrats erect to rights exercising can take the form of a rejection based on a mistake regarding a valid claim, or by allowing only a small sum as a benefit, or by an arrogant or belittling attitude, viewing the claimant stereotypically (Van Oorschot, 1995). Active rights exercising aims to overcome these barriers by enriching the standard practices of mediation and advocacy that social workers employ in social services departments with political meaning.

My claim is that although social workers in social services departments deal regularly with, for example, a request for a psychosocial report to support a claim for social housing, a subsidy for paying for a daycare centre for a child or for advice about dealing with debts, they lack the theoretical and ethical framework to guide them in this work. Consequently, they treat this aspect of their professional encounters as merely a technical activity. What is unique about the PAP is its aim to introduce a radical drive for social justice, to which the profession's values are committed, into this seemingly bureaucratic practice.

Active rights exercising as a theoretical and ethical concept

We coined the term '*active rights exercising*' in order to create a distinction between the rights exercising that stems from a very firm ethical stance, and practice based on conservative or neoliberal interpretations that focus on its bureaucratic aspect. The practice of *active rights exercising* comprises the sum total of activities that emanate from a deep ethical commitment to social justice. It can range from policy practice as a means to overcome structural barriers to proactive practice at the level of the individual that includes examining what the relevant rights are, carrying out the necessary procedures with service users in order to apply for these rights, accompanying service users to the relevant administrative authorities when needed, appealing after the rejection of requests and processing the emotional experiences triggered. Active rights exercising is a basic stance that is not dependent on the cooperation of the service user, on their level of activity in the process or on the specific nature of the helping relationship. Since the PAP perceives poverty to be a violation of rights, merely dealing with exercising rights is part of the struggle against poverty and the limited opportunities that it creates for those who experience it.

Moreover, the understanding that poverty is not only a lack of material resources, but also a shortfall of symbolic resources, entirely changes the usual, technical practice of exercising rights with individuals. Recognising situations of micro-aggression (Pierce, 1970) is particularly relevant for the practice of rights exercising because it reveals the interpersonal interactions of service users with the administrative officials as an arena of struggle. People living in poverty are particularly vulnerable to experiencing micro-aggressions in those interactions, partly because of the unique character of their reliance on the authorities and partly because they have to deal with their inferior symbolic capital, expressed in the social image associated with them as 'exploiting, lying or manipulating'.

The professional tendency frequently treats service users' reports of their encounters with state officials as imagined experiences or as a problem of oversensitivity, a fragile self-image or a lack of skills. This tendency leads to practice based on providing service users with the skills to deal better with administration officials, and motivating them to do so. Underlying this version of exercising rights is a conservative assumption that the people themselves are responsible for the problem and thus have to change in order to solve it.

The PAP, on the other hand, recognises that the barriers to the actualisation of rights, including experiences of micro-aggression, are very real experiences that stem not from the inherent characteristics of service users, but from structural features. This dictates a practice in which social workers need to have a deep commitment to issues of rights and to taking an active stance on finding solutions for their realisation. Therefore, at the level of the individual, accompanying service users to the authorities becomes a necessary practice, the aim of which is not only to increase the voices of service users, but also to help the officials to be more attentive.

How is active rights exercising practised by caseworkers?

The direct practice of active rights exercising is a practical expression of the social worker's stance, based on a deep commitment to rights and actualising them. This does not mean that rights can be fully realised in every situation as the absence of services or other structural barriers can prevent this from happening. However, it is the social worker's responsibility to be fully involved in the attempt to realise rights through creative ways of working, a willingness to delve into the details of law, rules and regulations, a refusal to accept 'no' for an answer when it seems unjust, and accompanying services users to administrative offices. All of these activities stand on their own, of course, but, as will be detailed later, since they always involve the recognition of service users, they also serve therapeutic purposes. The practice of active rights exercising, then, is a proactive practice that includes three stages: (1) defining problems in terms of rights; (2) standing by service users; and (3) moving from an individual problem to policy practice.

Defining problems in terms of rights

According to the Naming, Blaming, Claiming (NBC) model, in order to classify a problem as a violation of rights, one needs to name a particular experience as injurious (naming), and to have the knowledge that will enable attributing it to the fault of a social entity (blaming). Only then might one claim a remedy for it (claiming) (Felstiner et al, 1980/81). The added vulnerability of people in poverty carries the risk of them not naming and blaming as required, that is, not defining their problems in terms of rights. Thus, the role of the social worker at the initial stage is to ask questions about aspects of the real life of the service users and to listen out for possible rights-related issues. Indeed, they have to translate personal problems into the language of rights.

Active listening to rights is expressed in two ways: first, the social worker assists service users to identify rights that they are not aware of. In order to do so, they have to be familiar with the laws, regulations, services, benefits and eligibility criteria, and they need to inform service users about them. For example, if the social worker recognises that the service user meets the conditions for a reduction of municipal taxes, they would ask them if they get this reduction.

Second, the social worker is prepared to listen to accounts in which service users report the non-exercising of rights. This refers to service users *telling* them that their rights have not been exercised, whether because of bureaucratic difficulties, a lack of knowledge, stuck processes that are incomplete or that ended with a negative answer, or inappropriate treatment. In this type of case, listening from the point of view of active rights exercising means examining the issue thoroughly, understanding what right has not been accessed and what the barriers are to exercising it, and urging the service user to exercise it while standing by them.

Standing by service users

The stage after employing active listening to rights is standing by service users. This means learning from them exactly what help they want and how they want to receive it, and providing this help. Service users might only need advice or guidance regarding the necessary procedures, and then perform the actions themselves. Alternatively, they might want to simulate with the social worker a situation in which they present their problem to administrative officials. In certain cases, they might want the physical accompaniment of the social worker to the service. Each of these scenarios can arise and would constitute a concrete response to needs. Moreover, all of these options are possible subjects for discussion later on that, as will be elaborated in a minute, are therapeutic in nature.

In reality, the social worker often cannot find a way to deal successfully with rights issues, which are complex and tend to give you the feeling you are in a 'dead end'. At the same time, if the social worker realises that the issue has not been fully resolved, standing by their service users means that they have to continue to look for ways to complete the treatment. At this stage, collaboration with other professionals, such as administrative officials, lawyers or a Rights Exercising Social Worker, is vital.

It is important for the social worker to be guided by their intuition as to whether the situation involves injustice. Whenever the social worker feels that a negative answer from the authorities is unjust, the active rights exercising stance should lead them to refuse to accept 'no' for an answer, even if it comes from an authorised official and appears decisive. In order to overcome barriers at this stage, the social worker can address a 'higher level' – a higher-level official in the administrative hierarchy or someone outside the service (for example, an ombudsman) – or they can use their privileged position, namely, personal contacts, to 'open doors' (for a good method for negotiation, see Lens, 2004). They can also formally address an authorised appeal body.

Moving from an individual problem to policy practice

Since the active exercising of rights is based on the understanding that individual problems are an expression of systemic flaws, it follows that alongside case advocacy, there is a need to check to what extent the issue with this specific service user is common to other cases. Usually, the Rights Exercising Social Worker takes the lead at this stage. I will say a bit more about the role of the Rights Exercising Social Worker at the end of this chapter.

Active rights exercising as a therapeutic process

Since the bridging of the material and the emotional worlds is a basic concept in the PAP, rights exercising is understood to occur in the external reality, helping to solve concrete problems, as well as in the inner world of service users. Hence, it has the potential to make a significant contribution to curative experiences and to the strengthening of therapeutic relationships. The possibility of converting active rights exercising into an aspect of therapeutic relations depends on the orientation of the caseworker and the way in which they work in practice. In this sense, active rights exercising is similar to what the psychoanalyst Maxwell Sucharov (2013) calls 'therapeutic advocacy'. Sucharov argues that advocacy can become therapeutic because accompanying clients to encounters with various bureaucratic agents not only fulfils real social needs, which are essential in themselves, but also serves to create a space for the unique voice of the clients, which is frequently silenced by destructive social power structures. The ability to make your voice heard in the echelons of power can be a therapeutic experience. Coming from social work, Lorraine Tempel (2009) takes a similar approach, using intersubjective theories to understand the impact of active case advocacy on the alliance between social workers and single mothers at risk of physically abusing their children. She uses Kohut's (1971, 1984) self psychology, as well as more recent developments in contemporary psychoanalytic theory like those of Mitchell (1988) and Stern (1985), to emphasise the curative aspects of therapists' and service users' mutual involvement in case advocacy. Advocacy helps the mothers to overcome the initial trepidation felt towards social workers that may result from past experience. In this regard, advocacy is uniquely powerful because it involves the shared interactions between the service user and the worker, in which the worker visibly sides with the service user and is attuned to her. Examining the experiences of social workers, Tempel concludes that they described encounters that focused on advocacy as opportunities for enhanced potential to experience, communicate empathy and mutuality with service users, and emphasised the potential of these 'non-clinical encounters' to strengthen the helping relationship.

Whether manifested explicitly or not, issues of rights violation are always accompanied by strong emotions, to which social workers need to respond appropriately. In service users, they might arouse feelings either of anger, fury and aggression, or of despair and surrender. These emotions can be directed at the various administrative institutions, at street-level workers in those institutions and at the social services department, or even at the social workers themselves. They need to be dealt with in each of the three stages: defining problems in terms of rights; standing by service users; and transitioning from individual problem to policy practice. In fact, the practice in each of the stages should be linked to the specific way in which the service user experiences themselves and to the unique relationship established with them. In this context, a service user's willingness or refusal to accept help, their rhythm, their fears and their needs become very important. Any practice of rights exercising that does not take account of the personal experience of the service user or does not respect their rhythm or the way in which they want to operate can turn out to be less productive, even if it leads to exercising rights. Let us look now at examples of the therapeutic dimension in each of the three stages of active rights exercising.

Interviews with service users complement this picture. Research shows that service users frequently describe the physical accompaniment of social workers to administrative authorities as the important moment when they felt the social worker to be standing by them. At those times, they felt that the social worker believed them even in the face of others who doubted them (Saar-Heiman et al, 2016; Brand-Levi and Malul, 2019).

Thinking therapeutically when defining problems in terms of rights

To think therapeutically when dealing with rights presents challenges for social workers. One common challenge is how to understand service users who do not do what is needed in order to exercise their rights even though they say that they want to and know what to do. Keren, a social worker on a special programme aimed at preventing children from being removed from their homes, related that she has a close relationship with Oshrit, a young woman who struggled with alcohol addiction, who had had one child taken out of her care and a second child under threat of being removed. Through her close relationship with Keren, Oshrit has recovered from her addiction, has started working and has been cooperating fully with the treatment programme. Despite these important changes, she refused to deal with one thing: her large debts. She continued to say that she would deal with them "tomorrow", and "next week" and "later" but never did anything about it. When Keren asked Oshrit for the reasons for postponing dealing with the debts, Oshrit was unable to give answers. Keren said that she naturally saw the repeated postponing as an expression of Oshrit's weakness and her lack of full commitment to the treatment process. She could not think of any other reason for Oshrit's behaviour.

In an attempt to make a change, Keren asked Oshrit if she wanted her to accompany her to the bailiffs. To Keren's surprise, Oshrit agreed. On their journey together, Oshrit told Keren that she was happy that she had joined her "because if they arrested her at the bailiffs, Keren could inform her family and care for the children". Keren could not believe what she was hearing. She did not have the slightest idea that Oshrit was dealing with such a terrible (and unrealistic, in this case) fear. Oshrit went on to tell Keren that she had been arrested in the past for the non-payment of debts and constantly thought that were she to enter the bailiff's office, she would likely be arrested. Hearing of Oshrit's fear, which she had not dared to verbalise prior to this, allowed Keren to finally understand why Oshrit kept postponing dealing with the debt. In this case, Keren's offer to accompany Oshrit to the bailiff's office was a breakthrough in handling the debts, as well as in their relationship.

The principle underlying this and other similar stories is that when avoiding exercising rights, service users generally have good reasons. Usually, these reasons are not indifference or laziness, but linked to earlier, unprocessed traumatic experiences. In order to find out more about these reasons and to deal with them, the social worker should trust service users, be persistent and be patient.

Social workers face a different challenge when meeting service users who express intense anger towards administrative officials (these can include social workers from various services or from the social services department). Social workers often find it difficult to accept that this anger stems from an experience of injustice, so they feel the need to 'calm' the service user or to 'make them see the other side of the argument'. The PAP suggests viewing these cases as a test in which the service user is obliquely asking the social worker: 'Are you on my side or on the side of the system?'; 'Are you prepared to see injustice or are you overwhelmed by it?'; and 'Are you willing to see my pain?'

In this context, the role of the social worker is to refrain from trying to change the service user's emotional experience and instead to be sincerely curious about this experience. What really happened? How did it happen? What role do power relations play in the incident? Asking these questions with the intention of validating the service user's experience makes this listening to the story a primary step in the experience of recognition.

A further challenge is having to deal with service users who express apathy and helplessness when talking about their efforts to exercise rights. Here, the role of the caseworker is to make it clear to the service user that the situation is unjust, and to actually express it vocally. In cases like this, it is very important therapeutically for service users to hear the social worker express in words that they have suffered injustice and that their feelings about the situation are understood and justified.

In these situations, when service users are angry, blaming officials and expressing helplessness, the explicit verbal statement by the social worker 'You are right', displaying their recognition of injustice and their willingness to name it, would appear to be a simple act but it is sorely lacking in the lives of service users. Its effect on the experience of the self can be profound. When hearing that what they have had to undergo is not just and not proper, they achieve recognition both for what they feel and for the way they perceive reality. This recognition, which makes power relations visible, is necessary in order for service users to be able to experience and express new feelings that are hidden by anger or apathy. The processing of these feelings is a crucial step that allows the social worker and the service user to turn to considering the best way to counter the injustice.

Thinking therapeutically when standing by service users

At the second stage, it is important to identify and respond to the real difficulties facing service users when encountering street-level bureaucrats, particularly incidents of micro-aggression. The key issues here are: how can one make the officials listen to service users? How can they be made to treat service users with respect? How can they be enlisted to side with the service user? A discussion of these issues with the service users is a clear expression of standing by them.

Our experience shows that the answers that service users give to these questions vary. As I have already mentioned, they might ask for advice or guidance regarding what to say to the officials and how to say it, or they might ask for a simulation of the future meeting with officials. In some cases, they might ask the social worker to accompany them to the authority. Here, our experience indicates that the situation of going together enhances their relationship. For the social worker, these meetings are an opportunity for creating relationship-based knowledge, namely, an opportunity to get to know the service user in a new way. Sometimes, in these meetings, the social worker sees that the service user has better ways of coping than they were aware of: they might find that the service user is able to get organised, represent themselves, recognise opportunities and use them. Sometimes, the difficulties of the service user are revealed: fear of authority; confusion about social expectations; difficulty understanding the world of bureaucracy or to express themselves; or coping by being assertive. In addition, these situations are an opportunity for the social worker to understand the service in question and to experience at first hand the structural barriers entailed in poverty.

For the service users, it is an opportunity to include another person in their experiences of micro-aggression, which they often experience with no sympathetic witnesses. Micro-aggression might be expressed openly and directly, as in the case of an Arab woman who applied for social assistance and was asked by the clerk how come she had more children with her ex-husband after they had divorced (Saar-Heiman and Ruso-Carmel, 2019). In other cases, micro-aggression might be concealed in an apparent compliment. This happened to a social worker in the MAPA programme who accompanied her service user to a meeting for the purpose of getting a psycho-diagnostic report for her daughter, and was witness to the psychologist saying, "They sent you here at the tax payers' expense ... but you don't seem to me to be a typical welfare case. I don't understand what you are doing here."

Situations like these can be important experiences when they are shared. The social worker who sees and hears at first hand what micro-aggression is, might be shocked, puzzled, helpless or angry and furious, and at the same time has to cope with similar emotions felt by the service user. This becomes a unique opportunity for using self-reflection to enable better use of the self as a therapeutic tool (Fook and Gardner, 2007; Rossiter, 2007).

An important aspect of standing by is processing what was experienced. Whether the social workers accompanied the service user or not, a discussion of the experience of the visit to the administrative authority and its significance for the service user is an important part of the therapeutic relationship. Its importance lies in the fact that although those experiences are emotionally powerful, their banality makes them invisible and in normal life, they do not usually receive any processing. The possibility of speaking about them and examining their imprint on the soul is a valuable therapeutic resource, which cannot be accessed without having previously been involved in the active exercising of rights. Irit, a social worker, described a conversation with a service user, Sivan, in which Sivan proudly said that for the first time in years, she went to the public housing authority and managed to conduct herself without having an outburst or being aggressive. When Irit asked her, 'What was different when compared to past times?', Sivan answered, 'I went there feeling that I was not alone although you weren't with me ... I didn't even need to raise my voice, which is strange in itself. Generally, wherever I go I get what I want by shouting' (Krumer-Nevo et al, 2015: 24–5). The discussion that followed about the issue of 'shouting gets you everything you want' could not have taken place if Sivan had not experienced Irit as actively standing by her.

An additional, important aspect of discussing experiences of exercising rights is its contribution to the strengthening of the experience of self. This aspect has not yet been discussed in detail in the professional literature, though, in our experience, it is very important and requires research to explore it further. The experience of the service user who has had a professional who is prepared to stand by them, call injustice by its name and struggle to correct it allows them to feel that they exist, that they are worthy and significant for somebody else, and that they are right. Experiences of this sort nourish the self and are critical for creating a positive, coherent self-experience. This type of experience is particularly important for people who have encountered numerous traumas in the course of their lives.

Thinking therapeutically when moving from case advocacy to policy practice

At the third stage of the active exercising of rights – the transition to policy practice – therapeutic relations are also important. Having established a close and trusting relationship in which micro-aggression experiences were processed, some service users seek to be effective at the policy level by voicing their opinion and relating their experiences publicly. The caseworker can do this with them, either by means of steps that they take together or by directing them to a group or community action centre in the framework of the welfare services or rights organisations. For example, Danit was referred to the Centre for Parents and Children because she had difficulties parenting her child. Yuval, who worked at the centre, helped her with her difficulties with emotions regulation but also helped her to solve the problem of a debt that she had to her son's crèche. Before resolving the problem, the boy was expelled from the crèche and the staff were not prepared to let him return until the debt was paid. The situation persisted even though it meant that Danit lost the salary of the working days that she had to spend with the boy at home, though they knew that she was trying to solve the problem. Danit shared with Yuval her rage and helplessness in the situation. A couple of months later, with Yuval's support, she became active in policy practice to prohibit schools from expelling children because of debts. She gave media interviews and gave testimony at a parliamentary committee. The move from parental guidance to policy practice was natural for Danit and for Yuval because, as they perceived it, it was all about promoting social justice (for a fuller account of the story, see Saar-Heiman, 2019).

The role of the Rights Exercising Social Worker

I will finish this chapter by briefly describing the new role of the Rights Exercising Social Worker. It is evident that the active exercising of rights practice that we expect from caseworkers is very demanding. It requires them to be competent in a number of different spheres. They have to be familiar with the laws, regulations and bureaucratic procedures in various areas, such as health, regular and special education, debt, employment, culture, disability, rehabilitation, and more. They also have to be familiar with the workings of numerous bodies, such as the NII, Receiver of Revenue, Legal Assistance, bailiff, health services, education services, and the water, electricity and gas authorities, as well as the municipal authorities. In addition, they need to be familiar with the relevant formal and informal bodies operating in the framework of civil society. These may range from small, local suppliers of services in the community, to permanent, institutional bodies, whose operations are more easily traceable. For each body or content world, they have to be able to identify resources for their service users. In other words, they need to be familiar with the procedural and bureaucratic side, entailing ever-changing forms and procedures, as well as with the clerks and managers with whom personal contact can speed up answers, open doors and remove barriers.

Of course, we cannot expect caseworkers to be familiar with and able to operate effectively in so many different contexts. Moreover, active rights exercising demands time that is not available to caseworkers. For these reasons, we created the function of a Rights Exercising Social Worker. Their role is to encourage and assist caseworkers to adopt the stance and practice of active rights exercising in their routine work. The Rights Exercising Social Worker needs to be a specialist in the field. They need to keep updated on changes in regulations, laws and resources at the local and national levels, and to serve as an address for rights exercising issues for caseworkers who maintain direct contact with the families. Furthermore, because the Rights Exercising Social Worker is in possession of a lot of information, they are able to bring about change at the organisational, local and national levels.

The broad canvas of work done by a Rights Exercising Social Worker is evident from the fact that during the course of two years, one Rights Exercising Social Worker[5] intervened in 34 different issues, of which the most outstanding were: children's rights in arrangements outside the home; divorce; national health insurance; transport to medical treatment; a committee dealing with exceptional health requirements; dental treatments; medical assistance for non-status people; child support debt; TV licensing; wage stoppages; religious conversion; a rehabilitation budget; the income guarantee as a benefit replacing child support; a supplement to disability benefit; disability benefits for people who have been sexually assaulted; nominating a beneficiary; cancelling a national insurance debt; social status; making an apartment accessible; changing a public housing apartment because of crowding; help with rent; employment; and various legal inquiries. For these interventions, she made contact with 31 different organisations, some of which were local government, non-profit associations, rights and social change organisations and self-help groups. The work of a Rights Exercising Social Worker focuses on three principal spheres: the sphere of the department of social services; the sphere of the locality; and the national sphere.

In the sphere of the social services department

The Rights Exercising Social Worker operates proactively to increase the output of the caseworkers dealing with active rights exercising. They do this by gathering knowledge on the subject of rights exercising through their familiarity with a range of knowledge related to various spheres of life, as well as by means of their familiarity with efficient ways of searching for new knowledge. They are familiar with and use a range of knowledge sources, from Internet sites to consultation with various officials and people with specialist knowledge in various spheres of life, for instance, a lawyer specialising in family law, bailiff laws, specialists in the area of health and more.

In addition, they initiate easy access to knowledge and encourage the caseworker to use it. For example, they: regularly distribute information on rights and collate local knowledge for the use of the workers; create opportunities for shared consideration about advancing solutions to problems in complex cases; and initiate inviting people in key positions in administrative organisations to team meetings in order to establish close relationships with both their organisations and key people. They also present success stories at team meetings. Access to and the availability of the Rights Exercising Social Worker by the team of caseworkers are critical for the success of their role in this sphere.

Our experience proves that the introduction of a Rights Exercising Social Worker can make the caseworkers and the service users feel more optimistic about their situations. The fact that there is an expert in the social services department who takes responsibility for understanding complex systems and removing barriers allows the caseworker to feel that they can also operate effectively in the area of rights exercising. When the system is working well and success is achieved, it contributes to the development of activity in the field.

In the sphere of the locality

The Rights Exercising Social Worker works to create cooperation between services and administrative systems in order to promote rights exercising. This is achieved by creating beneficial relationships with officials in the administrative authority, and maintaining contact with them. This involves: initiating and motivating meetings between administrative authorities and the social workers at the social services department; initiating and motivating a local forum for rights exercising on which organisations and services sit; or writing a rights exercising column in the local newspaper.

The sphere of the locality was also identified as an important area in the struggle against poverty in Israel in the report by the National Committee to Combat Poverty (2014: 14), which recommended the establishment of a local organisational platform to deal with poverty, with the participation of all the relevant agencies and headed by a town coordinator. Experience teaches us that action in this sphere is decisive for improving routine ways of working and for solving complex problems.

The national sphere

The Rights Exercising Social Worker employs a tactic of policy practice at the national level and oversees this activity in the social services department. In this framework, they initiate and oversee professional activities aimed at creating new policy in order to bring about change in the existing policy or to prevent change for the worse in existing policy (Gal and Weiss-Gal, 2013). They also manage group work with service user-activists who help them in this regard. This practice is based on the recognition of service users as active citizens who can promote and influence rights discourse in society. The involvement in policy practice empowers the participants, enhances their sense of belonging and also enables the caseworkers to get a new perspective on their service users.

To summarise, during the last five years, there has been a tremendous change in social services departments in Israel in terms of their treatment of service users' rights. The discourse of rights and the practice of the active realisation of rights have revitalised practice at both the level of direct practice and the level of policy practice. The establishment of the role of the Rights Exercising Social Worker is a dream come true. It is important to celebrate the achievements of the active realisation of rights, both in terms of changes in service users' lives and in terms of changing the general ethos regarding rights in the social services departments. However, there is one word of caution. I have not said a word about the limitations of this kind of practice, stemming from its position within the institutional framework of state services. One major limitation is the restrictions on the areas of intervention. For example, there was no promotion of rights exercising on issues of child protection because this was regarded as contradicting institutional policy. I am saying this at the very end of the chapter because there is much to be proud of and to celebrate; however, I invite you not to forget what is still to be done, and to go on searching for solutions for realising rights — *all of them* — in the fight against poverty.

Notes

[1] As of 2012, Professor Dafna Barak-Erez is a supreme court judge in Israel.
[2] See, for example, Ife's (2012) inspiring proposal for human rights social work, and Gabel's (2016) call for a rights-based approach for social policy.
[3] For many years, discourse on social rights has dealt with issues regarding universal versus selective benefits and the level of support that they should provide. However, over time, it was realised that it is not enough to legislate social laws as this does not ensure that the rights will reach those for whom they are intended. This is the gap between the 'law in books' and the 'law in reality' (see Benish and David, 2018).
[4] Van Mechelen and Janssens (2017) build upon the classic contribution of Van Oorschot (1995) and add a third type — tertiary non-take-up — which is linked to the design of the benefit scheme, for example, the default settings that are used in administrative procedures.
[5] I thank Michal Noam-Alon for the information.

11

Material help and a flexible budget

The subject of material needs and a flexible budget is very fraught because it deals directly with money and the powerful emotions that it evokes. In 2002, in the early days of the student programme Casework for Social Change, we dealt with a woman who was thought to be difficult to reach. Nevertheless, she established a close relationship with the student, and shared her difficulties with her. There was one aspect of her life that she did not share: her material difficulties – she never asked for help in this regard. It took a year and a half before she dared to ask for help with food when the holidays came. We viewed her request as an expression of her growing ability to reveal her vulnerability, to trust and to accept help. However, there was no formal channel at the social services department for presenting requests for financial aid for food and there was no designated budget for it. Service users who needed this kind of help were referred to the soup kitchen that operated in the town. The woman, who until then had hidden her distress, did not want to go to the soup kitchen. Together with her, we wrote a letter of special request to the director of the social services department. The request was refused. Three reasons were given: giving material help is not professional work; help with food encourages dependence in the service users; and giving help with food once will open a Pandora's box of similar requests that the social services department will be unable to meet.

We had answers to each of these claims: giving material help is both humane and professional; the request for help with food is the expression of a need and is not dependence, and so much more so in the present case of this woman, who had never asked for anything; and if answering the request creates an opening for similar requests, it will be an important lesson that we should be willing to learn about people's needs. However, our reply did not convince the head of the department.

This case made it clear that as long as there is no structural change that enables people to make ends meet, if we wanted to stand by service users, we needed to equip ourselves with a flexible budget that would allow us to respond to urgent material needs immediately. We obtained a small budget from an external source that we used as a response to pressing material needs. It was only a minimal sum but since we developed the practice of active rights exercising in parallel, it enabled the students to listen carefully for evidence of material problems and to respond to them. At this stage, we developed some of the basic principles of using a flexible budget.

When the reports on the success of the students in establishing close relationships with service users, who were regarded to be 'beyond our reach' until then, reached the steering committee of the student programme in its first years, the head of the department claimed that we had succeeded only because we had a small budget. She did not realise how small the budget was, and that the change in the students' attitudes and practice with regard to material needs was no less important than the money itself.

In 2013, when the MAPA programme adopted the model of the student programme in full, we included in it a component of a flexible budget. Since this was a national programme run by the Ministry of Welfare and Social Services, it had to receive the approval of the Finance Ministry and, at that stage, the ministry representative vehemently opposed the request for a flexible budget. Following a protracted argument, we got what we asked for, and each family on the programme was allocated a budget of 2,900 shekels/year (about US$810). This was a small sum relative to the problems that service users were facing, but the idea of a flexible budget no longer seemed 'unprofessional'. In fact, quite the opposite: the discourse changed and, the Families First programme started only a year later, with a flexible budget of 8,000 shekels per family/ year (about US$2,250), which was agreed upon without any major battles. Two years later, other programmes started with a much larger flexible budget.

In 2017, three years after the first allocation of a flexible budget was approved by the Finance Ministry, a meeting took place with stakeholders from the Ministry of Welfare and Social Services and the Finance Ministry to summarise the experience and discuss policy regarding flexible budgets. This chapter is based on the lecture I gave at that event and on a research report that I wrote with colleagues later on (Gal et al, 2019).

It is natural that social workers working with people living in poverty are exposed to numerous material shortages and to the importance of material responses. Experience indicates that material assistance is a very fraught subject, partly because it is often a source of conflict between service users and social workers, and partly because it is also a source of internal conflict between the social workers themselves as it exposes personal and professional attitudes towards poverty, intervention and money. Sadly, these attitudes are seldom discussed and clarified in professional circles. To start our discussion, it is worth saying a few words about the history of the policy towards material assistance in Israel. I will then analyse a case study and establish some general principles for possible policy and practice.

Israel has gradually developed as a welfare state since its inception but it was only during the 1970s that a social-democratically oriented social security system was fully implemented. At that time, a disability allowance, unemployment insurance and a universal child allowance were introduced but, as yet, there was no guaranteed income for people in poverty who were not entitled to the other benefits. People with no income used to visit the social services departments (which were called 'welfare offices' at the time) asking for assistance with their basic needs, and were provided with limited material assistance from social workers, at their discretion.

Abraham Doron (2019), an expert on the history of the Israeli welfare state, found that even before the establishment of the state of Israel, there was tension between psychosocial treatment and material assistance. In 1958, a decade after Israel was established, Professor Phillip Klein, a UN advisor to the Ministry of Welfare, wrote an incisive report, stating: 'In the areas of family treatment and financial aid (relief), the foundation stones of the social services, there are serious flaws and shortcomings to the extent that these areas are lagging decades behind the achievements of the state in other areas' (Klein, 1958: 8). His criticism did not only relate to bureaucratic inefficiency, but also addressed the patronising attitude of the political leadership of the period and of the heads of the Ministry of Welfare towards needy groups, who consisted mainly of Jewish immigrants from Arab countries.

In the same year (1958), the Welfare Services Law was passed in Israel, which formed the basis for the establishment in local authorities of social services departments for the social treatment of people in need. The provision of material assistance served social workers as a manipulation to get service users into treatment. The broad framework of rules that regulated the use of this assistance and the limited existing resources left social workers discretion as to who would receive assistance and how much.

Given this situation, social workers had to decide what criteria to use – whether to help service users according to the severity of their needs, or according to their chance of overcoming poverty, or according to their level of cooperation with other aspects of the psychosocial treatment. The last option was appealing: it was assumed that if service users cooperated with the psychosocial treatment, they might have more chance of undergoing a fundamental change and improving their life situations, and they should thus also be supported with material assistance. Moreover, the 'cooperative' service users made social workers feel competent in their capacity as therapists. However, combining psychosocial treatment and material assistance strengthened the assumption that a disadvantaged person needing financial aid had some sort of personal flaw, and would necessarily also need treatment.

At that time, the discussions in the field regarding social workers' involvement in material assistance ignored the political-economic context in which those problems arose.

In 1982, the Income Support Law was enacted. It provided a safety net that offered a minimal level of income that was conditioned upon means and employment testing. The law separated the income support function, now provided by the NII, from the psychosocial treatment function, provided by the social services departments. This distinction was in line with the distaste felt by social workers for dealing with money as it "contaminates the psychosocial treatment", as a social worker once told me.

Any hope that the income support benefit would free social workers from dealing with material distress and allow them to deal only with treatment was ultimately dashed (Gal et al, 2019). Cuts in benefit budgets, the heavy caseload and the neoliberal ideology of the 1980s led to a rise in the incidence of poverty and an increase in hardship. In addition, at the beginning of the 21st century, the income support benefit level was cut drastically and the criteria for receiving it were stiffened, causing people in poverty to increasingly frequent social services departments with requests for material aid.

Social workers had two problems when facing these requests: first, they had access to only very limited resources provided by the Ministry of Welfare and Social Services for crisis situations, not for long-term poverty; and, second, they did not have any systemic body of knowledge regarding the way in which to use material assistance and, as a result, were guided mainly by their personal values and attitudes. This is where we are now: on the one hand, the income support benefit fails in its original goal of assisting people to maintain adequate living conditions; on the other hand, social workers in social services departments do not have the budget required to provide for service users' requests and are, at best, ambivalent or, at worst, hostile regarding the use of the small budget that they do have.

To illustrate how this set of circumstances is manifested in the practice of social workers, let us look at a vignette from a case study. Edva is a 23-year-old mother of three children. She was removed from her home when she was a young girl, and grew up in various hostels for at-risk children. When she reached adolescence, she rebelled and ran away back home, and having no choice, the authorities agreed to formally return her to her mother. There, she got to know the brother of her mother's husband, who was a lot older than her, and married him.

When she was pregnant with their third child, they got divorced. She was 22 years old. She then applied to the social services department for material assistance. She was not working and received the income support benefit, but it did not suffice to cover her basic needs. She needed help with payments for the registration fee at the crèche, for food and for disposable diapers. She told the social worker that she was having regular difficulties related to her financial situation. She had debts to loan sharks and her mother was pressing her to panhandle. Given the absence of an available budget at the social services department, and since Edva was not interested in attending a financial literacy programme, the social worker could not help her.

A few months later, worrying reports began to arrive about her parental functioning. The nursery teacher reported that Edva was arriving late to fetch the children, was dressed provocatively and was accompanied by a woman who was suspected of running a brothel. When Edva was asked by the nursery teacher about her clothing and her friend, she became defensive and said that her mother was pressing her to help with paying a fine for her brother, who, at the time, was in prison for forging cheques and identity cards. The social worker could not help her with this problem either.

After more reports arrived stating that Edva had not brought the children in for inoculations, a Youth Justice Social Worker was brought in, and social services decided to set up a Planning, Intervention and Evaluation Committee (Alfandari, 2019). This committee serves a crucial function in the child protection process, where professionals from different services and the family come together to decide on an intervention plan. The committee can recommend that the family needs treatment in the community or an out-of-home placement. If recommendation is not agreed by all the participants, the final ruling is made by the juvenile court (Alfandari, 2019).

Edva was very agitated by the committee, saying that the worst thing that could happen was that her children would be removed, as had been done to her when she was a child. She said that she did not want her children to remain at the crèche and had no interest in any further treatment or help from the social services department. My interpretation was that what Edva was actually saying was that she could not trust the social workers to help her anymore and that she preferred to cope with her problems on her own, without their involvement.

From her point of view, she was right. Every time she talked about her needs, she was ignored. Moreover, although they knew how extreme her material predicament was, the social workers never initiated any contact with her until they were worried about her children.

The minutes of the committee go on to note that one of the social workers made it clear that all three children were obliged to attend the crèche daily in order to make sure that they were safe and getting the treatment they needed. If Edva did not cooperate with the crèche staff, the committee would have to consider the removal of the children. Then, the crèche social worker, who attended the meeting, mentioned that Edva was in debt to them and because she had not settled it, the crèche could not continue to provide services for her children. Two days later, Edva settled the debt and the children returned to the crèche.

I know it is hard, but please listen to what happened at that meeting. This is a very painful situation; Edva's history is painful, and her poverty is painful. However, what makes it unbearable for me is the betrayal by the social workers, and the betrayal of the system that makes them act in what I consider to be an unethical way. The committee members, who included Edva's caseworker, the Youth Justice Social Worker and the crèche social worker, all knew that she had severe material shortages, that she had debts and that she had difficulties paying for diapers and food. They knew that she was not working and had no resources besides the very limited income support benefit. They knew that her mother was pressurising her to panhandle and to help pay her brother's fine in order to release him from prison. They knew that she had a friend who might be urging her into sex work. They did not offer her any help to deal with these issues. I am sure that they ignored her material predicament not because they are 'bad' social workers, but because they had no resources, and they were used to hearing similar stories without being able to help. We can assume that a system that does not give social workers the tools to deal with such a severe material shortage blinds them to seeing the pain that comes with poverty. However, they were not blind to the pain of the children, and they were justifiably worried about their safety and development.

The way in which our services are designed leads social workers to see one solution for keeping the children away from risk, insisting on sending them to the crèche. The ironic consequence of that decision is that it inevitably takes us back to dealing with Edva's lack of money. Here, again, Edva is supposed to deal with this issue on her own. The committee's decision that she should send the children to the crèche, or otherwise risk her custody of them, is like putting a gun to her head. By accepting this decision, we are collaborating with those forcing her into prostitution and panhandling.

Thinking psychologically, what happened in the committee must have been traumatic for Edva. In terms of attachment theory, her efforts to communicate her pain failed. In terms of object relations theory, the social workers were not 'new good objects' in Edva's psyche; instead, they joined the list of 'bad objects' that she had encountered throughout her life. The first time Edva approached the social worker after she got divorced from the father of her children and shared her material problems with her is a critical moment in this analysis. This was her first voluntary opening up to professionals. She desperately needed those professionals to recognise the efforts that were involved in requesting help and to stand by her in order to fight the injustice and pain she had experienced throughout her life. Unfortunately, the social worker ignored Edva's effort. The possible solutions that she had for dealing with a problem such as this were either referring Edva to a welfare-to-work programme in which she would acquire skills for integrating into the labour market, or sending her to a financial literacy programme. However, a young mother living such a chaotic life, on a minimal budget, could not realistically regard these options as answering her needs.

The second point of failure occurs when Edva arrives at the department for a clarification talk after it was reported that she had not fetched the children from the crèche. Here, too, she gave the social worker an opportunity to help her with her material needs. Again, her efforts were not acknowledged and her difficulties were ignored. She could reasonably have interpreted this as an expression of the social worker's indifference towards her, or that she was not worthy enough for anybody to care about her, or that nobody believed her. All these possibilities are terrible in terms of the experience of the self and in terms of their effect on the helping relationship that is so critical to develop here.

Given her distress and the lack of help, it is not surprising that we reach the third point of failure. Here, the professionals – the state – use their power to draw a red line. They did not use their power when she said she had no food, that she had debts to loan sharks and that her mother asked her to panhandle. However, they were very explicit when they decided that she must send the children to the crèche. The intervention of the crèche social worker, who made it a condition that Edva pay her debt before they would let the children in, is an example of the banality of alienation. By not stopping to ask Edva whether she was able to pay the money, and how she was going to do so, the committee totally ignored her situation and her as a person.

Thinking about it in terms of policy we should ask: could things have been done differently? Yes. However, for that to have happened, social workers needed a flexible budget that would have enabled them to respond to Edva's acute material problems. Once those problems were heard and responded to, they could have continued with the treatment process. I say *continued* because, in my view, giving material aid is a form of psychosocial treatment practice. In order to explain what I mean, I will outline four principles for using a flexible budget in the PAP.

The first principle is that material aid is essential. I suggest thinking about it as a form of humanitarian aid that is necessary in order to respond to the violation of rights that is poverty. Thus, in this framework, the assistance that Edva is requesting is an answer to the violation of her right to education, employment and personal security. Following the PAP's ontological stance, Edva's approach to the social worker to request help is perceived as resistance to her poverty, that is, an expression of her wish to improve her situation independently from her husband and mother.

The second principle is that in order to identify the struggle of people living in poverty, we need to agree on the limits of the real alternatives available to them. Once we do so, we begin to understand how critical a flexible budget is for offering these alternatives. Edva is a good example of this because the alternatives open to her to raise money – from panhandling to sex work – are all so bad that it would be better if she did not actualise them. Urging her to raise money to pay her debt to the crèche without examining with her what real alternatives were open to her is unprofessional and unethical.

The third principle demonstrates how material and emotional needs are linked, thus combining material assistance and psychosocial treatment in a fundamental way (see, for example, Schiettecat et al, 2017). This is a call to drop the distinction between 'fish' and 'hooks', and to accept that fish can be hooks and hooks can be fish. It depends on how the professional sees them and delivers them. In poverty-aware practice, providing material assistance is always viewed as an answer to both material and emotional needs, just as for a baby (and, in fact, throughout life), food carries both material and emotional meaning and it fills (or does not fill) the stomach and the heart at the same time. Human experience of needs always entails both the material and the emotional. Contrary to Maslow, who arranged needs hierarchically, I argue that the moment we ask for help with material needs, we are also dealing with questions of self-value, self-respect, belonging, trust and self-realisation. This is a universal experience, not unique to people living in poverty. However, the context of poverty generates proportionally more experiences of need for basic assistance and creates vulnerability in experiences of the self and in interpersonal relations.

The fourth and last principle concerns the design of specific regulations related to material answers. If we agree to recognise poverty fully, to stand by those people experiencing it and to struggle against it, it needs to be done in full view, without apologising. This has significance for the regulations governing the budget: it must be flexible, available and immediate.

Immediacy is important because as Joseph Wresinski, the founder of ATD Fourth World, an international movement fighting against poverty, used to say: "The poor can't wait."[1] They cannot wait because they are often dealing with a crisis or trauma, not with the serenity of established routine. When Edva does not know where she is going to get money for food, she does not have time to wait for budgetary approvals.

Flexibility is important because the budget is needed for a variety of needs: to pay an electricity bill; to pay for babysitters for toddlers during school holidays in order to enable their mother to go to work; to pay for the moving of donated furniture; or to purchase medicines or contraception. From our experience on the MAPA programme, we know that immediacy and flexibility are important not only for the service users, but also for the social workers. For both sides, this alleviates the feeling of helplessness and opens possibilities for creating bridges where frustration and suspicion usually reign.

In summary, basic needs and material aid challenge the profession. At the policy level, the shift in the management of material aid raises fears of a return to the pre-income support benefit period. It confronts us with the possible danger of abandoning our commitment to rightful income support benefit, which so desperately needs our firm commitment as its social legitimacy is waning. The big question is how to preserve and even reinforce the income support benefit as a right while, alongside it, providing other material resources to people living in poverty and to the professionals working with them.

At the level of direct practice, dealing with material aid forces practitioners to take a stand on issues like technocracy/clerical work and therapy, material and emotional needs, and dependence and independence. We are now taking our first steps in the development of a complete doctrine of providing material aid. It is strange to think that over the many years of the existence of the profession, a doctrine of this sort was not developed. However, the absence of a detailed doctrine should not prevent us from recognising the importance of material aid and the great advantages of providing it. Here we are, and we are prepared to work.

Note
[1] Personal communication with Jona Rosenfeld who knew Wresinski in person.

12

Active rights exercising: advanced

Entry into the field of rights exercising with a political commitment to social justice required us to take an unmarked route. When we started, we thought that our main goal was to educate social workers to use rights discourse and to support them in finding ways to realise the rights of the service users. An important aspect of the work was to allay their fears of entering the bureaucratic maze. This meant supporting them to be persistent when dealing with negative answers and to help them understand the relational aspects of this work, as well as its contribution to the therapeutic process. At the same time, the social justice perspective compelled us to understand the significant role that micro-aggression and (the lack of) symbolic capital played in encounters between service users and street-level bureaucrats, as well as to view our role as not being limited to realising the rights of a single person, but to changing policy and the attitudes of the street-level workers involved. Very quickly, we understood that the idea of realising rights is based on the assumption that there are rights that are grounded in law and that can be realised. However, the practice of viewing private issues as problems of rights, and the existence of new Rights Exercising Social Workers, opened a space for the emergence of complex issues that challenged our preconceptions. We realised that we were dealing with human situations that were not covered by law at all – the problems of migrant workers, refugees or asylum seekers, and other undocumented people appeared first. However, the problems of citizens that were not covered by existing laws and regulations also left the social workers helpless and frustrated. What could be done? What is the role of social workers in cases where there is no marked route for them to take? We were entering new social spheres of promoting social rights where legal rights did not exist. This chapter describes what this advanced realisation of rights looks like.[1]

Introduction

Since exercising active rights is a practice that stems from identifying life situations entailing poverty as a violation of human rights together with a firm commitment to correct it through a close relationship and solidarity with service users, what is needed for exercising rights is a willingness to enter the unknown – to take unmarked routes. In this chapter, I would like to differentiate between three types of active rights practice. They differ in the level of complexity of the problems that they pose, and as a result, in the degree of persistence, creativity, determination and imagination that the social worker has to employ in order to correct or fight injustice. In all three types, the relationship with the service user is extremely important, and the way in which rights exercising is woven into this relationship is vital for the effectiveness of the practice.

However, there is a caveat here: exercising rights is not dependent on the relationship, meaning that a social worker should also endeavour to realise the rights of service users with whom they do not have a close relationship, or have a very short or superficial relationship. A service user has the right to ask for advocacy or mediation in order to exercise their rights even if they are not interested in establishing a deep or long-term relationship with the social worker. Having said this, the practice of the social worker should be based on the assumption that everything that happens between them and the service user has relational significance. The social worker is always both a concrete, real person who should act with respect, and, to use a psychoanalytic concept, an object of transference, that is, an imagined persona that echoes experiences with figures of authority from the past, mostly negative (Tosone, 2004; Tempel, 2009). With this in mind, the social worker should find ways to stand by service users in their struggle to realise their rights.

As noted earlier, there are three types of active rights exercising practice. The first type is the simplest. It requires relatively straightforward mediation and advocacy, and what is important is that it is based on the realisation of *existing* rights. However, even this simple type requires the social worker to be familiar with a number of systems, procedures and regulations, and to know how to use them effectively.

The second type involves complex and unfamiliar processes. These are special cases that challenge the caseworker. Even if they do have some idea about the body or bodies that are supposed to provide the said rights, they cannot deal with the matter alone and need help from experts, whether a Rights Exercising Social Worker, lawyer or other professional.

The third type of active rights exercising necessitates special action in cases where there are no rights, in other words, in cases where the service user has a clear need but the answer to the need is not a statutory right. In these cases, the social worker's axiological stance becomes critical. If they perceive themselves to be a representative of the system, they might shirk their responsibility for actualising the need (because the need is not defined as a right, we refer to it as a 'need') and would, in the best-case scenario, refer the service user to another body. However, if they perceive themselves to be in solidarity with and standing by the service user, and if they believe that material and emotional needs are linked, they cannot disregard the service user and they have to embark with them on a search for an answer. In this case, what motivates them is to promote justice, not necessarily to realise rights. Let us look at these three types in more detail.

Active rights exercising: the simple version

Even this version of active rights exercising, supposedly the simplest, is not self-evident, and the social worker needs support to manage it successfully. The main challenge is overcoming past tendencies of inattentiveness with regard to issues of rights. For example, until three years ago, social workers in Israel did not deal at all with debt problems, which is a painful area that social workers felt was beyond their professional role. However, with increased awareness of the debt issue and its influence on the lives of people in poverty, it has become clear that once social workers were willing to regard it as part of their role, they could be active in this area, with the tools they have available. For instance, one caseworker described the Levine family, who approached her concerning a large debt that they had with the NII. Together with the family, she composed a letter to the claims officer at the NII, in which they detailed the reason for the debt and their difficult current financial situation. In addition, she enclosed a psychosocial report that she had written. About two months later, the family received a positive reply. Most of their debt had been written off.

In this case, what stood between the family and the reduction of the debt was the social worker's willingness to intervene. The family did not know to whom to apply and what to write. They live in a small, peripheral town where they did not have access to rights' organisations or to any other bodies that they could consult on the matter. They came to their caseworker with this request not knowing if she could help them, but trusting her to treat their problem seriously and to do everything that she could to find ways of doing so. They approached her not as an expert in debt, but as an expert in helping them and standing by them. The fact that she did not judge them and, together with them, looked for a solution fostered their relationship with her. Needless to say, the success in dealing with the debt led to a vast improvement of their material situation.

Besides the necessary change in her professional attitude, the practical challenge that the caseworker faced was locating the body to whom to apply, and finding out what the correct procedure was, since this was not part of her routine work. However, she was able to access this information quite easily through the Internet or other available sources of information.

Let us look at another example that required relatively simple advocacy but could not have been carried out in the same way had the caseworker not understood her role in terms of rights. In this case, Mr Shiff approached his social worker after not receiving the reduction in his water bill that he was supposed to receive by virtue of his receiving a disability benefit. The reduction in the water bill should have been automatic since the names of those entitled to a disability benefit are transferred directly from the NII to the water authority. However, Mr Shiff claimed that he did not get the reduction. He tried dealing with it by himself and called the water authority. They told him that his name did not appear on the list of those entitled to the benefit. He then called the NII, who insisted that his name had been included on the list and had been transferred to the water authority, as required. The caseworker contacted the two agencies and got the same replies. However, she did not relent and again addressed the NII, urging them to examine the matter further. Only then did it turn out that Mr Shiff's name was, indeed, mistakenly not included on the right list. Following the application, they settled the matter.

In this case too, it was clear which agencies needed to be contacted, and complicated procedures were unnecessary. The main challenge was to overcome the tendency to give up in the face of bureaucratic procedures and negative replies, to be willing to pursue a solution to problems, and to stay determined and unyielding. These latter factors are critical and are linked to the fact that active rights exercising does not end as long as the social worker continues to feel that an injustice has not been corrected.

Active rights exercising: complicated cases

The second type of active rights exercising requires more advanced mediation and advocacy procedures, and demands creativity and determination on the part of the social worker, and a prolonged follow-up of the case. These cases involve an elaborate mixture of laws, regulations and services that one has to negotiate in order to untangle the bureaucratic muddle. For the social worker, this requires competence in all these areas, creativity in solving problems and the willingness to use their personal privilege. They also often need the involvement of more than one professional. Moreover, the social worker might sometimes have to justify their actions in the face of criticism from their colleagues as they may be thought to be 'exceeding the boundaries of their role', 'fighting too hard' or 'identifying too closely with the service users'.

The story of Noga and Assaf is a good example of this sort. They are a young married couple and the parents of two small children. Assaf and the children are Israeli citizens, while Noga arrived in Israel as an immigrant worker and thus lacks Israeli citizenship, having only a residency permit and permission to work. The family's income is very limited, with most of it coming from social assistance benefits paid by the NII, including Assaf's disability benefit with a dependants supplement for the two children, and child benefits. The couple have separate bank accounts. All the social security benefits go directly to Assaf's bank account (since he is the only adult citizen in the family). Noga has a job as a cleaner that provides her with a meagre salary that goes into her bank account but she does not have access to Assaf's account. He manages most of the family's finances.

Noga first came to the social services department after Assaf was arrested following a domestic violence complaint that she filed against him. Since his arrest, he has refused Noga permission to withdraw money from his account. Noga was forced to stop working in order to take care of their children, and especially the baby, who suffers from health problems. At the same time, it was getting very close to the expiration date of Noga's residency permit in Israel. According to the regulations, in order to extend her residency permit, she had to go to the Interior Ministry office accompanied by her husband, by virtue of whose citizenship she was entitled to a residency permit. This was not possible since Assaf was detained at that time. At that point, Noga approached her caseworker and requested help.

Based on her initial appraisal, the social worker identified three urgent problems. The first of these was the immediate shortage of food. The small family had no source of income and had an acute need for food. The second problem was the expiration of the validity of Noga's residency permit. The third problem was the ongoing lack of income for the family.

The caseworker began to address these three problems. With regard to the first problem – the immediate shortage of food – she obtained food and baby formula from a special small budget that originated from a private donor as urgent humanitarian aid. At the same time, she and Noga tried to locate other sources of assistance with basic needs.

With regard to the second problem – the expiration of Noga's residency permit – the caseworker felt helpless. She had never dealt with a problem of this sort before and did not know where to start. In fact, there was nobody in the social services department with knowledge of or experience of the subject. She consulted a Rights Exercising Social Worker, who also did not have experience dealing with problems like this. However, at least the Rights Exercising Social Worker was more able to deal with problems that she had not had experience with before, and she could consult her network of Rights Exercising Social Workers. With the advice she received, she immediately approached the Israel Religious Action Centre, a non-governmental organisation (NGO), where a lawyer agreed to help Noga. The lawyer accompanied Noga to the Interior Ministry, and with his help, Noga got an extension of her residency permit.

The third problem needed patience and creativity. The only source of income available was the child benefits that were directed to Assaf's account. As noted, Assaf also received a disability benefit but this was directed to him personally, while the child benefits belonged to the children and were paid to his account only by virtue of him being their father, and their mother not being a citizen. Since he was not willing to give access to his account, the Rights Exercising Social Worker and Noga decided to apply to the NII on behalf of the children to receive the children's support benefits into Noga's account.

From the initial approach to the NII, it became clear that because Noga was not eligible for an identity card, they could not open a file for her. Hence, she could not receive the benefits. The Rights Exercising Social Worker, whose role included establishing personal contacts with the clerks at the various agencies that she worked with, approached her contact at the NII and asked her help to come up with a solution to Noga's problem. The Rights Exercising Social Worker and Noga, who knew very little Hebrew and so was accompanied by a specially enlisted interpreter, went together to meet the contact person at the NII. In the consultation they held, it was decided to take a number of steps that would enable them to circumvent the obstacle created by the fact that Noga could not receive the child benefits directly. They decided to put in a request to open a file at the NII in the name of the children (who are citizens by virtue of their father's citizenship) and to attach it to Noga's bank account number. At the same time, they submitted a request for income support for Noga, as well as a special request to recognise Noga as a recipient of a social security payment.

However, on the date that the benefits were due to go into Noga's account, they did not arrive. The Rights Exercising Social Worker again approached the NII. In the meantime, it became clear that the process of recognising Noga as a recipient of social security payments would take a long time; time that they did not have. The Rights Exercising

Social Worker approached the director of social security payments at the NII to explore the possibility of transferring the children's benefits and the dependency supplement directly to Noga without having to recognise her as a recipient of social security. As the reply to this request was also delayed, the Rights Exercising Social Worker approached the ombudsman at the State Comptroller's Office with a request to clarify the issue of transferring the benefits directly to Noga, without her receiving social security. Even with the involvement of the ombudsman, it took four months after the first request for the family to begin receiving income support payments into Noga's bank account through the file opened at the NII in the children's names. Later, a formal recipient of social security was nominated, and about two months after that, the family received the child benefits and the dependency supplement retroactively from the time of the first request.

For some of you, this example will engender hope; for others, despair. Hope springs from the relative success of Noga's treatment; despair results from the emotional roller coaster of shuttling between success and total failure when doing what seems to be the right and just thing. It also stems from the position that the caseworker and the Rights Exercising Social Worker found themselves in, torn between the intolerable, acute situation of Noga and her children, and an impersonal, indifferent bureaucracy. The caseworker and, to a lesser extent, the Rights Exercising Social Worker were close enough to Noga and the children to allow them to sense the urgency of the problems, as well as the level of hardship and the pain that the situation created. They knew the concrete significance of the fact that Noga did not have a source of income. They could not deceive themselves and think that Noga was exaggerating or manipulating because they knew her and could not therefore console themselves with the thought that she had 'got used to her difficult situation' and 'did not feel the pain' that it entailed (Rainwater, 1970). At the same time, they were close enough to the various services to be familiar with the impersonal way in which they behave and the administrative and bureaucratic time entailed in completing forms, getting approvals and then getting more approvals of one, two and three echelons that are out of touch with the urgency of the distress that was the lot of Noga and the children.

In this regard, the caseworker and the Rights Exercising Social Worker could not employ a discourse of rights because Noga's rights were not formally violated. They could have employed a discourse of justice but this would not have taken them far in the context of the NII. They had to translate the language of cruel injustice into a language that would convince anybody who could help.

When Noga lodged a complaint with the police against Assaf for his violence, it was an important act of defence of herself and the children. Normally, the social protection system should have provided her with a safety net in order to encourage her to defend herself and her children, and to support her after she did so. Moreover, we would have liked to see the professionals being impressed by Noga and praising her because they are aware of the difficulties entailed in revealing domestic violence, particularly in a situation of financial dependence, as in this case. In practice, the difficulties created by the complaint had the opposite effect and were liable to cause Noga to drop the complaint, or not to repeat it in the future. The role of the caseworker in a case like this is therefore critical. She is responsible for providing Noga with the required social safety net, for ensuring its effectiveness and for working with Noga so that she really feels safe. By doing so, she is supporting Noga in rebelling against private abuse and public patriarchy.

This example transforms the principles of active rights exercising into real actions: the involvement of Noga throughout the process; the closely linked working together of the Rights Exercising Social Worker and the caseworker; the consultation of the Rights Exercising Social Worker with colleagues; doubting every reply that was received, even when the source of the response was an authorised agency; the unwillingness to accept negative answers and the determination to 'go one floor up' to a more senior official in the system; close familiarity with key people in social security and other relevant systems, and the use of personal contacts; and proactive initiative and continuous follow-up and activity till some solution is achieved.

Active rights exercising in situations where there are no rights

The third type of rights exercising touches on issues in which rights do not exist at all in the given sphere. In fact, this type of practice makes the broadest interpretation of the idea that poverty is a violation of rights. This interpretation goes beyond the laws and regulations, and seeks to view the rights to housing, employment, education, health and welfare as rights that the social workers should work to actualise, including in cases and contexts for which the state does not regard itself responsible and does not offer any solutions. In these situations, the caseworkers and the Rights Exercising Social Worker base their practice on a basic sense of what is just and right, and what is wrong, and not in the discourse on rights.

Let us look at Fatima, a woman aged about 40 and a mother of six children, four of whom lived with her, of which three were minors. About five years ago, her husband died suddenly from heart failure. Until his death, they lived off his small income, but with his death, there was a deterioration in their economic situation. Fatima went into a depression and had difficulty functioning for four years. Throughout this period, she did not seek professional help and was helped by her older children. Only when she improved, started working a little and felt better mentally did she first request help from the social services department. Her state of health was not good at the time. She suffered from unbalanced diabetes, asthma and high blood pressure.

For years, Fatima has needed dental treatment but, over the years, she was able to postpone it. A few months before she came to seek help, she started having severe dental pain, to the point where she could not eat solids. This posed a serious danger for her because in order to keep her diabetes situation balanced, she had to eat carbohydrates regularly. Fatima approached the dental clinic of the health service (a state-mandated service) to which she was affiliated in order to get a quotation for the dental work she needed. The quotation she got amounted to the enormous sum of 35,000 shekels (about US$10,000), much more than she could afford. At this stage, she approached the social worker, asking help to raise the money.

In Israel, dental treatment is known to be a problematic issue for social workers. It is very expensive and although dental treatment for children up to the age of 18 was recently included in the health-care law, there is no provision for adult dental care. The social services department does not have any special budget for dental treatment either. They do have a limited budget that they can use for emergencies and it usually serves for basic needs such as furniture, electrical appliances and transportation to life-saving medical treatment. Theoretically, this budget could cover dental treatment as well but it is actually too small to cover the usual costs involved, so social workers have to make difficult decisions about whom and how to help. In this case, the social worker could help Fatima with about US$500. Since Fatima could not raise the balance of the money, this sum was, in fact, useless.

Social workers are accustomed to telling service users that they cannot help them with dental services, knowing that they are sending them to treat their teeth by themselves, mostly using painkillers and waiting for teeth to fall out. Fatima's case was somewhat different because she needed teeth in order to balance her diabetes, and this was perhaps partly the reason that motivated the caseworker to look for a better answer. The caseworker approached the Rights Exercising Social

Worker and together they approached the director of social services of the health service, who suggested approaching the Chief Enquiries Committee, the highest national authority of the health service that can approve requests for treatment, and advised them how to proceed.

As the caseworker, the Rights Exercising Social Worker and Fatima understood that they would have to wait a long time for an answer from the Chief Enquiries Committee and were worried that it would be negative, they started exploring alternative possible solutions. It turned out that at the Hadassah Medical School in Jerusalem, the dental students accept patients, with payment at cost. However, this solution seemed unworkable because of the distance between Jerusalem and the peripheral town where Fatima lived.

The Rights Exercising Social Worker knew about a small community dental clinic that operated in a nearby town, less than an hour's drive away. However, there was no direct public transportation; thus, the journey there would take more than two hours each way. The social worker suggested to Fatima that she approach this community dental clinic to get a quotation but Fatima had reservations about wasting money and time for one more quotation that she would not be able to afford. Fatima was also afraid that it was too far away and that she would not be able to afford to go there regularly for the ongoing treatment that she needed.

The Rights Exercising Social Worker felt desperate. She checked the lists of philanthropic funds that she had access to and located a number that might help; however, she realised that raising a contribution through them would take time, while she needed a quick answer. The only possible solution that she could think of was to contact the community dental clinic directly. She told the secretary about Fatima and the secretary asked her to email the quotation that Fatima had already received, as well as the X-rays that she had, and she promised to answer by phone about the estimated cost. After half an hour, the secretary phoned to say that the quotation Fatima received from the public health service was ridiculously high and that their quotation was one third of it. She suggested that Fatima should make an immediate appointment for an examination at a token cost. After the examination, she would get a detailed quotation and treatment plan, and would receive initial treatment to ease the pain.

When Fatima heard about it, she felt relieved. She was even happier after she visited the community clinic and received a final quotation of about 16 per cent of the original one. According to the doctor, the treatment planning included all the necessary treatments. Fatima paid half the amount and the department of social services paid the other half. Fatima immediately started a series of treatments that continued for a few months.

Once Fatima's problem was solved, the Rights Exercising Social Worker began to think about how to make this solution available to other service users. She got involved with establishing a group of activists who gave testimony at a parliamentary committee to protest the lack of responses to dental problems. In addition, the group was part of roundtable discussions with the Health Ministry, civil society organisations, the Ministry of Welfare and Social Services, and the municipality, aimed at setting up a community dental clinic in the nearby big town.

Clearly, advanced active rights exercising presents a real challenge for professionals. Some people might argue that it exceeds the boundaries of the profession and the role of social services departments. However, if we take the idea that poverty is a violation of rights seriously, the answer is clear: it requires solidarity and involvement with service users to create a better society.

Note
[1] I thank Sivan Russo-Carmel, the head of the MAPA programme, and Michal Noam-Alon and Yocheved Maayan, two of the first Rights Exercising Social Workers, whose work I refer to in this chapter.

13

In the face of social injustice: a panel

The conference day entitled 'What can I do in the face of social injustice?' took place at Ben-Gurion University in 2015. It was organised by the PAP student programme Casework for Social Change, and was attended by about 100 people, including service users, students and academics, social workers, and other professionals, most of whom stayed to listen to the panel discussion that concluded the day, much later than anticipated.

This chapter is an edited version of the concluding panel's transcript. It is a multi-voiced portrayal of the practice of the active exercising of rights that was first developed in the student programme, and later applied in other PAP programmes all over the country. The people who made up the panel were: Ruth, a service user; Rina, Adam and Shlomi, three students from the student programme; Idit, the programme's active rights coordinator; and Sivan, the head of the MAPA programme.

After the speakers had their say, two questions were taken from the floor. The first question caused a stir among the members of the panel and the audience. In fact, it was an extremely important question because it implied a return to the very conservative stances that the whole event sought to challenge. The answer to the question simply clarified the basic principles of the practice of the active exercising of rights that is based on the ontological assumption that poverty is a violation of human rights. Actually, the question constituted a living example of the ongoing need for the deconstruction and reconstruction of the basic concepts of the paradigm.[1]

Michal: 'There are three students here from the Casework for Social Change programme – Adam Cohen, Rina Bartz and Shlomi Michael ben Hamo – who can tell us something about their experience of engaging in the active exercising of rights. And also with us is Ruth Buzaglo, who belongs to one of the families that we have accompanied in the programme and who spoke in the Parliament on the World Day for Combating Poverty. Ruth also had a personal meeting with the Minister for Welfare and Social Services that day, who has since been replaced, though the meeting took place only a few months ago. Also with us are: Idit Zamir-Yaffe, the active rights coordinator of the student programme, on whose work the role of the Rights Exercising Social Worker is based; and Sivan Russo-Carmel, the head of the MAPA programme.

The first question I wanted to ask is addressed to you, Ruth. It relates to something that we want to convey here today: that the active advocacy we provide is important. The fact that we accompany clients to services is significant in people's experience. At least we think so. The subject of policy practice, as, for example, going to the Parliament, is important. And I wanted to ask you: what was it like in your experience? What did it mean to you?'

Ruth: 'For me, the experience was amazing. I have been on welfare for about 12–13 years and I have had contact with a number of social workers. Over all those years, I did not achieve what I have achieved this year with Adam, the student. Really. I want to say that there is a difference because when a person goes alone, with the documents and everything else that's required, she simply undergoes a runaround: go there, come here; go, come. When the administrators in those offices see that you're not alone, that you have a formal representative with you, and he introduces himself as a social worker, things change completely. It happened to me with lots of things I never dreamt of getting. But I got them with Adam during this year that is coming to an end. It's a pity. I would have liked it to continue because he helped me a lot. I achieved things I never dreamt I deserved. As a mother of two children, they always rejected me. I got into a situation in which I said I do not need a welfare file. If I cope alone, without your help, I do not need to have a social worker who comes to ask about the children, how they are and all that. I want to thank Adam because I received a lot because of him, which, before then, they said is not due to me as two children are not enough to qualify you for financial support. And he went with me to the municipality and to schools and to get glasses for the kids, which I didn't even know were available on welfare. Never! It's not as if I tried to exploit the system, but there were certain things I couldn't manage. I did buy one pair of glasses for my daughter but I didn't have enough money to get a pair for the other child. I want to mention that when I started to meet Adam, I did not work and now I do work. I'm having a good time. I'm enjoying myself. Today, they let me off early from work so I could come here. [Applause.]'

Michal: 'But not all the problems have been solved, right?'

Ruth: 'One problem has not been solved. The problem of the pergola, but I won't give up. [Laughter from the audience; Ruth smiles.] By chance, this week, Adam contacted my boss at work to say that he wanted me to come here. So my boss asked me, "Ruti, what are you going to the university for? Where will it lead?" So I told him my whole story because I have only been working there for two months and hadn't told them my life story, only briefly. And he said, "You come to work smiling and laughing, what's going on inside?" So I told him. It is hard for me to open up, but I told him a little, also about the housing problem. So he says, "You know that MP Elallouf is connected to the foundation that operates my workplace and we can talk to him, so don't worry, tomorrow we can see to it." [Laughter from the audience.] So I said, "Good." It's worked out well. I've got this problem and I won't give up. I won't give up on a place for my children to sleep. Absolutely. If it is not solved, I'll approach Elallouf from here. [Applause.] Thank you everybody.'

Michal: 'That is very moving. Thank you for that. I now want to address the students. I frequently hear heads of social services departments saying that it's impossible for them to practise active rights exercising. It's impossible to do it the way we do it. For example it is not possible to accompany families to organisations and services. First, they say it's not professional; you don't have to study at university for that; you can use a non-professional, an auxiliary. Second, they say it destroys the therapeutic relationship and can engender dependence. So, from your experience, can you say

	whether it is possible, why it's possible, what is the benefit?'
Rina:	'I'll start. First, it is possible but it depends on the circumstances. The huge number of families that each social worker has to work with nowadays creates an atmosphere that does not easily permit something like this.[2] I very much hope that things will change and we'll be able to do things a little differently. Besides the problem of the heavy caseload, it is also a matter of approach. From my experience, if you accompany the person without discussing it with her, it can possibly create dependence. Because you simply took her there and you took her away from there, you didn't create any change. But if you go with her and are really with her there, and speak to her afterwards about the experience, wonderful things can develop. Two of the families who could not come here today asked me to say in their name that the most important thing was that I accompanied them to all sorts of offices and services to arrange their rights, and if they had not had this accompaniment, they would not have achieved anything. I can say that very absorbing discussions, especially on emotional subjects, arise during the accompanying. I believe that when a social worker has the courage to stand alongside her clients, particularly in the presence of other people in power that she is dependent on, it brings out something different in the person. They develop trust and belief in the social worker that does not exist in the office of the social services department.'
Shlomi:	'The stories we have heard here this evening illustrate the significance of going with and standing by families. One of the things I have understood about the programme is that when you go together with families to administrative authorities, not only are you exposed to and experience what happens there, but a sort of relationship develops between you as well. That relationship is, in my view, the principal intervention tool. It is the principal tool for creating change. When you experience the pain together with the people, it creates a special bond between you that is very significant for the therapeutic process. It is

the very opposite of dependence. It strengthens and exposes the power of the people. And it is possible. If it happens here, I believe it can happen everywhere.'

Adam: 'I feel that accompanying is to be a witness to an important experience in the lives of the people I work with. When I go on my own to the various authorities, the electricity company, the housing company, the municipality, I am not sure what to do there. It is really difficult. When I went with Ruth to the municipal engineering department, for instance, and I was faced with a lawyer with many years of experience, and other professionals and technicians, I felt like an imbecile, actually. I can just imagine if Ruth were to go there alone, she'd be completely alone. It's so hard, almost impossible in the face of this enormous establishment. When I went with Ruth, I did not know what to do, but Ruth brought somebody else who *did* know. So we were three against three. [Laughter from the audience.] This improved the power imbalance a little. And we succeeded, in the small battle, not in the big war, but we succeeded a bit. I feel that accompaniment is like being a child who goes to some big place and it's hard for him. He needs somebody else. I don't feel that it is dependence. It is caring; it's concern.'

Michal: 'Thank you. Idit, I am now addressing you. You are the student programme coordinator and are responsible for helping the students with knowledge and advice to practise exercising rights. What have you learnt from your experience about why it is important to accompany clients to services and organisations? And also, what else is important in your view in rights exercising work?'

Idit: 'Before I became the programme coordinator, I was a student on the programme for two years. One of the experiences I remember from my time as a student was when I accompanied one of my clients, an Arab woman who wore traditional dress, to an interview at the employment bureau. We sat down in front of the clerk, she directly opposite him, and me a little to the side. He looked at the two of us and began to speak to *me*. He asked *me*, "Why have you come here and what is she doing here?" I looked at him and asked him to speak to her. So, first, on the individual level, the process with that woman was very significant – to gradually raise her voice and to help the clerk to listen to her voice. I remember that, at first, that woman did not speak at all. She waited for me to be her voice but I was insistent with her, and I said to her, "I am here with you but I am not the subject of the meeting." Slowly, her voice got heard more and more. The clerks we met began to give her space. So, in the process undergone by both the service users and the clerks, there is a very significant place for accompaniment, and social change can happen in those meetings of individuals.

I'll say a bit more about the social change and about the transition from active rights exercising to policy practice that we are attempting to promote in the programme. Ruth, for example, had the honour of speaking in the Parliament on the World Day for Combating Poverty. It's an important example. We routinely detect obstacles in the execution of policy and we swamp them with people we work with. This is important in terms of the process because of the people participating in it as individuals and the fact that action like this influences policy. I hope there will be more and more small successes like this.'

Michal: 'My last question is addressed to Sivan, the head of the Families Meeting Opportunities programme, who chose the first active Rights Exercising Social Workers and developed training for them. With the role of Rights Exercising Social Worker becoming more and more popular around the country, I am frequently asked about their role. From your experience, do you have to be a special type of person to be a Rights Exercising Social Worker? I ask this because there are people who say to me, "I'm not the type who fights and struggles and is able to be assertive in front of clerks." How do you become a Rights Exercising Social Worker?'

Sivan: 'That is a good question. We too are preoccupied by it. I think that social workers generally have to be special types. That special thing is the inability to

	accept injustice. I don't know how special it is, but this is what I'm looking for, and it's what develops and matures more and more in Rights Exercising Social Workers. The more you influence change and see things succeeding – that you have the power to do things – the more it increases the desire to continue to do them.'
Michal:	'But what if I am a quiet person, a little shy?'
Sivan:	'The inability to accept injustice does not mean shouting in the corridors of various services; rather, it requires a clear understanding that I am going to work on it and I am going to do what is necessary, and be willing to learn how to do it. There is no essential style; it can be done in different ways and you can learn how to do it.'
Idit:	'I would like to add something. The first thing I learnt in rights exercising work is not to be afraid of not knowing because rights exercising is a very broad field and we will never know everything about it. We will always be encountering new situations and questions. Accepting that you don't know means knowing how to ask, to consult and to constantly gather information.'
Michal:	'Thank you very much everybody. We still have a couple of minutes, so we can take two questions from the audience.'
Audience 1:	'I have a question for Ruthi. From the experience you underwent, do you think you could now do it alone? In other words, take care of your rights by yourself, go alone and speak on your own?'
Ruth:	'That is what I said at first. I went alone for 13–14 years and didn't get answers. I could speak, go alone, no problem. But the answer was negative because you are alone. When Adam introduced himself and said he is a social worker accompanying me, they began to talk differently to us. From the start they spoke differently. When you come alone, they can talk to you how it suits them. The fact is that after not getting anything for 13 years, I did get.'
Michal:	'Ruth, do you think that it will continue when Adam is not with you? Because he soon won't be with you.'

Ruth: 'That is what I meant to say earlier, that if I can get another student next year, I'll be very happy.'

Audience 1: 'Ruth, do you think that over the last two years, you have received a good toolbox that will allow you to function and succeed alone in what you are up against?'

Ruth: 'I do not think I'll manage. I don't think I'll manage on my own. Because the moment he leaves me, I'll have to go alone, and I'll go alone, that's not the problem. I'll be running a lot, but I won't get answers. [Commotion in the panel and the audience; people are all talking at once.]'

Rina: 'I'd like to deal with the question of the toolbox. It does not matter what toolbox you bring with you; it matters if you have someone backing you, and who is behind you. For instance, if Ruth were to come with a lawyer [cries from the audience.]'

Michal: 'Listen to what Rina is saying.'

Rina: 'If she were to come with a lawyer, it would also help. It's not that she will always need somebody; it's that the government institutions will change their behaviour slightly, then there will be less need for her to come with a social worker or a lawyer. And there are changes in this direction in some services; some of them already understand that they have to respond to people as if they are accompanied by a lawyer even when they come alone.'

Michal: 'So, what you are saying is that we need to ensure that various agencies need to understand that they have to behave differently.'

Sivan: 'The question is: *who* has to change? It's not the service users that have to change. Self-advocacy has always existed among service users. Our task is to enhance it, to strengthen it, to give people the feeling that what they have been doing up until now was quite right. The thing is that they lacked the resources and privileges that we bring.'

Michal: 'I have a real-life example that my students drew my attention to when they heard me speaking on the telephone. Sometimes, when I call to arrange things, I introduce myself as Michal Krumer-Nevo. And sometimes, when I come up against a wall,

I say, "This is Professor Michal Krumer-Nevo." The students who work with me call this: "Michal pulling out the professor." I bring it out when I need symbolic capital, when I need support to get a response. When I do it, it sounds natural, as if it's in my toolbox. But it is not in my toolbox; I am simply a professor. People who cannot haul out the professor have to bring something or somebody, a social worker. [Cheers from the audience.] And as Ruth said, she brought Adam, and it's fine because sometimes that is what is needed. And sometimes it is not needed, like in the story you heard earlier about Galit, who said she used to go to offices and shout to get what she demanded, and today she takes pleasure in going to offices and getting along without shouting, and to see that they relate to her. So, things change in people as well as in institutions, and the more things change in the institutions, the more we will talk about it, I hope. It is very important to be on our guard not to locate the problem in people's characteristics, but in their *real* relative power inferiority in the face of the institutions. And in order to deal with this relative weakness, they have to be strengthened, as do the services and the institutions. Just because somebody needs accompaniment for more than two years does not mean she is not alright. It is reasonable to require accompaniment for more than two years because you need as much as you need. Thank you for the question; it is an excellent question. One more question and we'll close the session.'

Audience 2: 'In one of the stories we heard earlier, a student mentioned that getting up in the morning to go to administrative offices with service users is something she hates to do. Where did you draw the strength to get up and do what you had to do?'

Adam: 'From anger. A boy in one of the families I worked with suffers from a severe and rare disease. He cannot attend school because there is no medication available from the health service. When I went to the health service, they told me the problem does not lie with them, but with whoever imports the medication from overseas. So, then I contacted the company that

	imports the medication from overseas and they said to me, "The problem does not lie with us but with the manufacturer overseas." All those people are faraway and they do not know the boy. But in the end, the child does not attend school. It makes me angry.'
Shlomi:	'For me, it is the friendship elements in the relationships we establish with the families on the programme. Perhaps it does not sound professional when I say there are friendship elements, but it is something internal, right inside your gut, that makes you feel you have to do something. You understand that it is not logical that the woman has to prove constantly and everywhere how much of a sad case she is, or how needy she is, or just how much she needs them to help her. It is this link that exists between you and the families that makes you act.'
Rina:	'When you are hosted at the home of a family once a week, and I say "hosted" intentionally, you think you are coming to perform an "intervention" or therapeutic meeting but, in practice, you are being hosted. They offer you something to drink and sometimes a meal. You are taken from a distant story, a story about someone who has a sick child, like in Adam's story, to a sick child right there. For example, in the family I work with, from a story about a family living in cramped conditions, you are *sitting* cramped. And you see the sewage. And you see the sick children every week. So, from distant problems, they become very, very pressing problems. And now it is no longer just *their* problem; it's also my problem. And when it is your problem, you have to solve it.'
Michal:	'We could continue but we will end with that. I want to thank the participants of the panel, and all of you who attended this evening. Thank you very much. [Applause.]'

Notes

[1] The panel (in Hebrew) is available at: www.youtube.com/watch?v=qSqiRssp8X4

[2] On average, a full-time caseworker's caseload consists of more than 100 families (see, for example, Alfandari, 2019a: 159–60).

PART IV

Solidarity

The fourth and final part of the book is dedicated to four examples of practice that present the theme of solidarity. In the PAP, solidarity is an ethical principle that dictates the positioning of the social worker vis-a-vis service users. By analysing situations in which social workers succeeded in standing by service users and other situations in which they were not successful, this part of the book aims to enrich the professional imagination and repertoire of solidarity in different contexts and settings.

Chapter 14, 'When Douby looked for a home: "standing by" within the establishment', tells the story of a woman who was evicted from her home, which she had occupied for many years, and the social work student who worked closely with her and tried to prevent the eviction. The story focuses on the response of the managers of the social services department to the event as an example of the difficulty of conducting a critical version of social work within the establishment.

Chapter 15, 'A babysitter for a dollar: community development', aims to draw conclusions regarding the appropriate community response to a case in which a fire broke out in the public housing apartment of a woman who had locked her children in when she left for work. Thinking about a response in terms of community development takes into consideration the structural barriers that this mother (and others) face, and challenges the automatic response that blames the mother for acting neglectfully.

Chapter 16, 'Between Othering and solidarity: crisis intervention with children at risk' builds upon a graphic description written by a social worker following a crisis intervention involving children at risk. The response of the social worker is analysed as an example of the 'standing against' position. The possibility of standing by is presented in the chapter as a tentative choice.

Chapter 17, '"I'm not that kind of person": solidarity in a group intervention', tells the story of a group I worked with for two-and-a-half years beginning in 2001. The chapter focuses on the first meeting of the group and the challenges of establishing solidarity during that first encounter. This challenge was intensified when one of the group members threatened to set himself and his children on fire as an act of protest in order to receive better housing. The response of the social worker is analysed in terms of giving recognition to service users and standing by them.

14

When Douby looked for a home: 'standing by' within the establishment

This chapter is based on a lecture written in a state of emotional turmoil linked to a crisis that occurred in relations between the academic students' fieldwork training programme, Casework for Social Change, and the social services department where the programme was run. The crisis occurred in 2012, the second year of the student programme. Nadia, who was treated by Ronit, a student in the programme, was evicted from her apartment, in which she had squatted for many years. When the bailiffs came to evict her, she contacted Ronit to request help. The student went to the apartment and tried to contact the social services department and even the mayor in order to repeal the eviction order. The director of the social services department argued that the presence of the student with the woman at the time of the eviction constituted assistance to the woman in contravening the law. Indeed, she was angry that the student, with the backup of her instructor, had approached the mayor's office directly after not managing to reach the social services department by telephone. She argued that the student had violated the rules of the department and she threatened to stop cooperating with the programme.

In retrospect, this event was important in the development of our relations with the social services department and helped us to mark the student programme as a critical programme. The event was woven into the lecture I gave a few weeks later at a conference on social activism and academia. Throughout the first part of the lecture, a home video showing the dog Douby was screened in the background.

Douby joined our family three weeks ago. She is a cheerful dog and about a year old. She wrinkles her forehead and inclines her head to the side in a graceful movement of strained attention when you speak to her. When she is happy, she jumps, with all four feet in the air. She rests her head on us, seemingly wanting to hug rather than requesting to be stroked. She only joined us temporarily because we already have Gurgur and Lola, and we decided we could not keep her. Only temporarily – until we find her a home. Home is a painful story in Douby's life because she came to us on the day I visited Nadia, the woman who was evicted from her apartment, which she had broken into 12 years ago and squatted in ever since. Nadia is treated by Ronit, a student on the PAP training programme Casework for Social Change. Ronit and Nur, Ronit's instructor, were called to Nadia's home when the bailiffs, about ten men, suddenly arrived there in the morning wielding an eviction order. The weather was terrible that day in Beer-Sheva, with sandstorms and haze. When I got there, all Nadia's possessions were already outside. Some had already been taken to the municipal storage site, and those that were outside waiting to be taken to the storage were covered in a thick layer of sand. Nadia went to sleep at the home of her 24-year-old son, temporarily. Later, she went to her sister's. Douby stayed behind and I could not resist taking her. I want you to imagine Douby as a dog looking for a home, and to think about Nadia.

Standing by, and here I am paraphrasing Michelle Fine (2006: 84), is a vision in which social workers remember the democratic and activist origins of the profession. It is a vision in which we as academics strive to be public intellectuals. Our purpose is to create a critical, pedagogic space in which we and our students are deeply involved in a debate that seeks to build a social work practice committed to democratic action.

Since my time is limited, I will only briefly mention what I would have liked to talk about if I had more time. I would have explained in detail the history of social work and explained something about the similarity between what is happening in academia and what has happened to the social work profession in this neoliberal era. While the institutions of knowledge are now subject to the principles of the market, to profit and loss, to donations and grants, social work is abandoning its values in the name of practice based on 'evidence', which is a professional concept that conceals the very neoliberal stance that I mentioned earlier. I would explain something about critical pedagogy, the challenges that it poses and the pleasure and the joy that it brings. I would say something about the ethical issues that arise as we strive to do casework for social change. Finally, I would perhaps ask why I am doing it when it is so demanding, requiring time, a lot of time, which is not rewarded in any form in the academic system. The last point is very important because, as Michelle Fine (2006: 103) (again) eloquently says, academia 'remains one of the few remaining spaces within which dissent is possible. Here social critique and outrage are recognized as forms of knowledge; inquiry is valued as oxygen for democratic sustenance; collaborations are possible and necessary for sustaining global movements of resistance.' We are fighting to preserve this quality of academia, this special place that academia has had in society, and to make it better. The fact that academic criteria do not grant this activity sufficient recognition is a badge of shame for academia.

Had I had more time, I would also have said a little about the forgotten and silenced history of social work aimed at social justice. It is important to remind ourselves that among the first women who began the voluntary activity that became the social work profession in the second half of the 19th century and the beginning of the 20th century were women-activists who were not afraid to go against the flow. Some of them endeavoured to create a practice that sought to stand by the most disadvantaged sections of the population from a deep social critique. Over time, in a long process of institutionalisation, the hard core of social work became closely connected to the establishment and the state system (Cloward and Fox Piven, 1975; Schram and Silverman, 2012; Reisch and Andrews, 2014). Today, social work services are predominantly financed and supervised, directly or indirectly, by the state, and an increasingly significant portion of professional practice has undergone a process of legalisation and managerialisation. This has led to greater and greater distancing from the possibility of work for social change, which was marginalised, and is now carried out by what are called community workers.

However, the connection between community work and social change is not the only connection that social work makes, and what I want to talk about a bit today is the attempt to politicise mainstream casework undertaken in the establishment. I want to tell you about the use we make of our privileged position in the university to create links between theory and critical practice in the field of the social services departments.

The Casework for Social Change programme began to operate about 18 months ago when I was joined by a group of experienced social workers: Mirit Sidi, Nur Shimei and Menny Malka. Before they joined me as instructors in the student programme, they had been working in the most difficult social areas, with young women living in wretched poverty, with Jews and Arabs, with physically abused women, and with violent men, and had managed to integrate critical social thinking into their interpersonal meetings with the people they met. They brought this experience with them and became student instructors in the PAP training programme. In the framework of the programme, the students do their practical training in social services departments, while taking theoretical and practical courses on the PAP. What is special, challenging and difficult about the programme is that we train the students to learn critical theory and practice, and, at the same time, to work in the social services departments that are perhaps the most conservative institutional spaces in the field of social work. We teach them to view the men and women that they meet not as bearers of scars of a personal pathology, but as the products of the iniquities of the social structures, and to devise a practice that manifests this understanding. We teach them, to use Johnson and Lawler's (2005) terminology, to replace 'the language of psychology' with 'the grammar of exploitation'. Yet, at the same time, they are operating in social services departments that are unaware of the grammar of exploitation and, consciously or unconsciously, promote it.

These situations of working in social services departments create tension but also offer opportunities. The tension is often so great that in order to release it, you need the patience of a skilled knitter who traces the individual threads in her tangle in order to undo it. The attitude of a knitter who simply cuts the knots to undo the tangle does not fit our programme because what we are dealing with is a tangle of interpersonal, institutional and establishment threads and relations, and although they create the oppression and the inequality, they cannot be cut in a single act.

For precisely this reason, these situations are sites for potential change, which occurs when they are politicised and the banality of bureaucratic and impersonal treatment exposes injustice. This injustice does not necessarily target a specific person, nor does it stem from personal motives; rather, it is the result of regulations and a chain of bureaucratic actions that are supposedly harmless. When viewed in this light, these places become the most fascinating and important places to be.

In order to illustrate two such situations, I will return to Nadia, who raised Douby until three weeks ago. Nadia is a short and slim woman aged 50. She has a special style of dressing and one can see that she used to be a beautiful woman. However, because she has no teeth at all, she now looks older than her age and is seemingly neglected. On the day the bailiffs got to her house, she immediately contacted Ronit, who had been working with her for the last couple of months. She also contacted David, who is an activist of the Movement for Living with Respect, a body of activists that assists in the prevention of evictions in legal, non-violent ways. In cases where the movement activists have not managed to prevent the eviction beforehand, they send a person to photograph and document the event. This course of action is based on the experience of other radical movements, according to which the presence of witnesses observing an event can change the way in which the oppressive action is executed. In addition, it can serve to encourage future political action.

In my view, the fact that Nadia contacted Ronit is very positive. It is evidence that she regarded her as relevant and helpful. It is like saying, 'I need you; I want you; come and be with me.' As institutional oppression takes place in the context of erasing the personal of both the oppressor and the oppressed, and of their relationship, any expression of a relationship and of the personal can be regarded as resistance to oppression.

Ronit hurried to get to Nadia's place. She informed Nur, her instructor, who joined them later that day. As the bailiffs had to pack up the whole house, which, while small, was filled with possessions that had to be loaded onto a truck, the eviction itself took a long time and only actually ended the following day. While doing this, they permitted Nadia to sort out her belongings and to keep some clothes and personal effects that she would need during the long period of life without a home that awaited her. Ronit and Nur stood by Nadia throughout this scene of tension, confrontation, heightened emotion, terrible anger, frustration, shame and pain. There was also a complicated legal matter here as Nadia possessed a document entitling her to social housing and they believed that delaying the eviction would allow her to exercise her right to vacate her apartment peacefully, without the use of force. They mediated between the highly agitated Nadia and the ten packers and transporters, and they spoke on her behalf while she sorted out her things. They served as lightning rods for her tremendous anger, humiliation and feeling of injustice, and they tried to stop the eviction while it was happening by means of phone calls to the director of the social services department and, when those were not answered, to the mayor's office. From the perspective of poverty-aware social work, they did exactly what they should have done. They behaved in an exemplary fashion.

When the director of the social services department heard that Ronit and Nur were present at the time of the eviction, she was furious. "Is that what you teach your students; is that what you do in academia?", she railed against me:

> 'It contravenes our regulations and agreements. We have an agreement with the police that we are not allowed to be present while a house is being vacated. Moreover, we are not allowed to report to our service users, namely, the people being evicted, of an impending eviction. We cannot operate against the police.'

To say that I was surprised when I heard this would not adequately explain my feelings. It was not that I was not surprised. It is true that I was unaware of the existence of this regulation, and as far as I understand it, it is a local initiative and not an obligatory national regulation. However, more than surprise, I felt pain, over my whole body: the pain of the service users, who are left totally alone; and the pain for the profession that I love, which has changed from being an instrument to create justice to an instrument of surveillance, and from a means of strengthening the voice of the disadvantaged to a means of oppression. For me, being there with Nadia was an expression of solidarity, of standing by her when she needed it the most. Not doing so would contradict the basic instinct of seeking justice. In addition, had we not been there, Ronit and Nur would not have had the intimate knowledge needed to go on working with Nadia.

Another week passes and Nur, Ronit and I are meeting with the senior staff and the director of the social services department, searching for ways to proceed. Nadia wants social housing. All inquiries by Nadia and Ronit into her eligibility have led nowhere. One day they tell her at the public housing authority that she is only entitled to a small subsidy to assist in paying her rent, not to a whole apartment; on other days, they say she is not eligible for any assistance. Nadia and Ronit's approach to the Women Lawyers for Social Justice has also led nowhere. "Nadia needs an apartment", I say to the department director, "And I want us to use every means possible, all your connections, to get her an apartment."

In fact, I am playing a game of cards with a very weak hand because I am unfamiliar with the people or the regulations at the Housing Ministry or the public housing authority. What I need is the goodwill of the director of the social services department, who has connections and influence. Nadia says that when the mayor is in favour, an apartment can be found. She says that homeless people who embarrass the mayor, who threaten the good name of the city, like those who camped out in tents and caused problems in the 2011 summer of social protest, do get apartments. I do not tell the director all this, but I try to remind her that she has power and she can use it for Nadia's benefit.

"I won't do it", she says:

> 'Do you know how many evacuees we have? We have got far worse cases. Do you know that just yesterday a young family was evicted, immigrants from Ethiopia, with two

small children and a baby, and they are in the street? They have nowhere to go. Nadia is 50 and she does not have young children. She can work, and she has some family, sources of support. She will manage. If I have to use my influence, I will do so for the family. On my list of priorities they are higher.'

I am shocked. "Oh dear", I say: "I support the family but I think that together we can apply pressure for both families. If there are so many families that have been evicted, what are you doing for them?" "Me?", she says:

'When I see a case that is really severe and justified, I go to speak to the regional director of the public housing authority and sometimes he listens to me. But if I go to him with every story that arises, he won't listen to me at all. I'll be left with no influence at all.'

I do not remember what exactly I said, but I remember what I was thinking:

'Are you taking on the role of the baddie in this story? Making a selection? To what end? In whose name? Don't you see that you are helping the public housing authority to create industrial peace, a false calm, in which you do not hear the crying of the Ethiopian family and Nadia? Do you not realise that you have become the censor of social pain? Instead of raising the voice of the evacuees and causing the housing minister and the director of social housing not to sleep at night because you send them the photos and the stories of all these families, you are keeping all this pain and all the injustice inside you. It's easy for the regional director to give you an apartment occasionally for some family. That's how he keeps the system quiet.'

What is unique about Casework for Social Change is its location. The location in the very heart of the establishment raises many difficulties but also creates opportunities. Here, I am going back to Michelle Fine (2006), who, based on Kurt Levin, asks what we have to do during a period of fear, authority and oppression, and with whom we have to do it. Our answer is that as researchers and social workers concerned about the fate of people living in poverty, we must position ourselves as close as possible both to our service users and to the establishment. In this way, we challenge the practice and the professionals operating there in the name of social justice.

15

A babysitter for a dollar: community development

For a number of years, I showed Ken Loach's movie 'Ladybird, Ladybird' to my graduate classes.[1] *The movie deals with the issue of social injustice in the child protection system, telling the story of Maggie, a single mother of four children, who was sexually abused as a young girl and grew up in institutions. As an adult, she maintained fleeting relationships with various men, four of whom are the fathers of her children. One evening, she goes out to sing in a local bar and leaves her children asleep, locking the door behind her in order to prevent a break-in by violent or drunken men. During the evening, a fire breaks out in the apartment, which causes serious injury to one of the children. After a number of additional incidents, including violent behaviour by her partner, social workers remove the children from her care. Maggie fights to get them back but does not succeed. At this point, she meets Jorge, an illegal immigrant from Paraguay. With him, for the first time in her life, she establishes a relationship based on love, care and mutual respect. Both Maggie and Jorge try to avoid any contact with social services. She is wary of the long arm of the child protection workers and he is concerned about being deported. However, when Maggie becomes pregnant, the social workers locate her. They interpret her suspicious attitude towards them as a lack of awareness regarding her parenting problems and, in due course, remove the infant from the parents' care. Not much later, this series of events occurs again. The movie is heartbreaking.*

Every year, the students were shocked by the movie, both by Maggie's story and by how they saw themselves reflected in the social workers' characters. And every year, they argued with me, claiming that the movie is one-sided in favour of Maggie and does not accurately describe the child protection system. One year, two students, who were Social Workers to the Youth Law – specialist social workers who have a legal role in criminal investigations of maltreatment and represent the child's interest in juvenile courts (Gottfried and Ben-Arieh, 2019) – were especially resolute, arguing that the movie was part of a public campaign to slander social workers by portraying them as 'child kidnappers'. They said that it was a terrible movie and that the situation in Israel is totally different.

Just three days after that class, Ziva, one of these two students, contacted me. In a voice filled with emotion, she told me that on the night of the lesson, she was on duty when she was called to the hospital to meet a woman and her two children who were scalded by a fire that broke out in their apartment when the mother had gone to work and left them locked in the apartment. Ziva said that although she took an oppositional stance in the class discussion regarding the movie, she felt that it had, in fact, influenced her response to the mother, and it was of a different nature from the way in which she would have responded to her in the past. The main difference was that she could see the mother's pain and anxiety, and responded to it. She calmed the mother and enquired out of warm curiosity about the circumstances that led to the incident. The story told by the woman is an excellent example of the impossible choice that frequently characterises life in poverty. You lose both ways: whether you go to the left or to the right. In order to make it a possible choice, changes in employment policy should be made and community services that support working women should be developed. I used this story to suggest a new community service – a babysitter for a dollar – in a column I wrote for a local magazine for the 2007 International Women's Day.

Women's day needs a symbol. I suggest choosing an anonymous woman, a citizen of Beer Sheva, who, about two months ago, left home in the early afternoon to work as an office cleaner and locked her two children, aged four and eight, in their public housing apartment. We can call her Rikki. Rikki left her children with her partner, but shortly after she left the house, he got drunk, the lights in the apartment fused and the children lit candles in order to provide light. One of the candles fell onto a pile of paper, setting it alight. The man, drunk and asleep on the sofa in the living room, did not realise what was happening. The children shouted for help, and the neighbour, who also called the fire brigade, helped to evacuate them from the house. When the children reached the hospital late at night, the medical team alerted the mother and a Social Worker to the Youth Law. The social worker's role in a case of this sort is to assess Rikki's competence as a mother. If the social worker concludes that the mother neglected her children by locking them up in the house without a responsible adult, they would be recognised as children at risk and the courts might be involved in order to decide on the necessary steps to protect them.

How can we understand Rikki's actions? Listening to her story revealed what poverty is and its impact on people's daily existence. This understanding can challenge her image as an irresponsible and neglectful mother. It appears that Rikki works for a minimum wage doing shift work for a manpower agency. A day before the incident, her employer had given her notice that in a short while, he intends to fire her. This tactic is commonly used in order to avoid providing employees with the full range of social service benefits that they are entitled to after working for the same employer for nine consecutive months. In addition, Rikki's cousin, who normally looks after the children when she is at work, informed her that she could not come over that evening. Rikki, who was loathe to forfeit the meagre wage that she was getting at her place of work, and feared that her dismissal would be brought forward, did not want to give up the day's work. Her concerns were eased by the presence of her partner, who seemed sober when she left the house. She knew that she could not fully rely on him or on her neighbours, who were liable to absentmindedly come into the house under the influence of alcohol or drugs, so she locked the door. The children did not have either a key or access to a telephone.

Is Rikki a neglectful mother? Can we judge her mothering without taking account of societal responsibility for her situation? After all, Rikki's job situation is insecure and she is insecure in the neighbourhood she lives in. Moreover, even at home, her situation is not secure as she cannot trust the electricity in her public housing apartment and she cannot rely on her partner to function as a responsible adult.

Do social services protect her from neglectful societal institutions? In the inquest made after the fire incident, it was found that some months earlier, she had approached her social worker and requested assistance with arrangements for the children in an afternoon childcare framework as she was beginning to work in the afternoons and evenings, after office staff leave their offices. Her request was denied because the budget was limited to assisting families with children at risk, and Rikki's children were not considered to be at risk at the time.

Although Rikki is a devoted mother as well as a responsible worker, and despite her isolation, lack of support, shortage of financial resources and gender inferiority, she is at risk of being accused of being an unworthy mother. This is a blatant case of inequality – between rich and poor, and between men and women – that leads to injustice. Society accuses Rikki of neglecting her children without taking responsibility for the range of situations in which society itself, so vast, self-satisfied and strong, has neglected, and continues to neglect, Rikki and many other women living in poverty.

This Thursday (8 March 2007) is International Women's Day. This day, dedicated to women all over the world who have struggled in the past and continue to struggle in the present for equal rights, is a wonderful opportunity to remember the struggle of women, known and unknown, workers in factories, cleaners and carers, women working to make ends meet, who struggle every day against poverty and the inferiority that stems from it. On this day 142 years ago, a strike broke out among the female workers at the textile factories of

New York to protest against their low wages and insufferable working conditions. This strike raised awareness of the exploitative situation endured by women working for low wages.

Today, many women are still exploited at work and their chances of being reduced to poverty are far higher than for men. In Israel, in 2007, 45.8 per cent of women over the age of 15 are in work. However, women earn less than men even when they do identical work. Two thirds of minimum wage earners are women, and 65 per cent of the recipients of income support benefit are women.

Poverty is a scourge. It is a scourge for those who experience it, women and men, as well as for society as a whole. However, women's poverty is not the same as men's. The life experiences of women living in poverty, the dangers inherent in poverty and the ways in which women cope are different from those of men. Women are the ones who find themselves in the centre of public criticism: why do they get married so young? Why do they have so many children? Why do they not work? And if they work outside the home, why do they neglect their children?

Yet, if you listen to the stories of women in poverty, you realise that they run contrary to the accepted stereotypes, according to which they are perceived as having adapted to their situation or as not seeking change. Their stories, by contrast, provide evidence of the emotional pain caused by poverty, the various ways in which they attempt to fight against their poverty and the restricted social opportunities open to them to succeed in those efforts.

As a society, we should learn to recognise the voice and knowledge of women in poverty as experts not only on poverty, but also on society's drawbacks, deficits and pathologies. If we agree to do so, we will be able to identify how exploitative working conditions, poor housing and gender inequality lead to situations in which children are left unprotected and women are accused of things over which they have very minimal control.

In the meantime, if the welfare system wants to express its commitment to women in poverty on Women's Day, I suggest setting up a voluntary service to provide *babysitters for a dollar* to women who need them. A babysitter for one dollar! For Rikki and for all the other women who find themselves alone in their struggle against poverty.

Note

[1] My colleague, Idit Weiss-Gal, also used the movie in her teaching (see Weiss-Gal, 2009).

16

Between Othering and solidarity: crisis intervention with children at risk

The intervention described at the heart of this chapter was written by Nurit, a family social worker, in the framework of an exercise in PAP training. Student social workers were asked to write a personal reflection on a meaningful, memorable incident from their experience. As you will see, Nurit writes very well and in a short text, she manages to describe an event in a way that gets under your skin. Since receiving it, I have regularly used Nurit's text in teaching. Some people think that my reading of the text is too critical. You can judge for yourself.

Introduction

This discussion is going to be difficult, both emotionally and cognitively. It is difficult emotionally because the example given, written very skilfully, manages in a few words to convey the tremendous hardship entailed in poverty. It is difficult cognitively because, at first reading, it seems that the description reflects both the social worker's understanding of the family's distress and her standing by them in their struggle against poverty. However, a second reading reveals the limitations of the professional choices described.

I have two aims in presenting this story. My first aim is to direct our attention to the moment when, under the influence of Othering, the willingness to help is translated into actions of saving that ignore the knowledge of people in poverty and their subjectivity. My second aim is to suggest alternative professional steps that are based on resisting Othering and on standing by service users.

The identification of moments of Othering is a critical aspect of the PAP. It refers to identifying the moments where social workers feel that their service users are 'Other', that is, fundamentally different and inferior to them, and consequently designate them as such by diverse actions or inactions. Othering is connected to interpretation processes: the social worker interprets the service user as Other, that is, as different from her, and, at the same time, attaches inferiority to that difference (Pickering, 2001). Othering is dangerous because it denies the Other's full human subjectivity, as well as their life context. It separates the Other from their knowledge and perspective, transforming them into an object that needs to be operated on from the outside by the self. Furthermore, Othering enables the self to ignore aspects of reality that are beyond the control of the Other. This way, the context – which is the matrix in which subjectivity is shaped – vanishes. An additional detrimental aspect of an interpretation governed by Othering is that it is perceived as self-evident truth. Taken together, these factors make regarding the other as Other seem so natural that the self does not realise that there is a process of interpretation involved and that other interpretations are possible.

Finally, the denial of the interpretive process also permits the denial of the fact that the process takes place in the context of power relations, in which the social worker defines the service user unilaterally, without the latter being able to define the social worker and without giving them the opportunity to define themselves, or to gain recognition of their self-definition.

The PAP aims to focus on those moments of interpretation in order to make the interpretive process overt and, through their deconstruction, elicit a new, more beneficial interpretation. This is very important: our goal is to arrive at a beneficial interpretation that will confront injustice where it exists and will enable the social worker to give compassionate, contextualised meaning to a service user's behaviour. This kind of interpretation that politicises the helping relationship will help the social worker to experience solidarity with service users and to stand by them.

I have already mentioned that Othering includes two processes: (1) identifying the other person as the Other; and (2) labelling them as such. Let us devote a moment to the first part: how, and in what circumstances, do we identify another person as the Other? Experience teaches us that Othering often occurs when what is most obvious is the pathology. In other words, when the social worker identifies the behaviour of the service user as pathological and it arouses strong feelings in then, then they will tend to see the service user as the Other. It follows that what is interpreted as pathology is likely to dominate and significantly distort perception. Thanks to the popularity of the strengths approach, social workers are able to focus on service users' strengths in order to balance the picture created by pathology. My experience shows that focusing on strengths is sufficient to preserve a balanced picture of people whose 'other' behaviour is not extreme or visible. However, in situations of poverty, the danger of interpreting various behaviours as pathology is too great for looking at strengths to balance it. For example, when a social worker meets a person whose speech is garbled and has missing teeth, she might feel that this person is different from and inferior to them. When they hear the life story of a woman who describes ongoing transitions between violent, intimate relationships, between prostitution and addiction, and between motherhood and losing the children to welfare, they might feel that the woman in front of them is totally different from them. If we were to ask the social worker about the strengths of those service users, they would probably be able to identify their strengths, but these would not change the whole picture of inferiority and the basic feelings of distance and unfamiliarity that the social worker might experience.

The second process is the process of marking the other person as an Other. As opposed to identifying the Other, which is internal and takes place in the mind of the self, the process of *marking* is interpersonal, occurring between the self and others. It can occur through embodiment, through using a specific look or gesture, or through verbal means, such as speaking or writing. The marking always emphasises the difference between the Other and the self, and gives it a negative meaning. After this long introduction, let us move on to the story written by Nurit, which describes a home visit to a service user, whom she calls B.

When poverty is in your face – written by Nurit

My team manager calls me to her room, together with another social worker. A report has arrived from the housing association about children walking barefoot, unsupervised, in an apartment flooded with water. The neighbours complained.

This is a family that I have been working with intensively. The mother, B, is a single mother of four children, aged four to nine. The father is in prison for drug dealing. On my instruction, the mother signed a rental contract and is getting help with the rent for two months, until we can arrange her entitlement for help with rent from the Housing Ministry. B has a key to the apartment that was furnished with a budget from the social services department, but the mother and her four children live at the grandmother's house and not in the rented apartment, contrary to what was agreed with the mother.

I got to the house at 11:30 in the morning, together with a social worker colleague who works with the grandmother. The area under the house is flooded. We go up the stairs. A neighbour opens the door out of curiosity with a look half of relief and half of blame, as if saying,

"You are finally here." At the entrance to the house S, the mother's sister, is mopping water down the stairs. "What happened?", I ask her. The door to the house is wide open. The other social worker and I enter. There is a mouldy smell of dampness. In the house – water with bits of rubbish floating in it, sweet wrappers, empty bottles and disposable cutlery and crockery. The water very quickly gets into my shoes, and my socks are soaking with a disgusting liquid. I am shivering. A cold winter's day. Outside, a cold wind and drizzle but it is even colder in the house.

I asked the grandmother, "What happened?" She replied: "It's not the first time. There is a problem with the sewage. It's not terrible. What can you do? They said they would fix it. What can you do, you see. We are getting rid of the water." I say to the grandmother, "Why didn't you say there was a problem?" and she replies, "What can we do? That's how it is."

Two representatives of the housing association are in the house; they ordered a tradesman to come, trying to establish the source of the flooding. In the lounge, torn sofas that seem to be more filling than upholstery; in the kitchen, a lot of rubbish. The counter is filthy. Between the fridge and the service room, piles and piles and piles of clothes are strewn that seem to have been standing there for a few months, mouldy, mouldy. Black. Damp. Stinking. The passageway of the house – a mix of things and bits of things placed in a disorderly fashion and blocking the way. Parts of things are floating towards the other rooms.

T, aged four, comes out of the bedroom. Dry snot on an old sore on her nose. Hair unkempt, adorned with dirt. Her pants bottoms are immersed in the water. She is wearing a thin shirt. She marches in the filthy water in sandals decorated with flowers. Little T smiles at me with a shy smile. "Who are you?" "I am Nurit. I am helping your mother." "Ah [amazed] Mummy is not here. When will she be back?" Grandmother answers, "She is at work. She'll be back in the evening." T continues, "Why isn't she here?" I feel the child's yearning for her mother, the lack of clarity and the great confusion she is in: "Mommy is not here and it's not clear when she'll be back. The house is filled with water. Strange people are wandering about. I am cold. But it was actually alright until the strange people arrived. Why did they come?"

The son D, aged five, is in the bedroom wearing shorts, a long shirt and trainers without socks. The mattresses in the bedroom are grimy, without bedding, with heavily contaminated blankets. The second bedroom looks similar. Two beds. On one of them, a rolled up figure under the blankets. The wooden doors of the toilet and shower have been eaten away by the dampness. I go back to the first bedroom and address the children, "What's your name?" T answers her name and chuckles. D says his name in a soft voice. I have to make an effort to hear. He looks anxious. I begin a conversation with T: "Do you want to go to the nursery with D?" The grandmother intervenes: "They didn't go today because D did not feel well. So I didn't take them." Then T, "I don't want to go to the nursery", and starts to cry. It seems she is not crying just because she does not want to go to the nursery, but that she is crying for much more than that. I asked T, "What is the nursery teacher's name?" "S", she answered. "What are the names of your friends at the nursery?" I turn to the grandmother and to T, "Let's dress you nicely. We'll wear clean, comfortable clothes and go together with D to the nursery."

    The grandmother rummages in the cupboard, looking for clothes. As she is looking some clothes fall from the cupboard into the water. The grandmother found tights, but there are no dry shoes. She wipes T's nose at my instruction and brushes her hair. While she is undressing and dressing the little one, a strong wind comes through the window. The window has a torn screen. I try to close it, but unsuccessfully. The grandmother explains that it broke and won't close. The police arrive. "What's this?", T asks. "They are police. They have come to help." "Ah," T chuckles. It seems the chuckles are an expression of the uncertainty and confusion that she is feeling. The policemen address me and the social worker with me, "Ah. You are from welfare. Ok." I wanted to close the bedroom door so that T has privacy while the grandmother is dressing her, but there is no door. I ask the police not to go into the room. For D, the grandmother finds dry shorts and some other warm items of clothing. The shorts are too big for him. Grandmother folds them. She rummages in the cupboard again. There are no other pants. I help her look. Can't find anything that fits. T is still crying that she does not want to go to the nursery. I chat with her and try to calm her. In the meantime, the mother's sister, Y, who was rolled up in bed under the blanket, arrives and addresses me and the grandmother, "Excuse me. Why is T crying?" Turning to T, "You don't have to go to the nursery. Don't cry. Stay with us." I say to Y while addressing the grandmother and T, "But see, it's wet here and cold; it's better to go to the nursery. There are games and lots of friends there." T continues to cry. I said to D and to T that I would buy them a sweet if they went with granny to the nursery. I ask them if they have eaten today. Both answered no. I asked the grandmother to prepare sandwiches for them. In the filth of the kitchen, she improvised sandwiches with yellow cheese, wrapped them with a piece of newspaper and put the two sandwiches into a supermarket plastic bag. We left the house. It's cold. D is wearing short trousers that the grandmother folds again and again but they fall from his slender body. T with tights and wet sandals.

On the way, I asked the grandmother to call the mother. She says that her phone is broken. I buy sweets for the children and they go into the nursery holding the sweets. They will spend a while in a pleasant and secure place and my team manager and I will figure out what to do. I so much want to hug the children, to take them home with me, to buy them new, warm clothes, to let them sleep in a clean bed, with sheets, to give them a hot, complete meal.

I leave there feeling discomfort, with intense pangs of conscience: what will those children go back to at 1 o'clock? What bed will they sleep in? What will they eat? Don't want them ever to go back to that house. There were tears in my eyes. And I was cold. I felt helpless in the face of all this dereliction, by the mother, by the educational and welfare institutions, by me. "What can be done? They said they would fix it." Giving up, no movement, emptiness, poverty is in your face. "What can you do? That's how it is."

First reading: risk and saving children

Nurit's text is vivid. Her words mercilessly describe the family's situation and the children's distress. After taking a deep breath, we can try to use the paradigmatic structure as an analytical tool for understanding this situation. Using this structure, we will seek answers to three questions: 'What did the episode describe?' (an ontological question); 'What kind of knowledge is it based on?' (an epistemological question); and 'What is the social worker's stance?' (an axiological question).

Analysing what the episode described, we can say that it is a story of pathology and risk. These are manifested in the sewage, in the dirt and neglect, in the fact that the children were at home instead of at nursery, in their unsuitable clothes, in the grandmother's helplessness, in the mother's decision to live with her mother and sisters instead of independently, and in the aunt rolled up on the mattress under the blankets late in the morning. 'The culture of poverty' is replayed right before our eyes, in the next generations as well, from the grandmother to her daughters and the grandchildren.

Thinking of the epistemological premise expressed in the text, one can say that it is clearly positivistic. Nurit alone is the knower and her knowledge is decontextualised and focuses only on the problematic behaviour of the family. She does not take account of the knowledge of the grandmother and the children, and does not contextualise the situation in terms of the family's economic and social conditions, or in the historical context of this family's life.

Her axiological stance, the answer to the question of what is good and right in her eyes, is simple. She wants the children to be in an orderly, clean house, wearing clothes that fit them and the weather, to eat breakfast, and to be in a formal educational environment. Apparently, from her practice, one can assume that in the particular situation, she felt that she was the only one who wanted these basic things for the children and the only one who could provide them.

The practice that Nurit employs stems from these three elements. Faced by the difficult situation, she wants to save the children, to extricate them in a single swoop from the depressing reality of their lives and to transfer them to the secure reality of the heated, clean, lit nursery.

However, I argue that the practice employed is governed by the impact of Othering. It is based on the perception that the adults in this family are Others, irrational or totally incompetent. This is evident from how they are depicted as people who live in a way that distances them from culture. They have seemingly got used to the dirt and filth, and they are portrayed as passive, weak and helpless. They have no understanding of the implications of the sanitary state of the house for the children and they are not aware of the importance of nursery education; therefore, it does not matter to them that the children stay at home. Othering is what makes Nurit think that she is the only one who can act on behalf of the children.

The wish to save children is a familiar motif in social work practice. This desire, as understandable and humane as it might be, becomes problematic when it prevents social workers from exercising critical reflection (Fook and Gardner, 2007; Mandell, 2008), making it difficult to get a better understanding of the children's needs and best interests, and blinds them from seeing the effect of the socio-economic context on the family (Lonne et al, 2008; Featherstone and Gupta, 2018). Thus, a preoccupation with saving becomes a form of social control that prevents the provision of social care (Featherstone et al, 2014; Gupta, 2017). Can the story be read differently and, if so, what is the benefit of a different reading?

Second reading: PAP analysis

Taking a social justice perspective and understanding poverty as a violation of rights draws our attention from the family's pathologies to the injustice that is inherent in the whole situation: the family is living in an apartment where the sewage is overflowing; it has happened more than once, actually it happened twice in two days; they approached the authorities who were supposed to fix it the first time it happened but they did not get an appropriate response; and when such a response does come after a complaint made by the neighbours, it is accompanied by social workers and police, as well as by an accusation from disgusted neighbours. By looking more closely at the neighbours' behaviour, we can gain a better understanding of the family's vulnerability and isolation. The facial expressions of the neighbours when they see Nurit on the stairs hint at their rejection of the family. The neighbours' attitude is also expressed in their initial report that brought the social worker to the building. This report of barefooted children going about unsupervised in a house flooded with water is false since the children were far from being alone in the house. One can assume that the neighbours knew that they were exaggerating the seriousness of the situation but chose to do so because they understood that the welfare authorities would respond immediately when they heard that it involved children at risk, whereas a report about a sewage overflow, a broken window, just shameful poverty and neglect for which the authority was responsible, not private people, would have remained unanswered.

To complete the picture of the vulnerability of the family and the injustice in the situation, we must identify the resistance of the family to it. In the face of the picture of general neglect, focusing on the family's agency and their struggle against poverty might appear superficial. However, especially because of the dominance of the impression of the neglect, the filth and the hopelessness, it is essential to identify the family's battle against poverty. If we fail to recognise their struggle, we are liable to adopt the pathological, Othering interpretation that prevents us from having an empathetic understanding, one that can be shared with service users and enriches the relationship with them.

Looking broadly at the family's daily struggle with adversity, we can say that in the face of poverty, exclusion and alienation, this family struggles in many different ways against all odds. First, the mother is working. In this sense, this is a very ordinary Israeli family in which the grandmother helps her working daughter with childcare. Second, the family actively try to solve the sewage overflowing: they reported it and they are busy mopping it up. They are not indifferent to it. Third, they are responsive to the children: the aunt arrives quickly when the girl cries and tries to protect her, and the grandmother attempts to meet their needs.

Nurit did not ignore all of these expressions of agency, but did not recognise them fully and did not interpret them as such. Instead, she describes the grandmother's actions as feeble and quiet, as expressions of helplessness and resignation. This is why she does not treat her as a partner in her intervention. In order to understand the grandmother better, we need to understand the harmful influence of ongoing Othering on the Other:

> In the face of this Other who is not-you, but taken-as-you by others, who can you become? This objectification of you is constructed as you as if you must continue to exist in its adamantine mould and shape your own self to it. It is to be imprisoned in an identity that harms you. You are both silenced and spoken for. You are seen but not recognised. You are identified but denied an identity you can call your own. Your identity is split, broken, dispersed into its abjected images, its alienated representations. (Pickering, 2001: 77–8)

Pickering proposes understanding the grandmother's response to the situation not as an acceptance of it, but as an expression of a considered understanding of it as power relations, in which Othering is enforced on her. Even if she is not capable of expressing it in words, she feels that her subjectivity is not taken into account and is not regarded as worthy.

Identifying the situation as one of injustice, and the behaviour of the family as an active struggle against it, is the answer to the ontological question. The epistemological question relates to the means by which professional knowledge is acquired. This leads us to see the various instances in which Nurit ignores what the family members tell her. When first entering the house she repeatedly asks the aunt and the grandmother "What happened?" This question displays interest but contains no real listening. Quite the contrary. When Nurit again asked, "Why didn't you say there was a problem?", it seems as if she did not hear that the aunt had said that it had also happened the day before and the grandmother had said that she had approached the authorities before.

The following dialogue regarding the children again expresses non-recognition of the grandmother's knowledge and the way in which she is disregarded as a partner in the process of change. Nurit asks T if she wants to go to the nursery but disregards the grandmother's response ("she is sick"), T's refusal to go to the nursery and the aunt's response supporting the child. Nurit understands all this as an expression of the family's problem, and her responses indicate to them that they are unworthy of a meaningful dialogue. This section ends with Nurit, who previously 'instructed' the mother to rent an apartment, again taking a supervisory stance, this time 'instructing' the young girl and the grandmother to get dressed and go to the nursery.[1]

The use of the verb 'instruct' in order to describe her intervention raises questions: what type of relationship is it in which decisions are taken in this way? What is the service user's opinion of this decision? It appears that B agreed with the first instruction to rent an apartment but she has not gone to live there. Why did she behave in that way? Perhaps she thought that her reservations about the move to the new apartment would not be accepted by Nurit and it was therefore better not to mention them, or she did mention them but was ignored. One can guess what her reservations were: she might have needed her mother's help with childcare or she might have preferred to be with her sisters and mother despite the poor conditions under which they were living because it was hard for her to be alone with four children. These are only two possible answers that might explain her decision. Anyhow, there is no indication in the text that her perspective was recognised.

Like the mother, the grandmother also complies with Nurit's instructions, at least outwardly. She wiped T's nose, combed her hair and took the children to the nursery "at my instruction". Since she correctly understands the relationship with Nurit as power relations, she knows that if she does not obey, she risks being regarded as uncooperative. In this messy and tense situation, the most evident resistance to Nurit's efforts to establish order is made by objects – the window does not close, the door is missing and the phone does not work – as if they express the opposition that the grandmother cannot afford to voice.

The PAP's axiological stance calls on social workers to show solidarity with service users through standing by them and assisting them to exercise their rights, both in the sphere of redistribution and in the interpersonal sphere of recognition. Taking a stance of solidarity is in itself an act of recognition, and of resisting the violation of rights. Hence, what would practice based on these principles look like?

PAP practice: mopping the floor as a practice of solidarity

Nurit's intervention was aimed at extracting the children from the chaotic house for a few hours. This kind of practice identifies the family as the major source of the problems, while poverty itself becomes blurred.[2] However, as Nurit herself writes, this kind of intervention is only an initial response that requires a further ongoing plan. I predict that even the best plan made by Nurit and her team manager will be useless if it is not built on a well-established helping relationship based on standing by the family.

PAP intervention would focus on doing just that. Standing by would be expressed through small, simple actions aimed at creating a close relationship and correcting rights violations. If we were to identify the mopping of the sewage by the grandmother and the aunt as an expression of agency and resistance against hardship, we would want to recognise it as such and to reinforce it. Instead of instructing them to act according to a plan of action that we have set, we would seek to regard their wishes and needs as worthy, good and important, and to take it upon ourselves to assist them to realise them. This type of intervention dispenses with the fantasy of saving the children and replaces it with a plan to enhance connection where there is isolation (see for example, Turney, 2012). In order to achieve this, we need to be prepared to get dirty. We need to ask for the mop and offer to help the grandmother to mop up the water. While doing so, we can tell her angrily that the fact that the authorities failed to repair the sewage amounts to awful negligence, and that it is shocking that they did not respond to her previous calls and that she has to deal with the situation alone. We would say that we are happy to be there to see it ourselves because that will encourage us to make sure that the authorities fix the problem. At the same time, we should smile at the children, tell them that everything will be fine and take a real interest in them and in their experiences at the nursery.

This kind of intervention will naturally be followed by a call to the grandmother or a visit to her a day or two later to ask if she approves of the repair and if we can help her with anything else. She may say, "No, thank you. Just one small thing." And we must take on that small thing as a project. Experience tells us that a few meetings like that with the grandmother, with easy talk, absent of any attempts to blame or correct her, will make Nurit relevant for the family. This is where a process of change can begin, in partnership with the family.

Summary

The story that Nurit wrote is disturbing because the description of the dirt and the neglect is so convincing and because her initial response, the wish to take the children and run away, is a perfectly humane response. Nevertheless, I claim that this is not a professional response; it does not really rescue the children, nor does it establish a helping relationship. In fact, I claim that the intervention undermines the possibility of helping the children and the family because it does not increase their trust in Nurit or in their ability to be aided by social workers. In a certain sense, this was a tragic intervention. In a situation where connections were needed, in which both the family and the social worker depended on each other in order to make a change, the intervention produced separation, severance and a sense of guilt and blame.

What caused Nurit to fail was, first, the link she made between the difficult external conditions and the people's qualities; the sewage and the filth, the helplessness and the despair all blurred into one. This perception, as if the people and the dirt are one, made it difficult for her to see the family's agency and their attempts, however weak, to live a decent life.[3] Moreover, it was difficult for her to even imagine that the people were unhappy with their situation and that, in their hearts, they might want a different life.

My contention is that one of the first tests of Othering, or, if you prefer, a litmus test of Othering, is the feeling that the person standing in front of us has no knowledge, that we do not really need them in order to plan an intervention, that we have nothing to learn from them and that there is no need for us to listen to them. For us to be able to stand by people living in poverty in cases where we experience them as 'strange' or 'different' to the point where we dismiss them as having knowledge, we must understand that we are operating in an area of interpretation. We must force ourselves to find, by means of critical reflection (Fook and Gardner, 2007), an interpretation that will release us from the Othering and convert us into allies that are relevant to the people who need our help. This is also essential in crisis situations when immediate action is needed. In these situations too, an action that stems from an Othering relationship will be less effective in the long run than an action based on solidarity. I am not suggesting that it is easy to enlist to the change process people who find themselves in difficult situations of isolation and lack of trust. However, we have to understand that that is our aim: to enlist, to join, to connect. I suggest viewing mopping the floor with the grandmother as an act of recognition and solidarity that facilitates the recovery of the experience of self – an act of correcting social injustice.

Notes

[1] A piece of vignette research found that the majority of social workers tended to use a confrontational style of communication (see Forrester et al, 2008).

2   A good contrary example is documented by Albert Camus (1995) in his autobiographical novel *The first man*. Camus was brought up in a very poor family in Algeria by his grandmother and mute mother, who waited for him to get to the age of ten in order to quit his studying and start working to support the small family. His teacher at the time saw his intellectual potential and offered to give him free extra lessons in order to help him continue his studies but his mother and grandmother refused to let him to do so. The teacher, Louis Germain, came to his home in the remote neighbourhood to try to persuade them to change their mind. What is so special in Camus's description of this visit is the teacher's attitude towards his mother and grandmother. He did not patronise them or criticise their decision, and chose to emphasise to the young Camus the esteem and respect he felt for them. When he left the house, he told Camus, who was waiting to hear how the meeting went: 'Your grandmother's a good woman. As for your mother … don't you ever forget her' (Camus, 1995: 163).

3   Julia Kristeva (1982) uses the term 'abjection' to describe the contemptible that lies outside the symbolic order, like body leaks, wastes and fluids. The fear and terror that the abject arouse stem from the abject being outside personal and social identity, but containing bits that did belong to the self. A corpse is contemptible because it is similar to the living body but fundamentally different from it. Nurit's terror of the sewage and the dirt links to the feeling that she is forced to confront the contemptible, and she tries to avoid it. The adults living in the house become identified in her eyes with the contemptible. As a result, they are deprived of their humanity, subjectivity and knowledge.

17

'I'm not that kind of person': solidarity in a group intervention

In 2001, Shula, the manager of a social services department in a small, nearby town, approached the Spitzer Social Work Department at Ben-Gurion University with an unusual request: to help her to work with the poorest and most excluded families in the municipality in order to 'wean' them off their 'long-term dependency' on social services. That request gradually led to the creation of a group of service users that met regularly once a week for two-and-a-half years, called 'The Light at the End of the Tunnel'. This chapter tells the story of that group and focuses on its challenging first meeting. At that time, the PAP was still only a theoretical outline that, through this intervention, started to develop as practice and to become more clearly delineated. Specifically, this chapter deals with the challenge of creating solidarity and making connections in divisive situations.

A few weeks before I joined the Spitzer Social Work Department at Ben-Gurion University, the department was approached by one of its graduates, Shula, with an unusual request. She had recently taken up a new post as the manager of the municipal social services department in a small, nearby town, and she asked the faculty of the academic department to help her to plan an intervention with the poorest and most excluded families in the municipality. I saw this as an opportunity to work on a challenging project and joined the steering committee, which comprised Shula, her senior team and two of my new colleagues in the school of social work.

Shula said that although the families had been known to the social workers for a long time, many of them since their childhood, meaningful helping relationships had not been established. Her team described a frozen situation in which service users had been coming to the department for years with requests for material aid that the social workers could not meet. Meanwhile, they had refused invitations from the social workers to begin meaningful therapeutic processes. Shula described a situation in which the best therapists that she had were wasting their expensive hours waiting for service users who did not show up to sessions.

Apparently, what they described was a fundamental conflict between two languages of need: the service users requesting material aid in order to cope with poverty; and the social workers viewing these requests as a 'fish'. For the social workers, the provision of 'fish' was an avoidance of the essential issue, 'hooks': the counselling and therapeutic processes that were supposed to solve the fundamental problems causing the material predicament. Moreover, the social workers insisted that the reason these people had been coming to the department for years was that they had developed 'dependency' on social services, and that in order to improve their situation, they had to be weaned off that dependency.

I understood the link that the practitioners made between poverty and dependency to be artificial.[1] To my way of thinking and according to a social justice perspective, the fact that people needed help for years was a result of their ongoing economic situation that they struggled against and was not the result of their psychological characteristics from which they needed weaning. At the stormy steering committee meetings, we argued about the nature and significance of prolonged poverty and 'dependency'. Finally, we decided to ask the families themselves for their reasons for maintaining long-term relationships with the social services department.

The social workers made a list of all the families involved and students were sent to interview each one of them. The interview contained four questions: 'What do you need from the social services department?'; 'Are you satisfied with what you have received over the years?'; 'If not, why do you continue to come to the department?'; and 'What message do you have for other people in your situation?'[2]

At the next meeting of the steering committee, we discussed the results of the survey: in reply to the first question, 'What do you need from the social services department?', the people answered that their main need was for money. They gave various reasons for needing money: to move from an apartment that was very damp; to repair front teeth; or to change rotten kitchen cupboards. A mother of six children said that she needed a washing machine because she was struggling to launder the children's clothes by hand.

In answer to the next two questions, they explained that they were only slightly satisfied with the assistance that they were getting from the local social services department because the majority of their requests for material assistance were rejected. Despite this, they continued to come to the department in the hope of benefitting from the limited resources distributed every now and again, like school bags at the start of the school year, heaters or blankets given out in winter, or food parcels distributed before the high holidays.

To the fourth question, the people answered with various messages, such as: "The department is bad news. You have to get by on your own" or "Be strong and apply to all possible sources; there's nothing to be ashamed of." Some service users directed their message to the social workers: "Relate to the people who apply to you, to those who are complaining. They're not coming there for no reason."[3]

Shula and her team were not surprised by the answers. They regarded them as confirmation of their perception that what the people wanted was money and not therapy because they were not aware of their inner psychological problems, and also that they were not ready to earn money by working because they had become accustomed to obtaining aid from the social workers. Everybody on the committee agreed that there were not many job opportunities in the area, and that the people's preference not to work was rational given the fact that formal, authorised work meant relinquishing their entitlement to the income support benefit that, though minimal, was their main and only fixed and dependable source of income. However, Shula and the other social workers still argued that "It's one's own responsibility to always look for a job."

The breakthrough in this discussion in the steering committee came as a suggestion made by one of my colleagues. She refused to view the situation as stuck and suggested backing the people's wish to increase the amount of money they had, even if they were not willing to work, as their wish was justified, saying:

> 'In fact, the things for which they are requesting money are worthwhile. We all want the families to have washing machines, healthy teeth and proper kitchen cupboards. Moreover, I can understand their unwillingness to relinquish income support. The benefit is regular and gives access to some additional benefits while the job market pays by the hour and is fluid.'

She had a radical idea: to invite the people who participated in the survey to join a group whose aim would be 'to raise money', not 'to work'. The idea was to 'raise money without jeopardising entitlement to the benefit in order to achieve what the people had mentioned as their basic needs'. After their long history of disappointments from attempts to invite people to participate in all sorts of therapy, Shula and her team were determined to find a solution and were desperate. They agreed to try the idea, though they did not believe that it would work.

Against their expectations, the first meeting was attended by 17 of the 35 people invited. It was very tempestuous. People were angry. They described their severe material hardship and expressed a total lack of trust in the social workers. At the same time, they agreed with the idea of setting up a group aimed at 'raising money to meet basic needs'. Nobody had any idea how this could be done, but we agreed that it was a worthy goal. Of the cluster of names suggested for the group, including 'The Depressives', the name chosen was 'The Light at the End of the Tunnel'. From the time of its establishment, the group met once a week, regularly for two-and-a-half years. It was made up of 15 service users (including both men and women), Shula and one of her social workers, my colleague Vered, and me.

The next meeting of the group was supposed to be for getting to know one another and establishing the group's rules. However, at the very beginning of the meeting, one of the men, named Efraim, who was very agitated, took over by telling his story while cursing furiously. What he said was that his apartment in the public housing project was full of mould and infested with rats and mice. His children had not been to school recently because it was impossible to shower in the mouldy bathroom and other children at school had been laughing at them. He had already applied several times to the housing authority to change his apartment but received negative responses. He went on to say that he had arrived at our meeting directly from the mayor's office, where he had spent the whole day trying to get the mayor to solve his problem. This was his plan: to continue to sit at the entrance to the mayor's office in protest at the state of his apartment until the mayor did something about it.

The whole group was enraged. They agreed that "Without connections and without threats you can't get anywhere." Among the ideas put forward to the group, the one that received the most attention was made by a women who suggested in no uncertain terms to Efraim that when he goes to the mayor's office the next morning he should take his children with him, together with a gas canister, and threaten to set them alight: "That's the only way to achieve anything", she said, and the others agreed.

Only a few minutes into the meeting, we found ourselves facing a serious challenge. Even if the threat of setting the children alight was only meant as a threat, and even if it was actually an effective way of getting the mayor involved in the case, both the social workers who were present, and we as academics, could not support the idea. How could we stand by him when we completely disagreed with the idea? What could we say that would express both our concern for him and our duty to protect his children? Thus, we gave a sigh of relief when we asked Efraim what his opinion of the suggestion was and he, who until that moment had been very angry and excited, calmed down, took a pause and said, "In truth, I'm not that kind of person."

This was a turning point. We said that we were happy to hear Efraim's response because the suggested solution, even if it were effective, scared us. We went on to think about other ways in which the group could support him. We explicitly said that we saw the group as a source of power. We were a special group because we were service users, social workers and academics together, and we needed to use our power as a group. Nevertheless, in order to work as a group, we had to agree on the path to take. We said that we could not personally do things that would jeopardise our own jobs because we also had responsibility to our families. We asked the group to come up with other solutions, of the sort that we could all support, and back Efraim. A lively discussion ensued.

One woman said that from her experience, the best way to deal with a problem like this is to make a complaint at the state comptroller. The state comptroller is the only person who can instruct the public housing authority and the Housing Ministry to change their decision. It was agreed that we all sign a letter to the ombudsman's office at the state comptroller, and that we would present ourselves as members of the 'Light at the End of the Tunnel Group.' As a form of first aid, Shula would send tradesmen to the apartment to deal with the rats and give it a coat of paint. Efraim agreed. He insisted that we all go to see the apartment, and at the end of the meeting, we all walked there and saw it with our own eyes.

As this all happened during the early days of the group, we did not yet have clearly agreed working methods. What guided us was the attitude of standing by service users, which was not even explicitly conceptualised at that time. However, standing by was the approach that guided us at the steering committee and led to suggesting the creation of a group under the umbrella of 'raising money' instead of the more obvious but less constructive idea of 'improving working motivation and skills' or 'weaning off dependency'. When meeting with the group, this same approach was manifested in our willingness to really acknowledge poverty and to express solidarity with Efraim in his struggle to reduce its impact on his life. The challenge that the group presented to us was to acknowledge Efraim's terrible poverty and to support him, while, at the same time, disapproving of a violent act involving children. To me, what was interesting about that tense moment when the suggestion was made was that we resisted the immediate impulse to directly oppose the proposed solution or to explain its disadvantages to the group.

That moment of resisting the impulse to 'take control' of the situation and instructing Efraim what to do, and instead simply asking him for his opinion, was an epiphany for me. At that moment the issue – 'What is poverty and what are the possible ways to resist it?' – became the focus of an interpretive struggle between people who hold different positions of power. For Efraim, poverty was a housing problem, compounded by: (1) having to depend on the authorities to solve it; (2) a shortage of the symbolic capital needed for his pain to be perceived as legitimate pain; and (3) needing his problem to be perceived by those in power as a problem they needed to solve. For Shula and her team, at that moment, the problem was protecting the children from their father. Although they agreed that the housing problem was a real problem, and deep inside they knew that Efraim's complaints about the housing authority were justified, the suggestion to threaten to set his children alight seemed extreme, and in fact, pathological. Since the professional team had the power to define the problem, they could have changed the definition of the problem from a 'housing problem' to 'a problem of a father endangering his children'. Of course, this definition would have meant intervention to prevent risk to the children, which would have made it more urgent than the housing problem. However, even before any decision regarding action could be taken, it is important to note that the moment another person's behaviour is interpreted as pathological, their subjectivity is erased, and they are perceived as lacking knowledge. In this case, the knowledge behind the idea of threatening to set fire to the children would not be acknowledged, and thus the person who suggested it would be perceived not as a person with knowledge, but as pathological. The fact that at the crucial moment, we refrained from using our power to dictate the way in which the problem was defined, and that we asked Efraim for his opinion, constituted recognition of him as having knowledge and subjectivity, and facilitated the easing of the power relations between us.[4]

At the next meeting, we signed letters to the state comptroller, to the Housing Ministry and to the public housing authority. Writing letters and following them up as a response to group members' needs became our way of working at the following meetings. We wrote letters of request to dentists to help with dental treatment and to private bodies asking for contributions of washing machines. All the group participants signed the letters.

Very quickly, our meetings were transformed from places of anger, mistrust and helplessness, to a place where pain and struggle were mixed with jokes, laughter and enjoyment. After only a few meetings, as we either rejoiced with the receipt of a new washing machine and with the beginning of a dental treatment, or lamented the refusal received in response to our letters or disappointment with donations that were discovered to be damaged, the group members began to say that they wanted to work. It was suggested that the work be done in a group, thinking that a group had more power than the total of its individual members. The situation was that some of the members of the group had never held out-of-home jobs, and because it turned out that what everybody had in common was the ability to cook, it was decided to set up a catering operation.

That is how 'Light at the End of the Tunnel Catering' was established. First, it supplied pastries and cooked food for conferences and cultural events at the university, and then it expanded. The organisation demanded a lot of goodwill, flexibility and initiative, a volunteering spirit, and willingness to work hard. A small budget was raised to get started. The mayor supported the group, came to one of the meetings and allowed the group to work in the kitchen of the old people's centre when it was unoccupied. All group members were involved, those who had fewer cooking skills helped with buying, peeling, preparation and cleaning.

The reactions to the first events were excellent and more orders followed. The profits were divided among the group members according to various criteria: for some events, the money was divided equally between all the participants; and for other events, the money was divided only among those people who had worked, or for each person relative to the amount of work that they had done. Decisions on the sharing of the money were taken jointly. As the earnings were not fixed and were not registered as personal earnings, they did not jeopardise the income support benefits that the participants received. Moreover, knowing that more money was due to come into the kitty when there were future orders led to greater financial freedom. For instance, one of the members who needed a sum of money to finance her husband's participation in a drug rehabilitation programme got the money as a loan in return for a commitment and guarantee from the whole group to return the money from future income. There were other similar instances. Knowing about future income and the willingness of the group as a whole to commit to making personal payments for its members became a real resource. At the same time, close relationships developed among the group members and between them and the social workers. From a situation of mutual mistrust, what developed was a relationship of solidarity and joint struggle against poverty.

Unfortunately, this story does not have a happy ending. In order to make the catering operation official, approvals, equipment and premises were needed. We might have complied with these requirements, but in the local elections, the mayor was replaced by a new mayor who did not appreciate the importance of the group. As a result, the catering group that had operated regularly for two-and-a-half years ceased its operation. Yet, all the people who were part of it had changed and we all remember the group for the good it achieved.

I learnt a number of important things from this experience. I learnt that, for me as an academic, prolonged collaboration with professionals in the field is a complex undertaking, yet possible and fascinating. I also gained important insights into power relations. I understood the fundamental existence of power relations on three levels: on the ontological level, that is, the way in which issues and problems that need to be solved are defined; on the epistemic level, that is, the question of how we know; and on the axiological level, that is, the question of what, in our view, is the desired, ethical solution.

With regard to the ontological level, I understood that when the group started, the social workers thought the problem of the service users was dependence, while the service users thought their problem was poverty and the paucity of realistic possibilities of being extricated from it. In the absence of a shared definition of the problem, the service users' definition, as true as it might have been, was meaningless. All they could do to demonstrate their perspective to the social workers was to refuse the professionals' offers of therapy. The social workers' ontological stance, their theory of the problem, was what determined what aid they would offer and the ways in which it would be offered.

With regard to the epistemic level, I understood the social workers' difficulty (which I shared) considering the question of 'How do we know?' in a crisis situation, as occurred when one member of the group suggested to Efraim to threaten to set fire to his children. Usually, a situation like this induces a knowing attitude among social workers. They know that just talking about it within the children's earshot would harm the children. Consequently, they believed that they should set clear boundaries to ensure that it did not happen. The option of asking Efraim his opinion of the suggestion was an epistemic moment because it implied that 'my knowledge as a professional is incomplete as long as I do not know what you think about it'.

On the axiological level, that is, on the question of what the ethical solution is, I learnt just how critical it is for practitioners to be able to recognise power relations and to be able to challenge them in any given circumstances. In fact, I experienced every moment of dead end or blockage in the relationship as a concentrated manifestation of imbalanced power relations. At times like these, professionals tend to use their privileged position of power to oppose service users, whereas at dead-end moments, the more productive way is to ease up on overt power and to find a way of using one's professional ability to strengthen the service users' power. In practice, it means to stand by them. Thus, the moment we asked Efraim for his opinion on the suggestion to threaten to set his children alight became a valuable opportunity for self-definition.

In retrospect, our experience with the Light at the End of the Tunnel group was guided by the principle of solidarity: it was our duty and our commitment. We did not know how far it would take us. In this sense, our intervention was not evidence-based; it was based on a real acknowledgement of poverty as a violation of rights and on a willingness to recognise its impact on people's lives without reducing the people's subjectivity and complexity. I was aware of the difficulties of creating solidarity but believed that solidarity could re-establish failed connections and that standing together in the face of poverty and adversity could open up unexpected possibilities for change for all the parties involved.

Notes

[1] For a thorough analysis of dependency, see Fraser and Gordon (1994).

[2] The last question was inspired by the Fourth World Movement, an international movement that fights poverty and puts the knowledge of people in poverty at the heart of its actions (see: https://4thworldmovement.org/). The question was received somewhat sceptically by the team, who thought that it was too abstract and would not elicit meaningful answers. However, interviewees responded without difficulty. The importance of the questions lies in its subtext that people do have a message (knowledge) and that they are connected to other people who experience a similar life context.

[3] For a fuller account of the questions and answers, see Krumer-Nevo et al (2006).

[4] For an insightful example of a similar moment of epiphany regarding power in a social worker–service user relationship, see Rose (2000).

References

Abramovitz, M. (1996) *Regulating the lives of women: Social welfare policy from colonial times to the present* (revised edn), Boston, MA: South End Press.

Achdut, N. and Stier, H. (2020) 'Welfare-use accumulation and chronic dependency in Israel: The role of structural factors', *Journal of Social Policy*, 49(1): 81–101.

Adams, J. (1920) *Twenty years at Hull House*, New York, NY: Macmillan.

Aldridge, H., Kenway, P., MacInnes, T. and Parekh, A. (2012) *Monitoring poverty and social exclusion 2012*, York: Joseph Rowntree Foundation.

Alfandari, R. (2019) 'Systemic barriers to effective implementation of child protection reform in Israel', in U. Klammer, S. Leiber and S. Leitner (eds) *Social work and the making of social policy*, Bristol: Policy Press, pp 155–67.

Alfandari, R. (2019a) 'Multi-professional work in child protection decision-making: An Israeli case study', *Children and Youth Services Review*, 98: 51–7.

Allen, G. (2011) *Early intervention: The next steps: An independent report to Her Majesty's Government*, London.

Altman, N. (2011) *The analyst in the inner city: Race, class, and culture through a psychoanalytic lens*, New York and London: Routledge.

Anastas, J.W. (2012) 'From scientism to science: How contemporary epistemology can inform practice research', *Clinical Social Work Journal*, 40(2): 157–65.

ATD Fourth World (1996) *'Talk with us not at us': How to develop partnership between families in poverty and professionals*, London and Paris: ATD Fourth World Publications.

Atkinson, A.B. (2015) *Inequality: What can be done?*, Cambridge, MA: Harvard University Press.

Bailey, R. and Brake, M. (eds) (1975) *Radical social work*, London: Edward Arnold.

Baines, D. (ed) (2011) *Doing anti-oppressive practice: Social justice social work* (2nd edn), Halifax: Fernwood Publishing.

Barak-Erez, D. (2003) 'Protecting expectations in administrative law', *Tel Aviv University Law Review*, 27(1): 209–56.

Bassok, D. and Galdo, E. (2016) 'Inequality in preschool quality? Community-level disparities in access to high-quality learning environments', *Early Education and Development*, 27(1): 128–44.

Beddoe, L. and Keddell, E. (2016) 'Informed outrage: Tackling shame and stigma in poverty education in social work', *Ethics and Social Welfare*, 10(2): 149–62.

Bell, K. (2012) 'Towards a post-conventional philosophical base for social work', *British Journal of Social Work*, 42(3): 408–23.

Ben-Rabi, D. (2019) *Evaluation of the MAPA pilot: Families Encounter Opportunities*, Jerusalem: Myers JDC Brookdale, Engelberg Center for Children and Youth (in Hebrew).

Benish, A. and David, L. (2018) 'The right to access social services: On (non-)take-up of social rights and the state's duty to make social services accessible', *Law & Governance*, 18: 1–37 (in Hebrew).

Benjamin, J. (1988) *The bonds of love: Psychoanalysis, feminism, and the problem of domination*, New York, NY: Pantheon Books.

Beresford, P. (2000) 'Service users' knowledges and social work theory: Conflict or collaboration?', *British Journal of Social Work*, 30(4): 489–503.

Beresford, P. (2001) 'Service users', *British Journal of Social Work*, 31(4): 629–30.

Beresford, P. and Croft, S. (2004) 'Service users and practitioners reunited: The key component for social work reform', *British Journal of Social Work*, 34(1): 53–68.

Beresford, P. and Turner, M. (1997) *It's our welfare: Report of the Citizens' Commission on the Future of the Welfare State*, London: National Institute for Social Work.

Beresford, P. and Wilson, A. (1998) 'Social exclusion and social work: Challenging the contradictions of exclusive debate', in M. Barry and C. Hallett (eds) *Social exclusion and social work: Issues of theory, policy and practice*, Dorset: Russell House, pp 85–96.

Beresford, P., Green, D., Lister, R. and Woodward, K. (1999) *Poverty first hand: Poor people speak for themselves*, London: Child Poverty Action Group.

Blair, C. and Raver, C.C. (2016) 'Poverty, stress, and brain development: New directions for prevention and intervention', *Academic Paediatrics*, 16(3): S30–6.

Blank, R.M. (1989) 'Analyzing the length of welfare spells', *Journal of Public Economics*, 39(3): 245–73.

Bond, M. (1999) 'Placing poverty on the agenda of a primary health care team: An evaluation of an action research project', *Health & Social Care in the Community*, 7(1): 9–16.

Boone, K., Roets, G. and Roose, R. (2018) 'Social work, poverty and anti-poverty strategies: Creating cultural forums', *British Journal of Social Work*, 48(8): 2381–99.

Boone, K., Roets, G. and Roose, R. (2019) 'Social work, participation, and poverty', *Journal of Social Work*, 19(3): 309–26.

Borden, W. (2000) 'The relational paradigm in contemporary psychoanalysis: Toward a psychodynamically informed social work perspective', *Social Service Review*, 74(3): 352–79.

Bourdieu, P. and Wacquant, L. (2001) 'NewLiberalSpeak', *Radical Philosophy*, 105: 2–6.

Bowlby, J. (1969) *Attachment and loss: Vol. 1. Attachment*, New York, NY: Basic Books.

Bowlby, J. (1973) *Attachment and loss: Vol. 2. Separation: Anxiety and anger*, New York, NY: Basic Books.

Brand-Levy, A. and Malul, M. (2019) 'Service users' perspectives of social treatment in social services departments: Differences between routine and poverty-aware treatment', *Bitachon Sociali (Social Security)*, 106: 157–88 (in Hebrew).

Brunner, J. (2008) 'An ethics of claiming and giving', in A. Honneth (ed) *Disrespect and recognition: Toward a new critical theory*, Bne Brak: Hakibbutz Hameuchad, pp 7–4 (in Hebrew).

Bullock, H.E. (1999) 'Attributions for poverty: A comparison of middle-class and welfare recipient attitudes', *Journal of Applied Social Psychology*, 29(10): 2059–82.

Bywaters, P. (2007) 'Tackling inequalities in health: A global challenge for social work', *British Journal of Social Work*, 39(2): 353–67.

Bywaters, P., Scourfield, J., Jones, C., Sparks, T., Elliott, M., Hooper, J., McCartan, C., Shapira, M., Bunting, L. and Daniel, B. (2018) 'Child welfare inequalities in the four nations of the UK', *Journal of Social Work*, 1468017318793479.

Camus, A. (1995) *The first man* (trans from French by D. Hapgood), New York, NY: Vintage Books.

Cates, C.B., Weisleder, A. and Mendelsohn, A.L. (2016) 'Mitigating the effects of family poverty on early child development through parenting interventions in primary care', *Academic Pediatrics*, 16(3): S112–20.

Chamberlayne, P. and Rustin, M. (1999) *From biography to social policy*, London: Centre for Biography in Social Policy.

Chase, E. and Walker, R. (2013) 'The co-construction of shame in the context of poverty: Beyond a threat to the social bond', *Sociology*, 47(4): 739–54.

Chaudry, A. and Wimer, C. (2016) 'Poverty is not just an indicator: The relationship between income, poverty, and child well-being', *Academic Pediatrics*, 16(3): S23–9.

Chetty, R. and Hendren, N. (2016) *The impacts of neighborhoods on intergenerational mobility I: Childhood exposure effects*. Working Paper 23001. Cambridge, MA: National Bureau of Economic Research.

Chubb, E.J. and Moe, M.T. (1996) 'Politics, markets, and equality in schools', in R. Michael (ed) *Reducing poverty in America: Views and approaches*, Thousand Oaks, CA, and London: Sage, pp 121–53.

Clarke, S., Hahn, H. and Hoggett, P. (eds) (2008) *Object relations and social relations: The implications of the relational turn in psychoanalysis*, London: Karnac Books.

Clifford, J. and Marcus, G. (eds) (1986) *Writing culture: The poetics and politics of ethnography*, Berkley, CA: University of California Press.

Cloward, R.A. and Fox Piven, F. (1975) 'Notes toward a radical social work', in R. Bailey and M. Brake (eds) *Radical social work*, New York, NY: Edward Arnold Publishers, pp vii–xxii.

Craig, G. (2002) 'Poverty, social work and social justice', *British Journal of Social Work*, 32(6): 669–82.

Crenshaw, K. (1989) 'Demarginalizing the intersection of race and sex: A black feminist critique of antidiscrimination doctrine, feminist theory, and antiracist politics', *University of Chicago Legal Forum*, 139–67.

Crenshaw, K. (1991) 'Mapping the margins: Intersectionality, identity politics, and violence against women of color', *Stanford Law Review*, 43(6): 1241–99.

Cummins, I. (2018) *Poverty, inequality and social work: The impact of neoliberalism and austerity politics on welfare provision*, Bristol: Policy Press.

Dalrymple, J. and Boylan, J. (2013) *Effective advocacy in social work*, London, Thousand Oaks, New Delhi and Singapore: Sage.

Daly, M. (2018) 'Towards a theorization of the relationship between poverty and family', *Social Policy and Administration*, 52: 565–77.

Davies, K., Gray, M. and Webb, S.A. (2014) 'Putting the parity into service-user participation: An integrated model of social justice', *International Journal of Social Welfare*, 23(2): 119–27.

Davis, A. and Wainwright, S. (2005) 'Combating poverty and social exclusion: Implications for social work', *Social Work Education*, 24: 259–73.

Deka, A. (2012) 'Local and global poverty: Insights using a rights-based approach', *Advances in Social Work*, 13(2): 471–83.

De Luca, E. (2002) *God's mountain* (trans from Italian by M. Moore), New York, NY: Riverhead Books.

Dibbets, A. and Eijkman, Q. (2018) 'Translators, advocates or practitioners? Social workers and human rights localization', *Journal of Human Rights Practice*, 10(2): 212–28.

Dodson, L. and Schmalzbauer, L. (2005) 'Poor mothers and habits of hiding: Participatory methods in poverty research', *Journal of Marriage and Family*, 67(4): 949–59.

Dominelli, L. (1997) *Anti-racist social work*, London: Macmillan International Higher Education.

Dominelli, L. (1999) 'Neo-liberalism, social exclusion and welfare clients in a global economy', *International Journal of Social Welfare*, 8(1): 14–22.

Doron, A. (2019) 'Social work in Israel: Light and shadows', in J. Gal and R. Holler (eds) *Justice instead of charity: Chapters in the development of social work in Israel*, Sde-Boker and Beer-Sheva: Ben-Gurion Research Institute for the Study of Israel and Zionism and Ben-Gurion University of the Negev, pp 394–408 (in Hebrew).

Dupere, S., O'Neill, M. and De-Koninck, M. (2012) 'Why men experiencing deep poverty in Montreal avoid using health and social services in times of crises', *Journal of Health Care for the Poor and Underserved*, 2(2): 781–96.

Edin, K. and Kefalas, M. (2005) *Promises I can keep: Why poor women put motherhood before marriage*, Berkeley, CA: University of California Press.

Edwards, R., Gillies, V. and Horsley, N. (2015) 'Brain science and early years policy: Hopeful ethos or "cruel optimism"?' *Critical Social Policy*, 35(2): 167–87.

Elbashan, Y. (2003) 'The access of disadvantaged groups in Israel to law', *Aley Mishpat*, 3: 497–530 (in Hebrew).

Featherstone, B. (2016) 'Telling different stories about poverty, inequality, child abuse and neglect', *Families, Relationships and Societies*, 5(1): 147–53.

Featherstone, B. and Gupta, A. (2018) *Protecting children: A social model*, Bristol: Policy Press.

Featherstone, B., Morris, K. and White, S. (2014) *Re-imagining child protection: Towards humane social work with families*, Bristol: Policy Press.

Felstiner, W.L.F., Abel, R.L. and Sarat, A. (1980/81) 'The emergence and transformation of disputes: Naming, blaming, claiming', *Law and Society Review*, 15(3/4): 631–54.

Ferguson, I. (2008) *Reclaiming social work: Challenging neo-liberalism and promoting social justice*, Los Angeles, CA: SAGE.

Ferguson, I. (2017a) 'Hope over fear: Social work education towards 2025', *European Journal of Social Work*, 20(3): 322–32.

Ferguson, I. (2017b) 'The new social work radicalism', *Aotearoa New Zealand Social Work*, 29(2): 131–2.

Ferguson, I. and Woodward, R. (2009) *Radical social work in practice: Making a difference*, Bristol: Policy Press.

Figueira-McDonough, J. (2007) *The welfare state and social work: Pursuing Social justice*, Thousand Oaks, CA: SAGE.

Fine, M. (2006) 'Bearing witness: Methods for researching oppression and resistance: A textbook for critical research', *Social Justice Research*, 19(1): 83–108.

Finn, D. and Goodship, J. (2014) *Take-up of benefits and poverty: An evidence and policy review*, London: Center for Economic and Social Inclusion, www.euro.centre.org/publications/detail/382

Fook, J. (1993) *Radical casework: A theory of practice*, Crows Nest: Allen & Unwin.

Fook, J. (2002) *Social work: Critical theory and practice*, London, Thousand Oaks and New Delhi: Sage.

Fook, J. and Gardner, F. (2007) *Practising critical reflection: A resource handbook*, Berkshire: McGraw-Hill Education.

Forrester, D., McCambridge, J., Waissbein, C. and Rollnick, S. (2008) 'How do child and family social workers talk to parents about child welfare concerns?', *Child Abuse Review*, 17(1): 23–35.

Foucault, M. (1995) *Discipline and punish: The birth of the prison* (2nd edn) (trans from French by A. Sheridan), New York, NY: Vintage Books, Random House.

Fourth World University Research Group (2007) *The merging of knowledge: People in poverty and academics thinking together*, Lanham, Boulder, New York, Toronto and Plymouth: University Press of America.

Fraiberg, S., Adelson, E. and Shapiro, V. (1975) 'Ghosts in the nursery', *Journal of American Academy of Child Psychiatry*, 14: 387–421.

Fraser, N. (1998) 'From redistribution to recognition? Dilemmas of justice in a "post-socialist" age', in C. Willett (ed) *Theorizing multiculturalism: A guide to the current debate*, Malden, MA: John Wiley and Sons, pp 19–49.

Fraser, N. (2003) 'Social-theoretical issues: On class and status in capitalist society', in N. Fraser and A. Honneth, *Redistribution or recognition? A political-philosophical exchange*, London: Verso, pp 48–70.

Fraser, N. and Gordon, L. (1994) 'A genealogy of dependency: Tracing a keyword of the US welfare state', *Signs*, 19(2): 309–36.

Fraser, N. and Honneth, A. (2003) *Redistribution or recognition? A political-philosophical exchange*, London: Verso.

Freire, P. (1970) *Pedagogy of the oppressed* (trans from Portuguese by M. Ramos), New York, NY: Herder and Herder.

Frost, L. (2016) 'Exploring the concepts of recognition and shame for social work', *Journal of Social Work Practice*, 30(4): 431–46.

Frost, L. and Hoggett, P. (2008) 'Human agency and social suffering', *Critical Social Policy*, 28(4): 438–60.

Fuchs, S. (2007) 'Agency (and intention)', in G. Ritzer (ed) *The Blackwell encyclopedia of sociology* (vol 1,479), New York, NY: Blackwell Publishing, https://doi.org/10.1002/9781405165518.wbeosa024

Fuchs, M. (2009) *Social assistance: No, thanks? The non-take-up phenomenon and its patterns in Austria, Germany and Finland after 2000*, Policy Brief 9/2009, Vienna: European Centre for Social Welfare Policy and Research.

Gabel, S.G. (2016) *A rights-based approach to social policy analysis*, New York, NY: Springer.

Gal, J. (2017) 'The Israeli welfare state system: With special reference to social inclusion', in C. Aspalter (ed) *The Routledge international handbook to welfare state systems*, London and New York, NY: Routledge, pp 332–46.

Gal, J. and Madhala-Brik, S. (2017) *The war against poverty: Where do things stand?*, Jerusalem: Taub Center (in Hebrew).

Gal, J. and Weiss-Gal, I. (eds) (2013) *Social workers affecting social policy: An international perspective on policy practice*, Bristol: Policy Press.

Gal, J., Krumer-Nevo, M., Madhala, S. and Yanay, G. (2019) *Material assistance to people living in poverty: A historical survey and current trends*, Jerusalem: Taub Center for Social Policy Studies in Israel. http://taubcenter.org.il/material-assistance-to-people-living-in-poverty/

Gans, H.J. (1971) 'Poverty and culture: Some basic questions about methods of studying life-styles of the poor', in P. Townsend (ed) *The concept of poverty*, London: Heinemann Educational Books, pp 146–64.

Garrett, P.M. (2010) 'Recognizing the limitations of the political theory of recognition: Axel Honneth, Nancy Fraser and social work', *British Journal of Social Work*, 40(5): 1517–33.

Garrett, P.M. (2013) *Social work and social theory: Making connections*, Bristol: Policy Press.

Garrett, P.M. (2018) *Welfare words*, London, Thousand Oaks, New Delhi and Singapore: Sage.

Gilligan, C. (1993) *In a different voice*, Cambridge, MA and London: Harvard University Press.

Giroux, H.A. (1983) 'Theories of reproduction and resistance in the new sociology of education: A critical analysis', *Harvard Educational Review*, 53(3): 257–93.

Goldberg Wood, G. and Tully, C.T. (2006) *The structural approach to direct practice in social work: A social constructionist perspective*, New York, NY: Columbia University Press.

Gottfried, R. and Ben-Arieh, A. (2019) 'The Israeli child protection system', in L. Merkel-Holguin, J.D. Fluke and R.D. Krugman (eds) *National systems of child protection: Understanding the international variability and context for developing policy and practice*, Cham: Springer International Publishing, pp 139–72.

Gray, M. and Webb, S.A. (2013) *The new politics of social work*, New York, NY: Macmillan International Higher Education.

Gray, M., Dean, M., Agllias, K., Howard, A. and Schubert, L. (2015) 'Perspectives on neoliberalism for human service professionals', *Social Service Review*, 89(2): 368–92.

Grell, P., Blom, B. and Ahmadi, N. (2019) 'Conditions for helping relations in specialized personal social services – A client perspective on the influence of organizational structure', *Nordic Social Work Research*, DOI: 10.1080/2156857X.2019.1596148.

Guba, E.G. and Lincoln, Y.S. (1994) 'Competing paradigms in qualitative research', in N.K. Denzin and Y.S. Lincoln (eds) *Handbook of qualitative research*, Thousand Oaks, CA: Sage, pp 105–17.

Gupta, A. (2015) 'Poverty and shame – Messages for social work', *Critical and Radical Social Work*, 3(1): 131–9.

Gupta, A. (2017) 'Poverty and child neglect – The elephant in the room?', *Families, Relationships and Societies*, 6(1): 21–36.

Gupta, A. and Blewett, J. (2008) 'Involving services users in social work training on the reality of family poverty: A case study of a collaborative project', *Social Work Education*, 27(5): 459–73.

Gupta, A., Blumhardt, H. and ATD Fourth World (2017) 'Poverty, exclusion and child protection practice: The contribution of "the politics of recognition&respect"', *European Journal of Social Work*, http://dx.doi.org/10.1080/13691457.2017.1287669

Handler, J.F. and Hasenfeld, Y. (2007) *Blame welfare, ignore poverty and inequality*, New York, NY: Cambridge University Press.

Hardcastle, D.A., Powers, P.R. and Wenocur, S. (2004) *Community practice: Theories and skills for social workers*, New York, NY: Oxford University Press.

Hawkins, L., Fook, J. and Ryan, M. (2001) 'Social workers' use of the language of social justice', *British Journal of Social Work*, 31(1): 1–13.

Healy, K., Darlington, Y. and Feeney, J.A. (2011) 'Parents' participation in child protection practice: Toward respect and inclusion', *Families in society*, 92(3): 282–8.

Heron, J. and Reason, P. (1997) 'A participatory inquiry paradigm', *Qualitative Inquiry*, 3(3): 274–94.

Hill, K.M., Ferguson, S.M. and Erickson, C. (2010) 'Sustaining and strengthening a macro identity: The Association of Macro Practice Social Work', *Journal of Community Practice*, 18(4): 513–27.

Honneth, A. (2001) 'Invisibility: On the epistemology of recognition', *Proceedings of the Aristotelian Society, Supplementary Volumes*, 75: 111–26.

Honneth, A. (2007) *Disrespect: The normative foundations of critical theory* (ch 3 trans from German by J. Farrell), Cambridge and Malden, MA: Polity Press.

Houston, S. (2015) '"When I look I am seen, so I exist to change": Supplementing Honneth's recognition model for social work', *Social Work and Society: International Online Journal*, 13(2): 1–17.

Houston, S. and Montgomery, L. (2017) 'Reflecting critically on contemporary social pathologies: Social work and the "good life"', *Critical and Radical Social Work*, 5(2): 181–96.

Howe, D. (1995) *Attachment theory for social work practice*, Houndmills and London: Macmillan International Higher Education.

Howe, D. (1996) 'Surface and depth in social work practice', in N. Parton (ed) *Social theory, social change and social work*, London: Routledge, pp 77–97.

Howe, D. (1997) 'Psychosocial and relationship-based theories for family and child social work: Political philosophy, psychology and welfare practice', *Child and Family Social Work*, 2: 161–9.

Howe, D. (1998) 'Relationship-based thinking and practice in social work', *Journal of Social Work Practice*, 12(1): 45–56.

Ife, J. (1997) *Rethinking social work: Towards critical practice*, Melbourne: Longman.

Ife, J. (2005) 'What is critical social work', in S. Hick, J. Fook and R. Pozzuto (eds) *Social work: A critical turn*, Toronto: Thompson, pp 3–8.

Ife, J. (2012) *Human rights and social work: Towards rights-based practice*, Cambridge: Cambridge University Press.

James, C., Este, D., Bernard, W., Benjamin, A., Lloyd, B. and Turner, T. (2010) *Race and wellbeing: The lives, hopes, and activism of African Canadians*, Black Point, Nova Scotia, Canada: Fernwood Publishing.

Johnson, P. and Lawler, S. (2005) 'Coming home to love and class', *Sociological Research Online*, 10(3), www.socresonline.org.uk/10/3/johnson.html

Johnson, S.B., Riis, J.L. and Noble, K.G. (2016) 'State of the art review: Poverty and the developing brain', *Pediatrics*, 137(4): e20153075.

Jones, C. (2001) 'Voices from the front line: State social workers and New Labour', *British Journal of Social Work*, 31(4): 547–62.

Jones, C. (2002) 'Social work and society', in R. Adams, L. Dominelli and M. Payne (eds) *Social work: Themes, issues and critical debates* (2nd edn), Basingstoke: Palgrave, pp 41–9.

Josselson, R. (2004) 'The hermeneutics of faith and the hermeneutics of suspicion', *Narrative Inquiry*, 14(1): 1–28.

Juhila, K. (2003) 'Creating a "bad" client: Disalignment of institutional identities in social work interaction', in C. Hall, K. Juhila, N. Patron and T. Poso (eds) *Constructing clienthood in social work and human services*, London and New York, NY: Jessica Kingsley Publishes, pp 83–95.

Kam, P. (2014) 'Back to the "social" of social work: Reviving the social work profession's contribution to the promotion of social justice', *International Social Work*, 57(6): 723–40.

Karjanen, D.J. (2016) *The servant class city: Urban revitalization versus the working poor in San Diego*, Minneapolis: University of Minnesota Press.

Katz, M. (1986) *In the shadow of the poorhouse: A social history of welfare in America*, New York, NY: Basic Books.

Katz, M. (1990) *The undeserving poor: From the war on poverty to the war on welfare*, New York, NY: Pantheon Books.

Katz, M. (1992) *The underclass debate: Views from history*, Princeton, NJ: Princeton University Press.

Katz, M. (1995) *Improving poor people: The welfare state, the 'underclass', and urban schools as history*, Princeton, NJ: Princeton University Press.

Kincheloe, J.L. (2005) *Critical constructivism primer*, Berlin: Peter Lang.

Klein, P. (1958) 'Welfare services in Israel', prepared for the government of Israel, Jerusalem.

Kohut, H. (1971) *The analysis of the self: A systematic approach to the psychoanalytic treatment of narcissistic personality disorders*, New York, NY: International Universities Press.

Kohut, H. (1984) *How does analysis cure?* (ed A. Goldberg, with P. Stepansky), Chicago, IL: University of Chicago Press.

Kristeva, J. (1982) *Powers of horror* (vol 98), New York, NY: University Presses of California, Columbia and Princeton.

Krumer-Nevo, M. (2005) 'Listening to "life knowledge": A new research direction in poverty studies', *International Journal of Social Welfare*, 14(2): 99–106.

Krumer-Nevo, M. (2006) *Women in poverty: Life stories: Gender, pain, resistance*, Tel-Aviv: Hakibutz Hameuchad.

Krumer-Nevo, M. (2009) 'From voice to knowledge: Feminism and participatory action research', *International Journal of Qualitative Studies in Education*, 22(3): 279–96.

Krumer-Nevo, M. (2015) 'Poverty aware social work: A paradigm for social work practice with people in poverty', *British Journal of Social Work*, 46(6): 1793–808.

Krumer-Nevo, M. (2017) 'Poverty and the political: Wresting the political out of and into social work theory, research and practice', *European Journal of Social Work*, 6: 811–22.

Krumer-Nevo, M. and Barak, A. (2006) 'Participatory action research: The perspectives of social service users regarding social services', *Social Security*, 72: 11–39.

Krumer-Nevo, M., Slonim-Nevo, V. and Hirshenzon-Segev, E. (2006) 'Social workers and their long-term clients: The never ending struggle', *Journal of Social Service Research*, 33(1): 27–38.

Krumer-Nevo, M., Weiss-Gal, I. and Levin, L. (2011) 'Searching for poverty aware social work: Discourse analysis of job descriptions', *Journal of Social Policy*, 40(2): 313–32.

Krumer-Nevo, M., Shimei, N. and Timor-Shlevin, S. (eds) (2015) *'If it's not enough for you': Realization of rights and active advocacy*, Beer-Sheva: Casework for Social Change Program, Ben-Gurion University of the Negev.

Kulka, R. (2005) 'Introduction', in H. Kohut (ed) *How does analysis cure?* (trans to Hebrew by E. Idan), Tel Aviv: Am Oved, pp 13–50.

Lavalette, M. (ed) (2011) *Radical social work today: Social work at the crossroads*, Bristol: Policy Press.

Lavee, E. (2016) 'Low-income women's encounters with social services: Negotiation over power, knowledge and respectability', *British Journal of Social Work*, 47(5): 1554–71.

Lavee, E. and Strier, R. (2018) 'Social workers' emotional labour with families in poverty: Neoliberal fatigue?', *Child and Family Social Work*, 23(3): 504–12.

Leibovitch, N., Danek, M., Shidlovsky, D., Ravid, G. and Ziv, Y. (2019) *Families First and Rights Centers: Final evaluation report*, Tel Aviv: ERI Research for Social Impact.

Leisering, L. and Leibfried, S. (1999) *Time and poverty in Western welfare states*, Cambridge: Cambridge University Press.

Lens, V. (2004) 'Principled negotiation: A new tool for case advocacy', *Social Work*, 49(3): 506–13.

Levine, L. (2009) '"Coalition of exclusion": Not take-up of rights among the poorest', in J. Gal and M. Ajzestadt (eds) *Access to social justice in Israel*, Jerusalem: Taub Center for Social Policy Studies in Israel, pp 225–55.

Lewis, O. (1966) 'The culture of poverty', *Scientific American*, 215(4): 19–25.

Lipsky, M. (1980) *Street level bureaucracy: Dilemmas of the individual in public services*, New York, NY: The Russell Sage Foundation.

Lissak, R.S. (1989) *Pluralism and progressives: Hull House and the new immigrants, 1890–1919*, Chicago: University of Chicago Press.

Lister, R. (2004) *Poverty*, London: Polity Press.

Lonne, B., Parton, N., Thomson, J. and Harries, M. (2008) *Reforming child protection*, London and New York, NY: Routledge.

Luby, J., Belden, A., Botteron, K., Marrus, N., Harms, M.P., Babb, C., Nishino, T. and Barch, D. (2013) 'The effects of poverty on childhood brain development: The mediating effect of care-giving and stressful life events', *JAMA Pediatrics*, 167(12): 1135–42.

Lundy, C. (2004) *Social work and social justice: A structural approach to practice*, Toronto: University of Toronto Press.

Mandell, D. (2008) 'Power, care and vulnerability: Considering use of self in child welfare work', *Journal of Social Work Practice*, 22(2): 235–48.

Mantle, G. and Backwith, D. (2010) 'Poverty and social work', *British Journal of Social Work*, 40(8): 2380–97.

Maslow, A.H. (1943) 'A theory of human motivation', *Psychological Review*, 50: 370–96.

McCoy, D.C., Fink, G., Shawar, Y.R., Shiffman, J., Devercelli, A.E., Wodon, Q.T., Vargas-Barón, E. and Grantham-McGregor, S. (2017) 'Early childhood development coming of age: Science through the life course', *The Lancet*, 389(10064): 77–90.

McDonagh, F. (2009) 'Introduction: Dom Helder in context', in H. Câmara, *Dom Helder Camara: Essential Writings*, Maryknoll: Orbis Books, pp 11–36.

McKernan, S.M. and Ratcliffe, C. (2002) *Transition events in the dynamics of poverty*, Washington, DC: The Urban Institution.

Ministry of Welfare and Social Services (2016) 'An outline for developing knowledge, theory and practice for social work with families in poverty/families with children at risk: A document prepared for a steering committee' (27.11.2016) Jerusalem (in Hebrew).

Mitchell, S. (1988) *Relational concepts in psychoanalysis: An integration*, Cambridge, MA: Harvard University Press.

Mitchell, S.A. and Aron, L. (1999) 'Preface', in S.A. Mitchell and L. Aron (eds) *Relational psychoanalysis: The emergence of a tradition*, Hillsdale: Analytic Press, pp iv–xx.

Moffatt, K. (1999) 'Surveillance and government of the welfare recipient', in A.S. Chambon, A. Irving and L. Epstein (eds) *Reading Foucault for social work*, New York, NY: Columbia University Press, pp 209–46.

Moraga, C. and Anzaldua, G. (eds) (1983) *This bridge called my back: Writings by radical women of color*, New York, NY: Kitchen Table, Women of Color Press.

Morley, C. and Ablett, P. (2017) 'Rising wealth and income inequality: A radical social work critique and response', *Aotearoa New Zealand Social Work*, 29(2): 6–18.

Morris, K., White, S., Doherty, P. and Warwick, L. (2017) 'Out of time: Theorizing family in social work practice', *Child and Family Social Work*, 22: 51–60.

Mullaly, B. (1997) *The structural social work* (2nd edn), Oxford: Oxford University Press.

Mullaly, B. (2007) *The new structural social work* (3rd edn), Oxford: Oxford University Press.

Murray, C. (1984) *Losing ground: American social policy 1950–1980*, New York, NY: Basic Books.

Murray, C. (1990) *The emerging British underclass*, London: IEA Health and Welfare Unit.

Narayan, D., Chambers, R., Shah, M.K. and Petesch, P. (2000) *Voices of the poor: Crying out for change*, New York, NY: Oxford University Press for the World Bank.

National Committee to Combat Poverty (2014) 'Final report', Jerusalem (in Hebrew).

Netting, F.M., Kettner, P.M. and McMurtry, S.L. (2016) *Social work macro practice* (6th edn), London: Pearson.

Niemi, I.P. (2015) 'The professional form of recognition in social work', *Studies in Social and Political Thought*, 25: 174–90.

NII (National Insurance Institute) (2017) 'Poverty and social gaps in 2016, annual report', Jerusalem (in Hebrew).

NII (National Insurance Institute) (2018) 'Poverty and social gaps in 2017, annual report', Jerusalem (in Hebrew).

O'Connor, A. (2009) *Poverty knowledge: Social science, social policy, and the poor in twentieth-century US history*, Princeton, NJ: Princeton University Press.

Parrott, L. (2014) *Social work and poverty: A critical approach*, Bristol: Policy Press.

Parton, N. and O'Byrne, P. (2000) 'What do we mean by "constructive social work"?', in N. Parton and P. O'Byrne (eds) *Constructive social work: Towards a new practice*, London and New York, NY: Macmillan and St Martin's Press, pp 6–26.

Patrick, R. (2016) 'Living with and responding to the "scrounger" narrative in the UK: Exploring everyday strategies of acceptance, resistance and deflection', *Journal of Poverty and Social Justice*, 24(3): 245–59.

Pease, B. and Fook, J. (eds) (1999) *Transforming social work practice: Postmodern critical perspectives*, Oxon and New York, NY: Psychology Press.

Peleg, E. (2013) *The poverty challenge of administrative law*, Tel Aviv: Resling (in Hebrew).

Perry, B.D. (2002) 'Childhood experience and the expression of genetic potential: What childhood neglect tells us about nature and nurture', *Brain and Mind*, 3: 79–100.

Peters, H.E. and Mullis, C.N. (1997) 'The role of family income and sources of income in adolescent achievement', in J.G. Duncan and J. Brooks-Gunn (eds) *Consequences of growing up poor*, New York, NY: Russell Sage Foundation, pp 340–81.

Pickering, M. (2001) *Stereotyping: The politics of representation*, Hampshire and New York, NY: Palgrave.

Pierce, C. (1970) 'Offensive mechanisms', in F.B. Barbour (ed) *The black seventies*, Boston, MA: Porter Sargent Publisher, pp 265–82.

Quigley, P.W. (2003) *Ending poverty as we know it*, Philadelphia, PA: Temple University Press.

Rainwater, L. (1970) 'Neutralizing the disinherited: Some psychological aspects of understanding the poor', in V.L. Allen (ed) *Psychological factors in poverty*, New York, NY: Academic Press, pp 9–28.

Rank, M.R. (2005) *One nation, underprivileged: Why American poverty affects us all*, New York, NY: Oxford University Press.

Regev-Messalem, S. (2014) 'Trapped in resistance: Collective struggle through welfare fraud in Israel', *Law and Society Review*, 48: 741–72.

Reisch, M. (2013) 'Social work education and the Neo-Liberal challenge: The US response to increasing global inequality', *Social Work Education*, 32(6): 715–33.

Reisch, M. and Andrews, J. (2014) *The road not taken: A history of radical social work in the United States*, New York, NY and London: Routledge.

Reisch, M. and Garvin, C.D. (2016) *Social work and social justice: Concepts, challenges, and strategies*, Oxford: Oxford University Press.

Reisch, M. and Jani, J.S. (2012) 'The new politics of social work practice: Understanding context to promote change', *The British Journal of Social Work*, 42(6): 1132–50.

Rigdon, S.M. (1988) *The culture facade: Art, science, and politics in the work of Oscar Lewis*, Urbana and Chicago, IL: University of Illinois Press.

Rigg, J. and Sefton, T. (2006) 'Income dynamics and life cycle', *Journal of Social Policy*, 35: 411–35.

Rojeck, C., Peacock, G. and Collins, S. (1988) *Social work and received ideas*, London: Routledge.

Roose, R., Roets, G. and Bouverne-De Bie, M. (2011) 'Irony and social work: In search of the happy Sisyphus', *British Journal of Social Work*, 42(8): 1592–607.

Roose, R., Roets, G. and Schiettecat, T. (2014) 'Implementing a strengths perspective in child welfare and protection: A challenge not to be taken lightly', *European Journal of Social Work*, 17(1): 3–17.

Rorty, R. (1989) *Contingency, irony, and solidarity*, Cambridge: Cambridge University Press.

Rose, S.M. (2000) 'Reflections on empowerment-based practice', *Social Work*, 45(5): 403–12.

Rosenfeld, J.M. (1993) 'Partnership: Guidelines for social work practice with and on behalf of defeated populations', *Hevra V'Revacha* [*Society and Welfare*], 13(3): 225–36 (in Hebrew).

Rosenfeld, J.M. and Tardieu, B. (2000) *Artisans of democracy: How ordinary people, families in extreme poverty, and social institutions become allies to overcome social exclusion*, Lanham, MD, New York, NY and Oxford: University Press of America.

Rossiter, A. (1996) 'A perspective on critical social work', *Journal of Progressive Human Services*, 7(2): 23–41.

Rossiter, A. (2007) 'Self as subjectivity: Toward a use of self as respectful relations of recognition', in D. Mandell (ed) *Revisiting the use of self: Questioning professional identities*, Toronto: Canadian Scholars Press, pp 21–33.

Rossiter, A. (2014) 'Axel Honneth's theory of recognition and its potential for aligning social work with social justice', *Critical and Radical Social Work*, 2(1): 93–108.

Rothman, J. and Mizrahi, T. (2014) 'Balancing micro and macro practice: A challenge for social work', *Social Work*, 59(1): 91–3.

Royce, E. (2018) *Poverty and power: The problem of structural inequality*, Lanham, MD, Boulder, NY, New York, NY and London: Rowman & Littlefield.

Ruch, G. (2005) 'Relationship-based practice and reflective practice: Holistic approaches to contemporary child care social work', *Child and Family Social Work*, 10(2): 111–23.

Ruch, G. (2018) 'The contemporary context of relationship-based practice', in G. Ruch, D. Turney and A. Ward (eds) *Relationship-based social work: Getting to the heart of practice* (2nd edn), London and Philadelphia, PA: Jessica Kingsley Publishers, pp 19–36.

Saar-Heiman, Y. (2019) 'Poverty-aware social work in the child protection system: A critical reflection on two single-case studies', *Child and Family Social Work*, https://doi.org/10.1111/cfs.12642.

Saar-Heiman, Y. and Krumer-Nevo, M. (2019). ' "You decide": Relationship-based knowledge and parents' participation in high-risk child protection crisis intervention', *British Journal of Social Work*, https://doi.org/10.1093/bjsw/bcz086.

Saar-Heiman, Y. and Ruso-Carmel, S. (2019) 'Is direct practice for social change possible? A critical examination and suggestions for practice', *Bitachon Sociali (Social Security)*, 106: 75–98 (in Hebrew).

Saar-Heiman, Y., Lavie-Ajayi, M. and Krumer-Nevo, M. (2016) 'Poverty-aware social work practice: Service users' perspectives', *Child and Family Social Work*, 22(2): 1054–63.

Saar-Heiman, Y., Krumer-Nevo, M. and Lavie-Ajayi, M. (2017) 'Intervention in a real life context: Therapeutic space in poverty-aware social work', *British Journal of Social Work*, 48(2): 321–38.

Saleebey, D. (1996) 'The strengths perspective in social work practice: Extensions and cautions', *Social work*, 41(3): 296–305.

Santiago, L. (1972) 'From Settlement House to antipoverty program', *Social Work*, 17(4): 73–8.

Scheper-Hughes, N. (1992) *Death without weeping: The violence of everyday life in Brazil*, California, CA: University of California Press.

Schiettecat, T., Roets, G. and Vandenbroeck, M. (2017) 'What families in poverty consider supportive: Welfare strategies of parents with young children in relation to (child and family) social work', *Child and Family Social Work*, 22(2): 689–99.

Schnitzer, P.K. (1996) ' "They don't come in!" Stories told, lessons taught about poor families in therapy', *American Journal of Orthopsychiatry*, 66(4): 572–82.

Schofield, G. (1998) 'Inner and outer worlds: A psychosocial framework for child and family social work', *Child and Family Social Work*, 3(1): 57–67.

Schram, S.F. and Silverman, B. (2012) 'The end of social work: Neoliberalizing social policy implementation', *Critical Policy Studies*, 6(2): 128–45.

Segal, E. (2013) 'Beyond the pale of psychoanalysis: Relational theory and generalist social work practice', *Clinical Social Work Journal*, 41(4): 376–86.

Sharlin, S.A. and Shamai, M. (2000) *Therapeutic intervention with poor, unorganized families: From distress to hope*, London and New York, NY: Routledge.

Shimei, N., Krumer-Nevo, M., Saar-Heiman, Y., Russo-Carmel, S., Mirmovitch, I., Zaitoun-Aricha, L. and Social Work for Change Group Members (2016) 'Social work for change: Performance ethnography on critical social work', *Qualitative Inquiry*, 22(8): 615–23.

Specht, H. and Courtney, M.E. (1994) *Unfaithful angels: How social work has abandoned its mission*, New York, NY: Free Press.

Spelman, E.V. (1997) *Fruits of sorrow: Framing our attention to suffering*, Boston, MA: Beacon Press.

Spicker, P. (1984) *Stigma and social welfare*, London: Croom-Helm.

Spicker, P. (2006) 'Definitions of poverty', in P. Spicker, S. Alvarez Leguizamon and D. Gordon (eds) *Poverty: An international glossary* (2nd edn), London and New York, NY: Zed Books, pp 229–43.

Stern, D.N. (1985) *The interpersonal world of the infant: A view from psychoanalysis and developmental psychology*, New York, NY: Basic Books.

Stevenson, O. (1992) 'Social work intervention to protect children: Aspects of research and practice', *Child Abuse Review*, 1: 19–32.

Strier, R. (2009) 'Class-competent social work: A preliminary definition', *International Journal of Social Welfare*, 18(3): 237–42.

Strier, R. and Binyamin, S. (2010) 'Developing anti-oppressive services for the poor: A theoretical and organisational rationale', *British Journal of Social Work*, 40(6): 1908–26.

Strier, R. and Binyamin, S. (2013) 'Introducing anti-oppressive social work practices in public services: Rhetoric to practice', *British Journal of Social Work*, 44(8): 2095–112.

Sucharov, M. (2013) 'Politics, race, and class in the analytic space: The healing power of therapeutic advocacy', *International Journal of Psychoanalytic Self Psychology*, 8(1): 29–45.

Sutton, E., Pemberton, S., Fahmy, E. and Tamiya, Y. (2014) 'Stigma, shame and the experience of poverty in Japan and the United Kingdom', *Social Policy and Society*, 13(1): 143–54.

Tardieu, B. (1999) 'Building a partnership with "fourth world families": The severely poor as leaders', in A. Ben Arieh and Y. Zionit (eds) *Children in Israel on the threshold of the new millennium*, Jerusalem: National Children's Welfare Council and Ashalim, pp 169–80.

Tempel, L.R. (2009) 'The intersubjective action of case advocacy and engagement in a working alliance', *Smith College Studies in Social Work*, 79(2): 125–38.

Timor-Shlevin, S. (2019) 'Controlled arena: Critical practice is state social services', in M. Krumer-Nevo, R. Strier and I. Weiss-Gal (eds) *Critical practice*, Tel Aviv: Resling.

Tosone, C. (2004) 'Relational social work: Honoring the tradition', *Smith College Studies in Social Work*, 74(3): 475–87.

Turney, D. (2012) 'A relationship-based approach to engaging involuntary clients: The contribution of recognition theory', *Child and Family Social Work*, 17(2): 149–59.

United Nations, Human Rights, Office of the High Commissioner for Human Rights (2012) 'The guiding principles on extreme poverty and human rights', www.ohchr.org/EN/Issues/Poverty/Pages/DGPIntroduction.aspx

Urek, M. (2005) 'Making a case in social work: The construction of an unsuitable mother', *Qualitative Social Work*, 4(4): 451–67.

Valentine, C.A. (1968) *Culture and poverty: Critique and counter-proposals*, Chicago, IL: University of Chicago Press.

Valentine, C.A. (1971) 'The "culture of poverty": Its scientific significance and its implications for action', in E.B. Leacock (ed) *The culture of poverty: A critique*, New York, NY: Simon and Schuster, pp 193–225.

Van Mechelen, N. and Janssens, J. (2017) 'Who to blame? An overview of the factors contributing to the non-take-up of social rights', CBS Working Paper, 17/08, University of Antwerp, Herman Deleeck Center for Social Policy.

Van Oorschot, W. (1995) *Realizing rights: A multi-level approach to non-take-up of means-tested benefits*, Aldershot: Avebury.

Van Oorschot, W.J.H. (1998) 'Failing selectivity: On the extent and causes of non-take-up of social security benefits', in H.-J. Andress (ed) *Empirical poverty research in a comparative perspective*, Ashgate: Aldershot, pp 101–32.

Vargas-Barón, E. and Grantham-McGregor, S. (2017) 'Early childhood development coming of age: Science through the life course', *The Lancet*, 389(10064): 77–90.

Wacquant, L. (2010) 'Crafting the neoliberal state: Workfare, prisonfare, and social insecurity', *Sociological Forum*, 25(2): 197–220.

Waldegrave, C. (2005) '"Just therapy" with families on low incomes', *Child Welfare*, 84(2): 265–76.

Walker, R. and Bantebya-Kyomuhendo, G. (2014) *The shame of poverty*, Oxford: Oxford University Press.

Walker, R., Kyomuhendo, G.B., Chase, E., Choudhry, S., Gubrium, E.K., Nicola, J.Y., Lodemel, I., Mathew, L., Mwiine, A., Pellissery, S. and Ming, Y. (2013) 'Poverty in global perspective: Is shame a common denominator?', *Journal of Social Policy*, 42(2): 215–33.

Wastell, D. and White, S. (2012) 'Blinded by neuroscience: Social policy, the family and the infant brain', *Families, Relationships and Societies*, 1(3): 397–414.

Wastell, D. and White, S. (2017) *Blinded by science: The social implications of epigenetics and neuroscience*, Bristol: Policy Press.

Webb, S.A. (2010) '(Re)Assembling the Left: The politics of redistribution and recognition in social work', *British Journal of Social Work*, 40(8): 2364–79.

Webb, S.A. (ed) (2019) *The Routledge handbook of critical social work*, London and New York, NY: Routledge.

Weiss, I. (2005) 'Is there a global common core to social work? A cross-national comparative study of BSW graduate students', *Social Work*, 50(2): 101–10.

Weiss, I. (2006) 'Factors associated with interest in working with the poor', *Families in Society*, 87(3): 385–94.

Weiss, I. and Gal, J. (2006) 'Poverty in the eyes of the beholder: Social workers compared to other middle-class professionals', *British Journal of Social Work*, 37(5): 893–908.

Weiss-Gal, I. (2009) 'Teaching critical perspectives: Analyses of professional practice in the film *Ladybird, Ladybird*', *Social Work Education*, 28(8): 873–86.

Weiss-Gal, I., Levin, L. and Krumer-Nevo, M. (2012) 'Applying critical social work indirect practice with families', *Child and Family Social Work*, 19(1): 55–64.

White, H. (1981) 'The value of narrativity in the representation of reality', in W.J.T. Mitchell (ed) *On narrative*, Chicago, IL, and London: University of Chicago Press, pp 1–24.

White, M. and Epston, D. (1990) *Narrative means to therapeutic ends*, New York, NY: W.W. Norton and Company.

Wilkinson, R. and Pickett, K. (2010) *The spirit level: Why equality is better for everyone*, London: Penguin.

Williams, F., Popay, J. and Oakley, A. (eds) (1999) *Welfare research: A critical review*, London: UCL Press.

Wilson, J.W. (1987) *The truly disadvantaged: The inner city, the underclass, and public policy*, Chicago, IL: University of Chicago Press.

Wilson, J.W. (1996) *When work disappears: The world of the new urban poor*, New York, NY: Alfred A. Knopf.

Witkin, S. (1991) 'Empirical clinical practice: A critical analysis', *Social Work*, 36(2): 158–63.

Zeytinoglu, I.U. and Muteshi, K.J. (2000) 'Gender, race and class dimensions of nonstandard work', *Relations Industrielles*, 55(1): 133–67.

Zurn, C. (2015) *Axel Honneth: A critical theory of the social*, Cambridge: Polity.

Index

Note: Page numbers in *italics* refer to illustrations. Page numbers followed by n refer to footnotes.

A

academia 204–5
active listening 51, 157–8
active rights exercising 153, 155–6, 179–81
  complicated cases 182–6
  and dependence 89–90
  direct practice of 157–9
  panel discussion 191–200
  Rights Exercising Social Worker 165–8
  simple version 181–2
  situations without rights 186–9
  as therapeutic process 159–65
Adams, Jane 152
administrative authorities 89–90, 151, 167
advocacy 151–2
  therapeutic 159–60
  see also active rights exercising
agency 137, 139–44, 225
  getting (back) at 141–2, 145–7
  getting by 141, 144–5
  getting organised 141–2
  getting out 141
Altman, Neil 98–99
Arab localities 14n5
Arab-Palestinians 3, 4
ATD Fourth World Movement 2, 47
autonomy 101

B

bad choices 86–7
banking model of knowledge 107
Barak-Erez, D. 151
basic needs 108, 121n2
benefits take-up 153–4
Benjamin, A. 9
Benjamin, J. 95
Beresford, Peter 47
Bernard, W. 9
Bourdieu, P. 21
brain development 21, 24
budgeting 85
  see also debt
bureaucratic problems 89–90

C

case advocacy 152
case studies *see* intervention stories
Casework for Social Change 169–70, 191, 205, 209
cause advocacy 152
Charity Organization Society 152
child abuse/neglect 8, 75
child protection 6, 211–12
childhood experiences 119
children at risk
  case study 217–20
  conservative paradigm 220–1
  Othering 221, 223, 226
  PAP analysis 221–4
  PAP practice 224–5
choice 86–7, 140–1
  see also opportunities
citizen rights 3
Cloward, R.A. 9
cognitive dissonance 49–50
community development 211–14
community social work 29
concrete needs *see* material needs
conservative paradigm 15, 18–26, *19*
  axiology 23
  crisis intervention 220–1
  epistemology 22–3
  Lev family intervention story 62
  ontology 18–22
  practice derived from 23–6
  rights exercising 156
  Sarit's story 114
constructivism 32
context 55, 61–2, 67–9, 73, 137
contextualisation 147–8
crisis intervention
  case study 217–20
  conservative paradigm 220–1
  Othering 221, 223, 226
  PAP analysis 221–4
  PAP practice 224–5
critical education 107
critical *habitus* 77–82
critical hope 9
critical reflection 17
critical social work 2, 98
critical thinking 137
critical writing 55–7
  guidelines *69*
  implications for practice 72–4
  Lev family intervention story
    first version 57–62

259

second version 63–9
  third version 70–2
cultural injustice 98
culture of poverty 19–20

D

De Luca, E. 95–6
debt 31, 161, 164–5, 173, 174, 175, 176
dependence 52–3, 85–6, 89–90, 108, 193–4, 230
dialogue 81, 107
  therapeutic 38
distributive injustice 98, 100, 102
Doron, Abraham 171
drugs addiction 125

E

education 107, 140
emancipation 56
emotional needs
  and material needs 48–9, 83–4, 90, 124, 176
  and physical needs 107–8
  Sarit's story 120
emotions 160
employment 84–5, 87, 212–13, 214
Este, D. 9
eviction 203–4, 206–9

F

Families First 6, 7, 170
Ferguson, I. 29
financial planning 85
  see also debt
Fine, Michelle 204, 209
flexible budgets 169–77
  case study 172–5
Fox Piven, F. 9
Fraiberg, Selma 119
Fraser, Nancy 93, 94, 96, 98
free choice 86
Freire, Paulo 107

G

Garrett, P.M. 9, 20–1, 98
getting (back) at 141–2, 145–7
getting by 141, 144–5
getting organised 141–2
getting out 141
'ghosts in the nursery' 119
Gilligan, Carol 46
Giroux, H.A. 140
God's Mountain (De Luca) 95–6
group intervention 229–37

H

habitus see critical *habitus*
hierarchy of needs 107–8, 121n2

higher needs 108
historisation 61–2
home visits 17–18
Honneth, Axel 93, 94, 96, 103n4
hope 8–9, 185
housing 110–11, 112, 114–16, 232, 233–4
  eviction 203–4, 206–9
Hull House 152
human rights 30, 32, 50

I

identity 120
immediacy 177
Income Support Law 172
inequality 26
injustice 98, 100–2, 158, 162
  panel discussion 191–200
  see also social justice
instrumental rationalisation 97
International Women's Day 213–14
intervention stories 55–7
  critical writing guidelines 69
  implications for practice 72–4
  Lev family first version 57–62
  Lev family second version 63–9
  Lev family third version 70–2
  see also crisis intervention; group intervention
invisibilisation 97
Israel
  employment 214
  hope 9
  poverty 4, 84, 85
  welfare state 3–5, 170–2

J

JAMA Pediatrics 24
James, C. 9
Juhila, K. 35
justice 98
  see also injustice; social justice

K

Katz, Michael 18, 19
Kettner, P.M. 28
Klein, Phillip 171
knowledge 68, 101, 105–7, 234
  and needs 108–9
    Sarit's story 109–21
  relationship-based 33–5
  Rights Exercising Social Worker 166–7
  v. voice 46–7
Kohut, H. 95

L

'Ladybird, Ladybird' (Loach) 211
language 45–6

knowledge v. voice 46–7
material/concrete and emotional
  needs 48–9
opportunities 49–50
opposition to poverty 50–1
pain 47–8
PAP course 77, 79, 81–2
resistance to poverty 51–3
Lewis, Oscar 19–20, 39n3
life stories 110–13, 125–36
listening 2, 47, 48, 90, 114, 118
  active 51, 157–8
Lister, Ruth 49, 98, 139–40, 141
Lloyd, B. 9
localities 167
location 209

M

macro-practice 28–9
MAPA [Families Meet Opportunities]
  programme 6, 151, 170, 177
Maslow, Abraham 107–8, 121n2
material assistance 38, 83–4,
  90, 229–32
  and flexible budgets 169–77
  case study 172–5
material needs
  and emotional needs 48–9, 83–4, 90,
    124, 176
  and recognition 100, 101, 102
McMurtry, S.L. 28
micro-aggressions 31–2, 156, 162–3
Ministry of Welfare and Social
  Services 105–6
misrecognition 97
  see also recognition
Mizrachi Jews 4
mothers 21, 135

N

Naming, Blaming and Claiming (NBC)
  model 157
National Committee to Combat
  Poverty 4, 6
National Insurance Institute (NII) 4
needs 107–9, 121n2
  Sarit's story 109–21
  see also emotional needs;
    material needs
neighbourhoods 123
neoliberalism 4, 21, 29, 86, 98, 139
Netting, F.M. 28
neuroenthusiasm 21
neurological-scientific research 24
New Labour 29
Niemi, I.P. 99
noise v. voice 46

non-take-up of rights 153–5, 157–8

O

object of transference 180
occupied territories 3
opportunities 49–50, 114
  see also choice
opposition to poverty 50–1
  see also resistance to poverty
organised self-realisation 97
Othering 15, 50, 88–9, 215–17
  children at risk 221, 223, 226
  conservative paradigm 20, 22, 35
  and knowledge 101
  and power relations 56, 91, 223

P

pain 47–8, 101, 123–5
  in life stories 125–36
paradigmatical thinking 16–18
paradigms 16, 19
  see also conservative paradigm;
    Poverty-Aware Social Work
    Paradigm (PAP); structural
    paradigm
parenting programmes 24
pathology 220, 234
Peleg, E. 154
physical needs 107–8
  see also material needs
Pickering, M. 223
Pierce, C. 31
policy practice 159, 164–5, 167–8, 196
political activity, social work as 2–3
politics of recognition see recognition
politics of redistribution 10, 28,
  37–8, 98
positivist approach 22–3, 27, 220–1
poverty
  culture of 19–20
  frequently-asked questions 83–90
  Israel 4, 84, 85
  opposition to 50–1
  resistance to 51–3, 101, 137–48,
    222, 225
  speaking about see language
poverty line 85
poverty wheel 30–1
Poverty-Aware Social Work Paradigm
  (PAP) 1, 3, 19, 30–9
  Arab localities 14n5
  axiology 35–6
  development 5–10
  epistemology 32–5
  ontology 30–2
  practice derived from 37–9
  power, abuse of 80

power relations 3
　children at risk 223, 224
　group intervention 236, 237
　knowledge v. voice 47
　Othering 55–6, 91, 223
　Poverty-Aware Social Work Paradigm (PAP) 32–3, 34, 35–6
　recognition of 94
　and resistance 139, 146, 147
　Sarit's story 114–15
priorities 85
psychoanalysis 137
psychodynamic approaches 90
psychosocial treatment 4, 83–4, 171, 172, 229–30
public services 99

R

Rainwater, Lee 49–50
reality 46
recognition 10, 15, 37–8, 93–7
　of injustice 162
　negation of 103n4
　of pain 124–5
　and the political 98–9
　and poverty-aware social work 99–102
　of resistance 143
redistribution, politics of 10, 28, 37–8, 98
reflection *see* critical reflection
reification 97
relational social work 99
relationship-based knowledge 33–5
relationships
　active rights exercising 160, 163, 180, 194–5, 200
　conservative paradigm 22
　and dependence 86
　and recognition 94–5, 101
　and resistance 51, 143
　structural paradigm 28
　see also power relations
research 123
resistance to poverty 51–3, 101
　and agency 139–44
　　getting (back) at 141–2, 145–7
　　getting by 141, 144–5
　　getting organised 141–2
　　getting out 141
　crisis intervention 222, 225
　strengths perspective 138–9, 142
respect 10, 37–8, 98, 151
responsibility 51, 52, 87–8, 126
rhetoric *see* language
rights
　citizen rights 3

human rights 30, 32, 50
　non-take-up of 153–5, 157–8
　social rights 168n3
rights centres 6
rights exercising 151–3
　active 153, 155–6, 179–81
　complicated cases 182–6
　and dependence 89–90
　direct practice of 157–9
　panel discussion 191–200
　simple version 181–2
　situations without rights 186–9
　as therapeutic process 159–65
　and poverty 153–5
Rights Exercising Social Worker 8, 151
　complicated cases 184–5
　panel discussion 196–7
　role 165–8
　situations without rights 186, 187–8, 189
rights-based practice 149
Roets, G. 139
Roose, R. 139
Ruch, G. 99

S

Saleebey, D. 138, 139
Scheper-Hughes, Nancy 123
Schiettecat, T. 139
self-control 101
Settlement House 152
social capital 89
social change 152–3, 196
social injustice 191–200
　see also injustice
social justice 28–9, 38, 50, 96, 98, 152, 153
　see also injustice
social rights 168n3
social security system 170–1
social services departments 4, 6, 166–7, 168, 171, 203, 206
social work 2–3
Social Workers to the Youth Law 6, 14n6, 211–12
solidarity 35–6, 201–2
　see also standing by
Spelman, Elizabeth 134
standing by 204
　active rights exercising 158, 162–4
　crisis intervention 225
　eviction 206–10
　group intervention 233
　and recognition 143
　see also solidarity
states 14n8, 23–4, 29, 98, 99, 153, 205
　see also welfare states

street-level bureaucrats 155, 162–3
strengths perspective 79, 138–9, 142
structural failures 87–8
structural paradigm 15, *19*, 26–30
Stuart, Mary 152
subjectivity 55, 60–1, 67, 68, 147, 234
subjugation 56
Sucharov, Maxwell 159
suffering 135
  see also pain
suicide 114, 127, 128, 129, 131, 133
support 81, 84
surveillance 25
symbolic capital 49, 72, 89, 140, 199

T

Tardieu, Bruno 2, 47
teaching 75–82, 205–6
  critical *habitus* 77–82
Tempel, Lorraine 159–60
therapeutic advocacy 159–60
therapeutic dialogue 38
therapeutic process 90, 159–65
therapy 93–5
Timor-Shlevin, S. 78
Tosone, C. 99
training *see* teaching
transference, object of 180
trauma 21
Turner, T. 9

U

UK 153

ultra-Orthodox Jews 4
underclass 20–1
'undeserving poor' 18–19
unique outcomes 62, 74n4
United Nations (UN) 30
US 154

V

Vager-Atias, Einat 77
voice 46–7, 105, 106
  see also knowledge

W

Wacquant, L. 21, 25
Wastell, D. 24
Webb, S.A. 98
welfare benefits take-up 153–4
Welfare Service Law 171
welfare services 99
welfare states 3–5, 170–2
welfare-to-work programmes 23–4
White, Hayden 127
White, S. 24
work 84–5, 212–13, 214
Wresinski, Joseph 177
writing 123
  see also critical writing

Y

Younghusband, Eileen 152

www.ingramcontent.com/pod-product-compliance
Lightning Source LLC
Chambersburg PA
CBHW070916030426
42336CB00014BA/2427